Lecture Notes of the Institute for Computer Sciences, Social Informatics and Telecommunications Engineering 486

The LNICST series publishes ICST's conferences, symposia and workshops.
    LNICST reports state-of-the-art results in areas related to the scope of the Institute.
    The type of material published includes

- Proceedings (published in time for the respective event)
- Other edited monographs (such as project reports or invited volumes)

    LNICST topics span the following areas:

- General Computer Science
- E-Economy
- E-Medicine
- Knowledge Management
- Multimedia
- Operations, Management and Policy
- Social Informatics
- Systems

Ana Lucia Martins · Joao C. Ferreira ·
Alexander Kocian · Ulpan Tokkozhina
Editors

Intelligent
Transport Systems

6th EAI International Conference, INTSYS 2022
Lisbon, Portugal, December 15–16, 2022
Proceedings

 Springer

Editors
Ana Lucia Martins (ID)
Iscte-Instituto Universitário de Lisboa
Lisbon, Portugal

Joao C. Ferreira (ID)
Iscte-Instituto Universitário de Lisboa
Lisbon, Portugal

Alexander Kocian (ID)
University of Pisa
Pisa, Italy

Ulpan Tokkozhina (ID)
Iscte-Instituto Universitário de Lisboa
Lisbon, Portugal

ISSN 1867-8211   ISSN 1867-822X (electronic)
Lecture Notes of the Institute for Computer Sciences, Social Informatics
and Telecommunications Engineering
ISBN 978-3-031-30854-3   ISBN 978-3-031-30855-0 (eBook)
https://doi.org/10.1007/978-3-031-30855-0

This Springer imprint is published by the registered company Springer Nature Switzerland AG
The registered company address is: Gewerbestrasse 11, 6330 Cham, Switzerland

Preface

We are delighted to introduce the proceedings of the sixth edition of the International Conference on Intelligent Transport Systems (INTSYS 2022) from the European Alliance for Innovation (EAI). We returned to presential mode, and the conference took place in Lisbon, Portugal, from 15th–16th December, 2022. This conference brought together researchers, developers, and practitioners from around the world who are leveraging and developing Intelligent Transportation Systems (ITS) to increase efficiency, safety, and mobility, and tackle Europe's growing emission and congestion problems.

The theme of INTSYS 2022 was "Intelligent Transportation Systems: Challenges for 2030". This edition received 45 submissions, from which the technical program of INTSYS 2022 accepted 15 full papers. All 15 papers were presented in oral sessions at the main conference tracks. All accepted papers were subjected to a double-blind peer-review process with a minimum of four reviews for each paper.

In this edition of INTSYS 2022 the presence of industry was reinforced by the two guest speakers sharing the innovative solutions of their organizations. Additionally, sustainability gained renewed space in the conference as innovative green initiatives were shared.

Concerning the committees, it was a great pleasure to work with the excellent organizing team of the EAI, which was essential for the success of the INTSYS 2022 conference. In particular, we would like to express our gratitude to Veronika Kissova and the EAI staff for all the support provided in all subjects. We thank ISTAR and ISCTE for their support in hosting the conference. We would also like to express our gratitude to all the members of the Technical Program Committee, who have helped in the peer-review process of the technical papers, as well as ensured a high-quality technical program. We thank the extensive list of external reviewers from several areas of expertise and numerous countries worldwide. A special acknowledgment must be addressed to all the authors for their effort in producing such good quality papers and for the extremely rich and positive feedback shared at the conference. We strongly believe that the INTSYS conference provides a good forum for all researchers, developers, and practitioners to discuss all science and technology relevant to ITS. We also expect that future INTSYS conferences will be as successful and stimulating as indicated by the contributions presented in this volume.

December 2022

Ana Lucia Martins
Joao C. Ferreira
Alexander Kocian
Ulpan Tokkozhina

Organization

Steering Committee

Imrich Chlamtac   University of Trento, Italy

Organizing Committee

General Chair

Ana Lucia Martins   Iscte – Instituto Universitário de Lisboa, Portugal

General Co-chairs

João C. Ferreira   Iscte – Instituto Universitário de Lisboa, Portugal
Alexander Kocian   Pisa University, Italy

TPC Chairs and Co-chairs

Ana Lucia Martins   Iscte – Instituto Universitário de Lisboa, Portugal
João C. Ferreira   Iscte – Instituto Universitário de Lisboa, Portugal
Alexander Kocian   Pisa University, Italy

Sponsorship and Exhibit Chair

Miguel Nunes   Iscte – Instituto Universitário de Lisboa, Portugal

Local Chair

João C. Ferreira   Iscte – Instituto Universitário de Lisboa, Portugal

Workshops Chair

Berit Irene Helgheim   Molde University College, Norway

Publicity and Social Media Chair

Carlos M. P. Sousa   Molde University College, Norway

Publications Chair

Ulpan Tokkozhina   Iscte – Instituto Universitário de Lisboa, Portugal

Web Chair

Bruno Mataloto   Iscte – Instituto Universitário de Lisboa, Portugal

Posters and PhD Track Chair

Luis Elvas   Iscte – Instituto Universitário de Lisboa, Portugal

Panels Chair

Luis Elvas   Iscte – Instituto Universitário de Lisboa, Portugal

Demos Chair

Frederica Gonçalves   University of Madeira, Portugal

Tutorials Chair

Ana Madureira   ISEP, Portugal

Technical Program Committee

Alexander Kocian   University of Pisa, Italy
Ana Martins   Iscte – Instituto Universitário de Lisboa, Portugal
Atilla Altintas   Chalmers University, Sweden
Berit Helgheim   Molde University College, Norway
Bruno Mataloto   Iscte – Instituto Universitário de Lisboa, Portugal
Carlos M. P. Sousa   Molde University College, Norway
Federico Costantini   University of Udine, Italy
Frederica Gonçalves   University of Madeira, Portugal
Gabriel Pestana   INOV, Portugal
Ghadir Pourhashem   University of Zilinska, Slovakia

Jason J. Jung	Chung-Ang University, Republic of Korea
João C. Ferreira	Iscte – Instituto Universitário de Lisboa, Portugal
Lorna Uden	Staffordshire University, UK
Lubos Buzna	University of Zilinska, Slovakia
Luis Elvas	Iscte – Instituto Universitário de Lisboa, Portugal
Marek Kvet	University of Zilinska, Slovakia
Maria C. Pereira	Iscte – Instituto Universitário de Lisboa, Portugal
Nuno Bettencourt	University of Porto, Portugal
Nuno Domingues	Polytechnic Institute of Lisbon, Portugal
Paolo Milazzo	University of Pisa, Italy
Sophia Kalakou	Iscte – Instituto Universitário de Lisboa, Portugal
Ulpan Tokkozhina	Iscte – Instituto Universitário de Lisboa, Portugal
Vitor Monteiro	University of Minho, Portugal
Vitoria Albuquerque	NOVA University, Portugal

Conference Manager

Veronika Kissova	EAI - European Alliance for Innovation, n.o., Belgium

Contents

Intelligent Transportation and Electric Vehicle

Smart City

Analysis of the Tourist's Behavior in Lisbon Using Data from a Mobile Operator

Bruno Francisco[1], Ricardo Ribeiro[1,2] (iD), Fernando Batista[1,2] (iD), and João Ferreira[3,4(✉)] (iD)

[1] Instituto Universitário de Lisboa (ISCTE-IUL), 1649-026 Lisbon, Portugal
{bamfo1,ricardo.ribeiro,fernando.batista}@iscte-iul.pt
[2] INESC-ID Lisboa, 1000-029 Lisbon, Portugal
[3] Instituto Universitário de Lisboa (ISCTE-IUL), ISTAR, 1649-026 Lisbon, Portugal
joao.carlos.ferreira@iscte-iul.pt
[4] Inov Inesc Inovação – Instituto de Novas Tecnologias, 1000-029 Lisbon, Portugal

Abstract. This paper aims to provide to all entities involved in Lisbon tourism activities a geospatial, statistical, and longitudinal analysis tool based on data provided by a mobile operator in cooperation with Lisbon City council, which allows obtaining knowledge about the behaviors and habits of tourists and visitors of the city. The main intention is to provide information that allows decision-makers to base their choices on real data and facts instead of empirical knowledge and non-sustained information The work was mainly developed in three distinct phases. On the first phase, it was necessary to create knowledge about the tourism business and understand the available data to understand whether they would be able to answer our questions. In the next phase, the dataset was prepared and adapted to our needs - the data given to us had information regarding both mobile phones belonging to Portuguese and foreign users. Considering that our focus was on second group, part of the information was discarded.

Through the work developed, it was possible to identify which countries and geographical areas come from Lisbon's tourists and visitors. Additionally, we were able to identify, through the available data, the most visited places, and parishes in the city, as well as the place where they eat and sleep when they are in the city. It was also possible to characterize how events such as the Web Summit or a football game influence the behavior and movements of visitors in Lisbon.

The analyses and information provided were duly validated by specialists from the Lisbon Municipal Council, through presentations and questionnaires to decision-makers and users of the developed solution.

Keywords: Tourism · Lisbon · Travel Behavior · Smart Mobility · Transportation Networks · Big Data · Data Analytics · Mobile Networks · Data driven

1 Introduction

According to [1], the Portuguese capital receives about 4.5 Million tourists every year. Considering that Lisbon has approximately 504 thousand residents, the city receives

A. L. Martins et al. (Eds.): INTSYS 2022, LNICST 486, pp. 3–22, 2023.
https://doi.org/10.1007/978-3-031-30855-0_1

around 9 tourists per resident, the same is to say that it receives nine times the fixed population. As a term of comparison, cities like Prague, Barcelona and London receive between 4 and 5 tourists per resident. Looking into this ratio and considering that when compared with any of the referred cities, Lisbon is much smaller, it is easy to understand that all the stakeholders need to have a deep knowledge of the behaviors and movements along the city, to provide the tourists, the best possible experience.

Considering this number of visitors, the empirical knowledge is not enough to manage and define the strategy for hotels, local accommodations, stores, restaurants, transports, museums, security and all the areas we can remember when we think about tourism. By providing to stakeholders like City Council and the entities responsible for tourism with the necessary information, we can have a very positive impact on the decision-making process, mitigating the risk of incorrect actions that can lead to an unpleasant stay in Lisbon and to the decrease of the financial income. The best ambassadors that Lisbon can have abroad are the previous visitors.

Cities are complex environments and there is a huge number of challenges that need to be addressed to provide everyone a better experience in a city like Lisbon.

Addressing these challenges assumes a decisive role, especially now that tourist activity begins to recover after the pandemic period. As of the second half of 2021, the recovery started, and in May (last data available), there was a recovery of around 162% [2], compared to the same month of 2021. Even so, we continue with a negative variation, compared to May 2019.

Considering the Big Data generated and available these days, it is perfectly unthinkable that this digital asset is not used and that is exactly what we intend with our work - use Big Data to respond to our challenges.

This work was developed in partnership with the Lisbon City Council [3], more specifically with the Lx Data Lab [4], which provided us with the data obtained through an established contract with a Mobile Operator.

Considering that it was not possible through the literature review to find the information available in previous works, with this work, we intend to create knowledge in relation to: 1) Where do the Top visitors of Lisbon come from? 2) What are the most visited areas of Lisbon? 3) Where are the Tourists during mealtimes and where they sleep?; and 4) Event Analysis. To achieve this, we apply a data science approach with CRISP-DM [17] using past data of mobile operators, where we use cellular grid areas with information about tourists' nationality (number only due to GRDP rules), and time stamps in periods of five minutes.

According to the General Secretariat for the Economy [5], the weight of Tourism on the Portuguese Gross Domestic Product is around 19%, being the 5th country in the world where the contribution of Tourism has the greatest weight. This fact is particularly relevant given the number of people that this sector employs in its various aspects, so any negative variations in this indicator have an extremely harmful influence, not only in economic terms, but also in social terms. Unfortunately, it was not possible to confirm from any source what percentage of financial income derived from Tourism is generated in Lisbon. Of course, we cannot just and only focus on the financial part, which is not always in the best interests of the "Customers", that, in our case, are the Tourists. It is important that whenever you visit Lisbon, you can be sure that you will find a safe city, properly sanitized, with a good transport network, enough accommodation and framed with the most visited places and events of interest that can properly complete all points of interest, such as monuments, gastronomy, climate and so on. We believe that from the moment we provide decision-makers with the data, they will be able to create a transport network that meets the demand of tourists, they will be able to better train police authorities and all professionals working in Tourism.

Given this scenario, it turns out to be simple to understand that the motivation to carry out this research work lies in the possibility of carrying out an academic work that can have practical applicability and with a positive impact on the economy and, consequently, on the lives of all those who depend on tourism. The main intention is to avoid mistakes in decision-making by stakeholders.

The reminder of this document demonstrates, mostly through visualizations, that it is fundamental to to better understand how do tourists "behave" in the city of Lisbon. The focus of the analysis will be on the evolution over the five months of data we have available, considering the number of people and origin, with particular attention to the most represented countries and continents. Attention will also be paid to the places where tourists spend the most time and where the largest numbers of visitors are found, where they sleep and where they are at mealtimes (for the time being, our datasets do not make it possible to specify the commercial establishments). Finally, the influence of events in Lisbon will be highlighted, in relation to volumes and origins by comparison with a baseline that will always be the same period of the previous or subsequent week, to understand how events such as the Web Summit (https://websummit.com/) or the games Football League of Champions League (https://www.uefa.com/uefachampionsleague/) change the usual panorama of Tourism in Lisbon.

2 Related Work

The high rate of use of mobile phones combined with mobility makes the data generated through the signaling exchanged between the terminal and the network a tool through which analyzes can be carried out that make it possible to identify patterns and behaviors related to mobility. According to the GSM Association [19] there were 460 million mobile subscribers in Europe in 2021, covering around 86% of the population; according to data provided by ANACOM [20], in Portugal there are around 13 million active sim cards. Therefore, this information can effectively be one of the best probes that exist for the analyses. It should also be noted that since roaming within the European Union started to have costs like those in the country of origin, people began to enjoy their mobile services much more when they are visiting another European country, which now allows them to have a sufficient volume of data and potential also to carry out research work related to tourism using this information. Therefore, the use of such a kind of data has been applied to study the way how people move in the cities.

Mariem Fekih et al. [5], 2021, explored and made use of data generated through signaling exchanged between a mobile operator in order to create Origin-Destination matrices, with the main objective of assessing whether the amount of data generated through signaling can or cannot be a reliable source of analysis of the commuting movements of individuals, proposing a system capable of transforming the data generated by the mobile network into flows that allow typifying the Origin-Destination, having these validated through inquiries made by the local authority responsible for transport. This study was conducted in Rhône in the French Alps and the data used were provided by the mobile operator Orange. Through this work, the authors showed that these data can be used to estimate the pendulum movements, having been possible to prove through the questionnaires that the conclusions are valid. It was also possible to prove that this method can be automated and that after a few days, it may be possible to typify these movements successfully, being possible to avoid the constant questionnaires. Thus, the group of researchers proved that the use of this information allows the means of transport to be optimized, benefiting users through optimizations that allow a higher quality of service.

In the article "Enhancing pedestrian mobility in Smart Cities using Big Data", Ebony Carter et al. [6], 2020, proposes the use of different datasets generated through sensors installed on the Internet of Things network of the city of Melbourne to improve accessibility and the sustainability of the Municipality. The datasets used for the study include diverse information, for example: about parking, mobility, departures and arrivals at the airport and pedestrian traffic, having been estimated that in a period of 24 hours, data of around 650 thousand people. The results and analyzes were produced through heatmaps and various graphics, which allowed interpreting and contextualizing the analyses. Through the work carried out, it was possible to characterize pedestrian movements in Melbourne, and it was proposed to City officials that they continue to develop the sensor network and Internet of Things, since it is an essential source for the continued development of knowledge. Necessary information on pedestrian movements to improve sustainability and accessibility.

Continuing the study of the work carried out using the data generated by the signaling generated by cellular networks, Claudio Badii et al. [7], 2021, developed several metrics that allow us to perceive whether a given individual is or is not in mobility and if he is in motion, how you are doing it (on foot, by bicycle or in your own or public means of motorized transport), with the objective of sending each person personalized messages that can raise awareness of issues related to sustainable mobility and healthy living habits. To achieve their goals, the authors created a multi-class classifier that proved to be more accurate than resorting to a hierarchical approach and able to handle and manage data in real time. The developed solution was implemented in Antwerp and Helsinki.

Data generated through social networks are also an important source of information for the topic of mobility and behaviors in cities, Saqib Ali Haidery et al. [8], 2020 made use of data from Weibo, a Chinese social network in the sense of analyze and typify the number and density of Weibo users in the city of Shanghai using estimation techniques with one or more variables. With this work, it was possible to use the referred data to conduct different vectors of analysis: points of concentration of people and from their location develop personalized recommendations and typify the different volumes in the 10 districts of Shanghai. From this information, it is possible to develop disaster mitigation plans as well as manage security and emergency resources.

Chiara Mizzi et al. [9], 2018, in the article "Unraveling pedestrian mobility on a road network using ICTs data during major tourist events", also used the data provided by the Italian mobile operator TIM to study the characteristics of pedestrian mobility on the road network, using the City of Venice as an example to study the impact of tourists on the lives of local citizens as well as preserving the city's cultural heritage. After having worked and transformed the data, they developed an algorithm capable of reconstructing pedestrian movements through the streets of Venice and from there, they were able to distinguish mobility patterns between tourists and locals. Additionally, it allowed stakeholders to be given important and relevant information for decision-making based on data and not on empirical knowledge.

Entering in the field of machine learning, Jaeseong Jeong et al. [10], 2021, presents a model in which people's mobility predictions are made from the traffic seen from the core side and the 5G radio. With this approach, it is possible to analyze mobility in real time and with data being generated in real time. The contribution of this work focused on the concept of NWDAF (Network data analytics function), having proposed an approach a predictive model capable of adapting the 5G network to each user and their needs, allowing to give the user a better experience regarding internet connection speeds and the reduction of latencies.

Continuing the study of the state of the art, the work developed by PENGZHAN GUO et al. [11], 2021 is also relevant, who in their article "Route Optimization via Environment-Aware Deep Network and Reinforcement Learning" studied and developed an adaptive system that allows optimizing taxi services, proposing a deep learning system capable of optimizing routes on which these vehicles provide service, identifying the "optimal path", especially in abnormal cases and unexpected situations. For this case study, the researchers used data from "yellow taxis" circulating in New York City in the pre- and post-Covid period. The model created was able to detect anomalous events such as unexpected concentrations of people and, from there, adapt its recommendations on the best route to follow between two points, having been able to increase the weekly profitability of the vehicles by 98%.

Martin ŠAUER et al. [12], 2021, developed knowledge about the intra-regional flow of tourists in Central Europe and its implications, having listed that understanding and typifying these movements is essential for strategic planning and sustainable development, particularly at the level of the most visited cities. In carrying out this work, data provided by entities responsible for tourism in various cities in Germany, Austria and the Czech Republic were used and from these data it was possible to conclude that the factors that most influence the distribution of tourists are: air connections, the attractiveness of the chosen destination and the size of the tourism market in the place where visitors come from, given that, as in the case of Lisbon, the Germans are the ones who most influence tourism.

Continuing with the study of work done in relation to mobility, Xin Lao et al. [13], 2021, in the article entitled "Comparing Intercity Mobility Patterns among Different Holidays in China: a Big Data Analysis" made use of data provided by Tencent, a Chinese Internet-related service company to model mobility patterns between Chinese cities on holidays, identifying the differences between different more traditional festive seasons such as Spring Festival, Tomb-sweeping Day, Dragon Boat Festival, and Mid-Autumn Festival and the less traditional ones in China, like Christmas and New Year's Eve. Through the work carried out in this article, they were able to prove that: a) movements are different depending on the type of holidays, b) the cities of Pearl River Delta and

Xi'an are those from which more people leave for their hometowns during the traditional festive periods and c) during less traditional holidays, travel is mainly for recreational reasons, unlike traditional holidays where people travel mainly for cultural and traditional reasons.

Xin Li et al., 2018 [14], through the article entitled "Position prediction system based on spacial-temporal regularity of object mobility" proposed the creation of a system that makes predictions regarding the mobility of a given object, using historical data of the referred object that could be any type of "connected device" with GPS, from a mobile phone, to a car or any type of wearable - from the past data, the proposed model is able to predict which will be the next positions occupied by the referred object, and each possible position to be occupied in space is classified according to a score calculated on historical data, with the one with the highest classification being displayed. It should be noted that when evaluating the accuracy of the model proposed by Xin Li et al., it obtained accuracy rates 44% higher than those obtained with an algorithm based on Markov time series, thus proving the capacity of its model for predictions.

In the article entitled "The path of least resistance explaining tourist mobility patterns in destination areas using Airbnb data", Umut Turk et al. [15], 2021, resorted to data provided by the Airbnb local accommodation platform to identify which are the 25 most attractive tourist destinations the world, having as motivation to do so the fact that a lack of knowledge on the topic was identified. Initially, an assessment was made of the quality of Airbnb's offer and prices in each of the locations and subsequently the prices and quality of the transport network were evaluated in each of the locations studied. The authors confirmed that the asking price for local accommodation is directly related to its geographic location and the quality of public transport to the places of interest in each city that one of the reasons that most weigh in choosing accommodation is the proximity to good transport, especially in cities like Berlin and Frankfurt (Table 1).

Table 1. Keywords definition

	Number of documents		
Concept	453106	3156	44
Data Analysis			
Behavio#r Analysis			
Population	220301		
smart cities			
cellular network			
Touris*			
Roaming			
Context	642769		
Mobility			
Limitations			

(continued)

Table 1. (*continued*)

	Number of documents	
Period: 2018 - 2022		
Only Journal papers, articles and reviews		

This is demonstrated by the 44 documents returned by the query (Concept AND Population AND Context AND Limitations) when we use the keywords from each column.

After completing a manual approach to identify the key subjects for their research questions and specify the outcomes, 16 publications were identified. Our study's systematization considered the year, the region, the RQ subject, and a succinct description. The 16 studies that were reviewed were selected based on the standards. The trend line in Fig. 1 reveals that the subject we're looking at is becoming more and more popular, underscoring its significance.

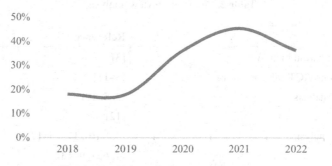

Fig. 1. Evolution of relevant studies per year

Given that the goal of this study is to identify how tourist behavior analysis and tourism mobility are used in smart cities, Table 2 and Fig. 2 provide theoretical explanations of the topics mentioned in each of the papers that were evaluated, with a focus on the use of mobile phones and tourist behavior analysis when using mobile devices. Figure 2 demonstrates how most studies examined how people used mobile phones and other ICT infrastructure and their behavior (ICT). Our research is based on both ideas since we not only analyze human behavior utilizing Lisbon's communication infrastructure as an operator, but also grasp it and develop a plan to satisfy their needs.

Table 2 provides a summary of a more thorough analysis of this review. The problems were plainly stated; therefore, it was unnecessary to ask the publications' authors for clarification. Since the studies' results were categorized based on their inclusion or exclusion in the research, they are not mutually exclusive.

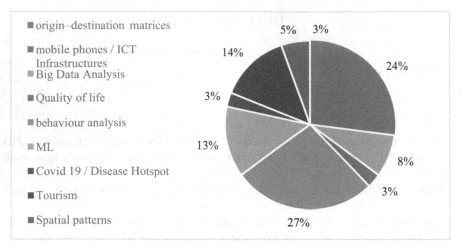

Fig. 2. Relative weight by document subject

Table 2. Summary review analysis

Topic	Reference
(1) origin–destination matrices	[3]
(2) mobile phones/ICT Infrastructures	[3–11]
(3) Big Data Analysis	[3, 5, 10]
(4) Quality of life	[12]
(5) behaviour analysis	[4, 8, 10, 11, 13–17]
(6) ML	[4, 6, 7, 9, 13]
(7) Covid 19/Disease Hotspot	[13]
(8) Tourism	[11, 13]– [15, 17]
(9) Spatial patterns	[14, 15]

3 Knowledge Extraction Approach

CRISP DM stands for Cross Industry Standard Process for Data Mining [19]. The goal of CRISP DM is providing us with a structured way of planning and executing a data mining project, ensuring that the best insights are retrieved from the available data. During the present work we followed this methodology as it has proven to lead to a more efficient data mining. Given the relevant data and our primary objectives, we chose a modified version of this methodology for our project that consists of 3 phases, due the need of visual dashboards for decision makers: 1) Business understanding; 2) Data understanding 3) Data preparation and 4) Visualization

3.1 Business Understanding

In this first stage, the emphasis is on comprehending the project's requirements and goals from a business standpoint. Using this knowledge, a data mining issue definition and a rough project schedule are then created to meet the goals.

Understanding the project's goals and requirements is the focus of the business understanding phase and it is divided in 4 sub-tasks. Except for the third task, the remaining three tasks in this phase are fundamental project management procedures that apply to most projects:

a) Define business objectives
b) Assess situation
c) Define data mining goals
d) Create a project plan

In our specific case, and considering that we have no knowledge regarding the tourism business, in addition to what is common sense, we mostly resort to the help of the Lisbon city Council and the LX Data Lab. This was the way found to ensure that we were able to obtain enough knowledge to allow us to interpret the data and the results obtained, this would not be possible without knowing the business or, at least, the analyzes would be more superficial and eventually with less added value.

3.2 Data Understanding

The data made available by Lisbon city Council (Câmara Municipal de Lisboa) is supplied under an agreement with a mobile operator and is generated using the information provided by the cellular network and the mobile devices of each user. The information contained in the dataset is duly anonymized for legal and privacy reasons. In this way, it is not possible in any way to make any specific analysis of a particular user. There is not even any key that relates a given user to an event, and it is only possible to carry out analyzes involving volumes.

All the data available is aggregated in 3743 grids of 200 × 200 meters, being collected in periods of 5 minutes. Due to privacy constraints, if a certain grid doesn't have at least 10 users in the 5 minutes frame, it won't be reported. Data is made available on the big data platform, for a period of about 45 minutes after being collected. This means that we can have a maximum of 1 hour delay between the collection and the availability of the data. However, it is important to say that for the scope of the present work, we will use a snapshot of the data and, therefore, we will not be leverage of the online data stream. Although we won't be using them all in our project, Table 3 presents the 24 indicators/dimensions available in the data provided by the Mobile Operator.

In addition to the dataset that contains the data provided by the city Council through the agreement established with Mobile Operator, a dataset that contains information related to each of the 3743 grids was also used. These are the data that allow us to geo-reference the main dataset since it contains the coordinates of the centroid of each grid, the parish, or parishes in which the grid is inserted, the name, the geometry and the WKT. With this information and using the "Grid_ID" key, it becomes possible to

Table 3. Mobile operator dataset variables

ID	Name	Description	Type
0	Grid_ID	Number of the grid There are 3743 squares of 200 by 200 m to cover the metropolitan area of Lisbon	Nominal
1	Datetime	Time and date of occurrence	Datetime
2	C1	Number of distinct terminals counted on each grid cell during the 5-min period – Measured every 5 min	Metric
3	C2	Number of distinct terminals in roaming counted on each grid cell during the 5-min period– Measured every 5 min	Metric
4	C3	No. of distinct terminals that remained in the grid cell counted at the end of each 5-min period	Metric
5	C4	No. of distinct terminals in roaming that remained in the grid cell counted at the end of each 5-min period	Metric
6	C5	No. of distinct terminals entering the grid	Metric
7	C6	Terminals leaving the grid – These are the distinct terminals that left the grid. The calculation is made using the previous 5-min interval as reference, also considering the crossings of the grid in the same interval	Metric
8	C7	Number of entries of distinct terminals, in roaming, in the grid	Metric
9	C8	Number of exits of distinct terminals, in roaming, in the grid	Metric
10	C9	Total no. of distinct terminals with active data connection in the grid cell – Measurement every 5 min	Metric
11	C10	Total no. of distinct terminals, in roaming, with active data connection in the grid cell – Measurement every 5 min	Metric
12	C11	No. of voices calls originating from the grid cell	Metric
13	C12	Entering the city: No. of devices that for 5 min enter the 11 street sections considered for analysis. For this purpose, a section of track is a route with	Metric
14	C13	Entering the city: No. of devices that for 5 min enter the 11 street sections considered for analysis. For this purpose, a section of track is a route with	Metric
15	D1	Top 10 origin Countries of the devices in Roaming	Metric
16	E1	Number of voice calls that ended in the grid within the 5-min	Metric
17	E2	Average download speed per grid within the 5-min	Metric
18	E3	Average load speed per grid within the 5-min	Metric
19	E4	Peak download speed on the grid within the 5-min	Metric
20	E5	Peak upload speed on the grid within the 5-min	Metric
21	E6	Top 10 apps used on the grid within the 5-min	Metric

(*continued*)

Table 3. (*continued*)

ID	Name	Description	Type
22	E7	Lowest permanence period on the grid within the 5-min	Metric
23	E8	Average permanence on the grid within the 5-min	Metric
24	E9	Maximum permanence period on the grid within the 5-min	Metric
25	E10	Count of devices sharing the internet connection in the grid within the 5-min	Metric

insert the events in the space and, from there, trigger our analyses, after collecting the data for our study, we carefully examined it and investigated each variable to understand its potential and how we could increase the added value of this research. As previously mentioned, our key objective is to comprehend how tourists move around. To do so, the Lisbon city Council provided us with a dataset about people's movement in the city of Lisbon (both roaming and non-roaming), based on mobile phone data produced. The mobile operator extrapolated the data to create the currently accessible dataset to provide a more accurate depiction of the mobility of all individuals who moved around Lisbon between September 2021 and January 2022.

3.3 Data Preparation

This process was oriented to the dashboard visualization of geographic and temporal data to obtain a clear image that would be able to help us understand the data and address the questions we set out to answer. In the course of our work, we realized that the result would be as rich as the more information we were able to provide to stakeholders

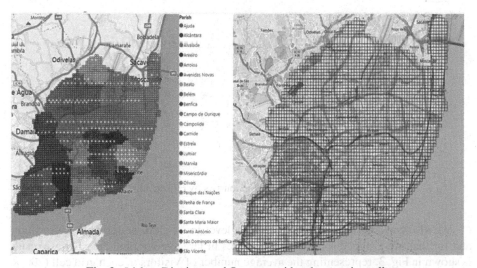

Fig. 3. Lisbon Districts, and Operator grid and respective cells

4 Insights and Visualizations

Once the data had been worked on and prepared, it was time to start creating the graphics and visualizations that effectively allow us to respond to the questions we set ourselves. Therefore, in this section, we will continue our analysis. For this phase, two "high-level" tools were used, namely, Microsoft Power BI (https://en.wikipedia.org/wiki/Microsoft_Power_BI) and Microsoft Excel (https://en.wikipedia.org/wiki/Microsoft_Excel). The latter, not being exactly a massive data analysis tool, with due work, allowed us to obtain interesting results.

At this stage, we portrayed the data graphically to make it easier to focus on the most crucial information and quickly identify trends and patterns in the tourist population's mobility. We can study and discover more about data using graphs and charts.

4.1 Where Do the Top Visitors of Lisbon Come from?

Bearing in mind that our work focuses on tourists in the city of Lisbon and their habits, it makes perfect sense that we start exactly by typifying their origins, whether from the country or from the Continent/Geographical Area where they come from. In Fig. 2, representing the average number of Visitors in each 200 × 200 meters cell from the grid, it is visible that the top six of the origin of the Tourists in the 5 months of analyzed data, are the same, although the rankings change between the months. According to available data, the largest number of visitors to Lisbon come from Germany, Spain, France, Italy, the United Kingdom, and Brazil. The analyzed month with more visitors was November, eventually due to Web Summit.

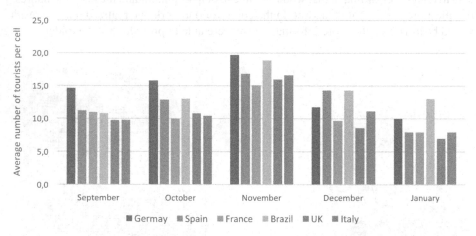

Fig. 4. Top six Lisbon tourists by citizenship

We also consider it important to go up a level in terms of geographic aggregation and for that, we grouped some of the countries in large geographic areas whose result is shown in Fig. 3, representing the average number of Visitors in each grid cell (200 × 200 meters). Through this visualization, we can see that the most represented areas of

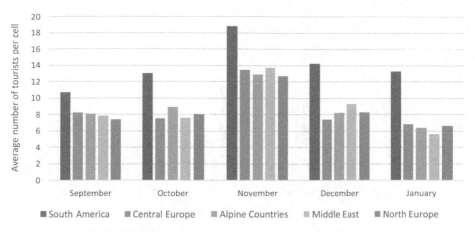

Fig. 5. Evolution of Lisbon tourists by geographic area

touristic origin are South America, Europe (South/North/Center), the Alpine Countries and the Middle East. This information is supported by the per Country analysis performed before. Once again, we can see that November was the month with more Tourists, most probably because of the *Web Summit*.

4.2 What Are the Most Visited Areas of Lisbon?

As previously mentioned, we grouped the parishes of Lisbon and our first analysis of the most visited areas of the city falls precisely on this grouping. Not surprisingly, the areas most visited by tourists are the Historic Center and the City Center of Lisbon (Fig. 4), representing the average number of Visitors in each of the 200 × 200 meters grids. Even so, it is interesting to check the average number of visitors in each of the grids and their evolution over the months.

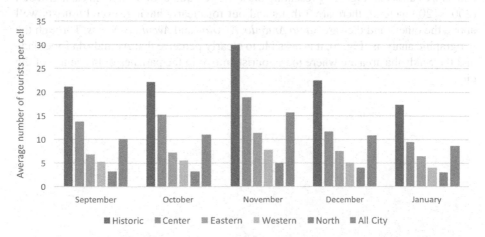

Fig. 6. Evolution of Lisbon Tourists by Month and City Area

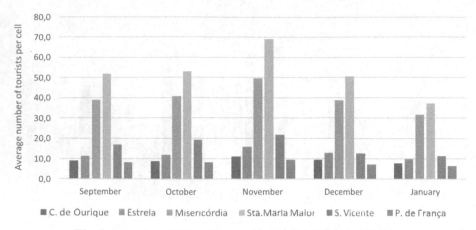

Fig. 7. Evolution of Lisbon Tourists by Month in Historical Parishes

According to the available data and through Fig. 5 and focusing on parishes in the Historic Center of Lisbon that receive the most foreign visitors we can see that *Santa Maria Maior* and *Misericórdia* are by far the most visited ones. This insight is consistent with the fact that it is in these parishes that very emblematic monuments of the city are located.

Through a georeferenced analysis, using the centroids included in the dataset of the mobile operator, we were able to understand the exact locations in the parishes of the historic center of Lisbon where Tourists travel the most. In Fig. 6, it is possible to see highlight in Castelo, *Alfama, Baixa Pombalina* and *São Vicente de Fora*. These visualizations provide useful insights to decision-makers detailed information at street and hourly level.

Continuing with the analysis of the Parishes most visited by Tourists in Lisbon, it is still very important to characterize those belonging to the City Centre. Among the 6, and as we can see in Fig. 7, representing the average number of Visitors in each grid cell (200 × 200 meters), there are 3 that stand out for clearly having several tourists well above the others and they are *Santo António, Arroios* and *Avenidas Novas*. Through the geographic analysis (Fig. 8), it is possible to clearly perceive that Avenida da Liberdade and the Saldanha area are where more tourists move in the parishes of the center of the city.

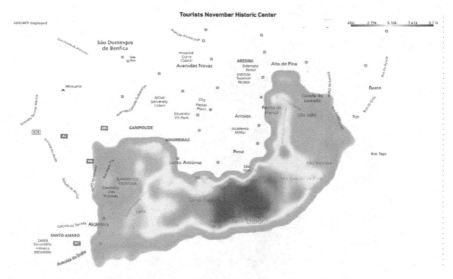

Fig. 8. Heatmap of Lisbon Tourists in Historical Parishes (November)

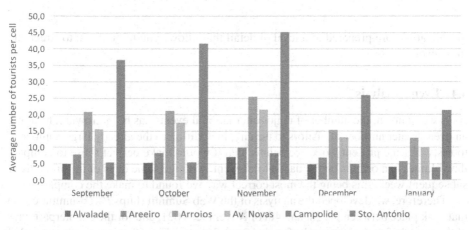

Fig. 9. Evolution of Lisbon Tourists by Month in City Center Parishes

4.3 Where Are the Tourists During the Mealtimes and Where Do They Sleep?

Using the centroids present in the dataset of the mobile operator again and applying a time filter to the data, considering that the lunch period is between 12am and 2.30pm and dinner is between 7.30pm and 10pm, we created the visualization in Power BI below (Fig. 9) which shows the concentration of tourists in the afore mentioned periods. Carrying out the exercise for the month of September, even though the data are prepared to do so for any of the months, we can see that, with the exception of the West zone of Lisbon (Belém/Alcântara), visitors have lunch and dinner in the same places in the city, which ends up making sense since it does not make much sense for them to travel to have their meals, unless the restaurant it is also a point of interest. Again, the data and

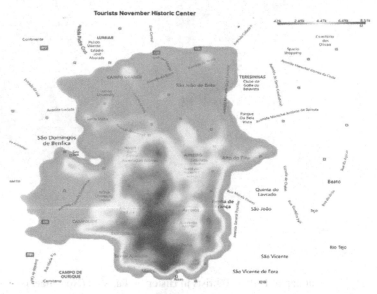

Fig. 10. Heatmap of Lisbon Tourists in City Center Parishes (November)

visualizations are prepared to a level of detail that allows you to go down to street and time level.

4.4 Event Analysis

As is well known, the number of major international events has been growing, bringing an even greater number of visitors to the city, in addition to the already large number of tourists. For the present work, we believe that it would make perfect sense to compare the volumes and origins on the days of the event, with the same days of the previous or subsequent week, this being the most correct way we found to make the comparison.

Therefore, we developed the analysis of the Web Summit (https://websummit.com/) that took place between the 1st and 4th of November 2021, and for the counterpart days of the week before and the week after the event. Through Fig. 10, it is possible to see that on the days of the event, tourists were mostly concentrated in the Lisbon International Fair (https://www.fil.pt/) while on the same days of the counterpart weeks were more spread out above by the points of interest of the Parish, namely in the Oceanário. It is also possible to see that the number of Tourists on the days of the event almost tripled compared to the same period last year. It is also possible to verify that, in percentage terms, the geographic areas of origin of the visitors are also quite different. During the Web Summit week about 21% of the Tourists were from South America while in the previous and following were from the Eastern Europe.

Additionally, we also analyze the influence of a sporting event, in this case a Champions League football match held on October 20th - Benfica - Bayern. For this case, we only use visitors from Germany, as Bayern Munich is a German Club. For this analysis, we applied a time filter between 07pm and 10pm, in the parishes of Benfica, Carnide and São Domingos de Benfica. On Fig. 11, it is noticeable that, compared to the same day and time of the previous and the after week, the number of Germans in the analyzed parishes grew almost 20 times and that their concentration was almost exclusively in the centroids of Estádio da Luz. The fact that there is a much higher than usual volume of German tourists in the area surrounding the stadium on the day of a Champions League game against a German team, does not represent anything new, being exactly what would be expected from find in this analysis. The exercise intends to demonstrate the capability of a tool like the one that was developed to help quickly and in real time take on events that may require, for example, the intervention of security forces (Figs. 12 and 13).

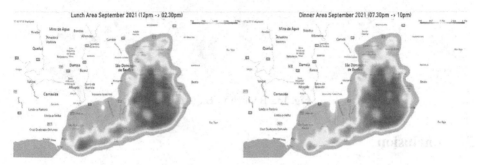

Fig. 11. Heatmap of Lisbon Tourists at Lunch and Dinner Time (September)

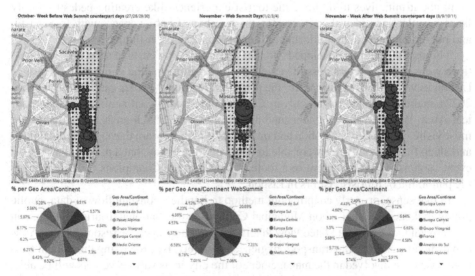

Fig. 12. Web Summit Analysis

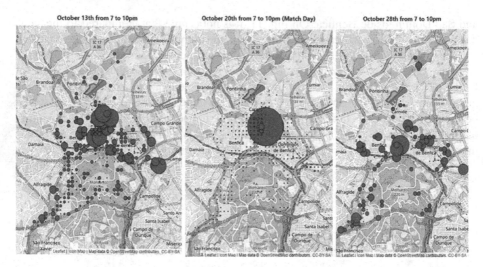

Fig. 13. Benfica vs Bayern

5 Conclusions

It is essential for public policy to comprehend the spatial spread of urban tourism. As a result, in areas where there is a high concentration of tourists, local authorities might think about initiatives to improve the tourist experience, like creating pedestrian-only lanes or enlarging sidewalks, increasing the number of public spaces with free Wi-Fi, and positioning new tourist information centres, among other things.

Through the method developed and the tools used, we were able to answer the questions we wanted to. It was possible to identify the origin, and the number of Tourists in Lisbon as well as the evolution over the period under study (September 2021 to January 2022), making a separation not only by Country but also by Continent/Large Geographical Area. We were able to understand and demonstrate which areas and parishes are most visited in the City of Lisbon and the places where they are during the typical meal and sleep times. Finally, we were able to understand in a way that a major international event such as the Web Summit or a football match in the Champions League changes the panorama of tourists/visitors in Lisbon.

In that sense, properly adapting our method to handle a constant flow of data, public policy makers, like the Lisbon Municipal Council or the National Tourists Office, can take advantage of an aggregated view that in real time manages the resources of various departments ranging from transport, hygiene, and safety. By processing this data in real-time, everyone involved in the management of the city in its various vectors will be able, on the one hand, to provide a much more pleasant experience for visitors, but also to avoid security breaches and any type of unwanted events Additionally, our work can encompass an analysis tool based on real data that allows, in the medium and long term, to plan accommodation and commerce.

It is also important to mention that with the available data, we can have much more insights than the ones we refer to in this work. However, due to scope limitations, we have chosen the one that seems to have the best fit. The developed tool was designed with the possibility of using a series of filters that allows the Lisbon City Council to make its own analysis on topics that were not explored in this dissertation, making more final analysis both from a temporal and geographical point of view. If users deem it necessary, they can still use the solution developed to load new data, if they follow the same structure, making it possible to use it in analyses with new information coming from the same source.

To process an amount of data of this order to obtain real value for the benefit not only of Tourism, but of all those who travel through Lisbon for work or leisure, it is essential that there is a large computational and analytical capacity. For the first case, there should be recourse to cloud technology, which, as is well known, although with high costs, allows processing large amounts of information, without delay and without the need to install local capacity. From an analytical point of view, it makes sense to develop machine learning mechanisms, capable of highlighting patterns and helping data analysis, providing decision-makers with automated reports and dashboards to support decision making.

References

1. LISBONEIDEE Homepage. http://www.lisbonne-idee.pt/p5358-lisboa-recebe-mais-turistas-poresidente-que-londres.html. Accessed 23 July 2022
2. Câmara Municipal de Lisboa Homepage. https://www.lisboa.pt/. Accessed 23 July 2022
3. LxDataLab Homepage. https://lisboainteligente.cm-lisboa.pt/. Accessed 23 July 2022
4. Secretaria Geral da Economia Homepage. https://www.sgeconomia.gov.pt/noticias/portugal-e-o-5-pais-com-mais-forte-contributo-do-turismo-para-o-pib.aspx. Accessed 24 July 2022
5. Fekih, M., Bellemans, T., Smoreda, Z., Bonnel, P., Furno, A., Galland, S.: A data-driven approach for origin–destination matrix construction from cellular network signalling data: a case study of Lyon region (France). Transportation **48**(4), 1671–1702 (2020). https://doi.org/10.1007/s11116-020-10108-w
6. Carter, E., Adam, P., Tsakis, D., Shaw, S., Watson, R., Ryan, P.: Enhancing pedestrian mobility in smart cities using big data. J. Manag. Anal. **7**(2), 173–188 (2020). https://doi.org/10.1080/23270012.2020.1741039
7. Badii, C., Difino, A., Nesi, P., Paoli, I., Paolucci, M.: Classification of users' transportation modalities from mobiles in real operating conditions. Multimed. Tools Appl. **81**(1), 115–140 (2021). https://doi.org/10.1007/s11042-021-10993-y
8. Haidery, S.A., Ullah, H., Ullah Khan, N., Fatima, K., Shahla Rizvi, S., Kwon, S.J.: Role of big data in the development of smart city by analyzing the density of residents in Shanghai. Electron. Switz. **9**(5) (2020). https://doi.org/10.3390/electronics9050837
9. Mizzi, C., et al.: Unraveling pedestrian mobility on a road network using ICTs data during great tourist events. EPJ Data Science **7**(1), 1–21 (2018). https://doi.org/10.1140/epjds/s13688-018-0168-2
10. Jeong, J., et al.: Mobility prediction for 5G core networks. IEEE Commun. Stand. Mag. **5**(1), 56–61 (2021). https://doi.org/10.1109/MCOMSTD.001.2000046
11. Guo, P., Xiao, K., Ye, Z., Zhu, W.: Route optimization via environment-aware deep network and reinforcement learning. ACM Trans. Intell. Syst. Technol. **12**(6) (2021). https://doi.org/10.1145/3461645
12. Šauer, M., Vystoupil, J., Novotná, M., Widawski, K.: Central European tourist flows: intraregional patterns and their implications. Morav. Geogr. Rep. **29**(4), 278–291 (2021). https://doi.org/10.2478/mgr-2021-0020

13. Lao, X., Deng, X., Gu, H., Yang, J., Yu, H., Xu, Z.: Comparing intercity mobility patterns among different holidays in china: a big data analysis. Appl. Spat. Anal. Policy (2022). https://doi.org/10.1007/s12061-021-09433-z
14. Li, X., et al.: Position prediction system based on spatio-temporal regularity of object mobility. Inf. Syst. **75**, 43–55 (2018). https://doi.org/10.1016/j.is.2018.02.004
15. Türk, U., Östh, J., Kourtit, K., Nijkamp, P.: The path of least resistance explaining tourist mobility patterns in destination areas using Airbnb data. J. Transp. Geogr. **94** (2021). https://doi.org/10.1016/j.jtrangeo.2021.103130
16. Data Science Process Alliance. https://www.datascience-pm.com/crisp-dm-2. Accessed 24 July 2022
17. GSM Association Homepage. https://www.gsma.com/mobileeconomy/europe/. Accessed 20 Dec 2022
18. ANACOM Homepage. https://www.anacom.pt/streaming/ServicosMoveis1T22.pdf?contentId=1722575&field=ATTACHED_FILE. Accessed 20 Dec 2022

Data Driven Spatiotemporal Analysis of e-Cargo Bike Network in Lisbon and Its Expansion: The Yoob Case Study

Bruno Gil[1], Vitória Albuquerque[2] (iD), Miguel Sales Dias[1]([✉]) (iD), Rui Abranches[3], and Manuel Ogando[3]

[1] Instituto Universitário de Lisboa (ISCTE-IUL), ISTAR, 1649-026 Lisbon, Portugal
{bruno_alexandre_gil,miguel.dias}@iscte-iul.pt
[2] NOVA Information Management School (NOVA IMS), Universidade Nova de Lisboa, Campus de Campolide, 1070-312 Lisbon, Portugal
[3] Yoob, Estr. de Telheiras 159 Z, 1600-769 Lisbon, Portugal

Abstract. The adoption of more environmentally friendly and sustainable fleets for last-mile parcel delivery within large urban centers, such as e-cargo bikes, has gained the interest of the community. The logistics infrastructure network, had to adapt to the requirements of this new type of fleet, and micro-hubs and nano-hubs emerged. In this paper we tackle spatiotemporal characterization of e-cargo bike fleet behavior, by conducting a data centered case study where we explore data from Yoob, a last mile delivery e-cargo bike logistics startup that operates in the Lisbon area and outskirts. We also address the identification of potential expansion locations to the establishment of new hubs. Our data was collected during a 4-month period (January to April 2022). By adopting state-of-the-art data science and machine learning techniques, and following the CRIPS-DM data mining method, our innovative approach discovered five clusters that are able to characterize the Yoob fleet, with variations in distances traveled, times, transported volumes and speeds. In the perspective of expanding Yoob's e-cargo bike network, three new locations in Lisbon were signaled for potential new hub installation. To the authors knowledge this is the first study of this kind carried in Portugal, bringing new insights in the field of last mile logistics.

Keywords: e-cargo bikes · micro-hub · K-Means · last-mile logistics

1 Introduction

The impact of urban logistics and logistics networks in urban mobility of the large cities are increasingly discussed by policy makers and logistics operators [1]. These last ones, along with service providers are beginning to introduce more environmentally friendly vehicles into their fleets. E-cargo bikes are one of the most widely implemented electric powered vehicles for deliveries within urban centers [2].

This study of based on data generated by e-cargo bike urban logistic operator, allows us to understand and find patterns and dynamics in the functioning of E-cargo bikes in urban centers, taking the example of the Lisbon case study.

© ICST Institute for Computer Sciences, Social Informatics and Telecommunications Engineering 2023
Published by Springer Nature Switzerland AG 2023. All Rights Reserved
A. L. Martins et al. (Eds.): INTSYS 2022, LNICST 486, pp. 23–39, 2023.
https://doi.org/10.1007/978-3-031-30855-0_2

1.1 Motivation and Topic Relevance

Performing last mile delivery with less impact on urban mobility in a sustainable and ecological way is the main goal of Yoob. This startup is a delivery logistics company operating in Lisbon's urban center, and it is the first of its kind operating in the city, and in Portugal. Operations started in the fall of 2021. At the time of this article writing, Yoob has a fleet of ten e-cargo bikes and two e-vans supported by five logistic hubs spread (referred to as micro and/or nano-hubs) throughout the city, including the city center. With the growth of their operations in the city, the need arose to get more insights on the behavior patterns of Yoob's e-cargo bike fleet. This data centered study provides insights for better strategic decisions for Yoob's future logistic operations and expansion of its network.

1.2 Research Questions and Objectives

This study aims to analyze and visualize the behavior patterns of e-cargo bike fleet based on anonymized real time data of a logistics company, collected in Lisbon from January 2022 to April 2022. It also intends, based on collected data, to evaluate the optimal sites for the new hubs locations to expand the e-cargo bike delivery area in Lisbon. Therefore, the following research questions are addressed by our research:

RQ1: How can we characterize the spatiotemporal traffic of the last mile logistic distribution performed with the e-cargo bike fleet, taking into consideration open data of the city and data collected during the performed routes?
RQ2: Based on the fleet behavior and the patterns detected, what are the best possible locations for the micro-hubs or nano-hubs expansion?

1.3 Structure

This paper is organized into four sections. In Sect. 1, we introduce the topic context, motivation and relevance, and we raise our research questions and objectives. In Sect. 2, we present a literature review by using the Preferred Reporting Items for Systematic Reviews and Meta-Analyses (PRISMA) methodology [3]. In Sect. 3, we apply the CRoss Industry Standard Process for Data Mining (CRISP-DM) [4] methodology to our case study, presenting the results of each phase. Finally, in Sect. 4, we present and discuss our conclusions, limitations, and future work.

2 Literature Review

2.1 Methodology

PRISMA [3] is a standard methodology for generating systematic and objective findings from literature reviews. It is an approach that assisted us in describing literature findings, as well as to contribute to our goals.

2.2 Results

To kick start PRISMA in our systematic literature review (SLR), we run the following logical query on academic data repositories: ("e-cargo bikes" OR "electric-assist cargo bicycles") OR ("micro-consolidation hubs" OR "hub location") OR ("Last mile logistic" OR "urban logistic") OR ("spatial patterns" AND "data mining"). 34 articles met the eligible requirements.

Analyzed literature methods applied strong emphasis on visualization, with focus on study and detection of transportation traffic patterns [10–19]. K-means [10, 11, 20] was used to perform clustering analysis regarding travel activity for taxis and bikes and to find the places that gave rise to shorter travel distances. DBSCAN was implemented to found travel paths made by users of public transportations [12] and to study private car trajectories in the city [15]. In the decision taking for hub location, the two principal algorithms implemented were Genetic Algorithm [2, 21] and PROMETHEE [20, 22].

Moreover, we found that the study of e-cargo bikes is still very limited and focused on the scope of environmental impact and benefit of cargo bike usage. Very few papers analyzed the behavior and performance patterns of last mile delivery of e-cargo bikes in urban centers. The importance of using spatiotemporal analysis in comparison to traditional data mining approaches that consider instances to be "distributed equally and independently", is due to the possibility to find existing links between the various instances of available data in space and time [23]. Ignoring these connections can lead to misinterpretation and results that are difficult to understand [18, 23].

We observe homogeneity in the applied spatiotemporal methods. The clustering technique for pattern detection was the most present in our SLR. Zeng et al. [14] characterized the taxi travel patterns of Chongqing residents from two perspectives, hot spots and hot paths, by applying the GRIDBSCAN and ST-TCLUS (Spatial-temporal trajectory clustering) clustering algorithms. It allowed to conclude that depending on the time of day, these areas varied according to their land use. Y. Huang et al. [15] studied the travel patterns of private cars to identify the most frequented sites using the Density-Based Spatial Clustering of Applications with Noise (DBSCAN) algorithm and Markov chains, allowed them to identify that 59% of car trips exhibit regular spatiotemporal mobility and repeated travel patterns. By applying the ST-HDBSCAN clustering algorithm (combination of ST-DBSCAN and HDBSCAN clustering algorithms) Li et al. [18] made a spatiotemporal characterization of the hotspot characteristics, through the study of "Spatiotemporal Distribution", "Travel Distance Distribution" and "Travel Direction Distribution", concluding that the most frequented areas are the ones where there is a higher density of points of interest. Toro et al. [10] studied the mobility patterns of users of Milan's bike sharing systems and using the clustering technique with K-Means, allowed him to identify which stations have the same usage pattern. In the exploitation of the most frequent paths made in the Singapore Strait Ron, Wen et al. [16] applied the K-nearest neighbors' algorithm, to perform clustering on time series of waterways, which allowed them to identify the most congested areas spatially and temporally. Atluri et al. [23] state that, in exploring problems with spatiotemporal data, finding the similarities or dissimilarities between instances is the key to solving most challenges. In the collected studies, the evaluation of the performance of cargo bikes is highly focused on comparing with the performance of the cargo vans in the last mile delivery [17, 24–26].

Cargo bikes showed a greater flexibility and advantage in the routes they made. Most of the time the chosen bike route is shorter than the route made by vans [24]. This difference can be up to twice as large on shorter trips [17]. Also, it was found that cargo bike riders easily break traffic regulations by riding in the opposite direction during short trips [24]. Amaral et al. [17] identified that travel times were not as important for cargo bikes as for motor vehicles, because bicycles can easily "outrun" traffic jams. An interesting observation by Conway et al. [24], showed that the speed of cargo bikes on the bike paths is lower than when on the road for motor vehicles, with a speed figure lower than 20% on some of the routes. The impact of street topography was mentioned in Amaral et al. [17] who defined a scale between the elevation and the impact on cyclist performance. This scale sets as a reference, below 2%, with no effect, between 2% and less than 5%, already considered with impact and above 5%, representing a substantial impact. The speed considered in the studies was not homogeneous, varying between 11.6 km/h [24] and 24.0 km/h [25]. A literature review done by Büttgen et al. [7] finds an average speed of this type of vehicles between 8.0 km/h and 25.0 km/h.

Overall, all studies conclude that cargo bikes represent a more viable and advantageous alternative in last mile delivery, with greater gains in more congested areas [24], but with some constraints. Sheth et al. [25] concluded that the distance and the number of deliveries, are the most impacting factors on viability and cannot exceed 3.2 km and 20 orders per stop. In Amaral et al. [17], the capacity of the vehicle was not considered, but authors concluded that beyond 3.0 km, it was no longer efficient to deliver with this type of vehicle. The combination of cargo bikes and the implementation of micro hubs has helped the green alternatives for last mile delivery, to gain momentum [9]. Distribution networks with micro-hubs do promote a more organized last mile delivery [8] and benefit from economies of scale [27].

The definition of micro hub in the literature is vast, and for our paper we adopted the definition by Katsela et al. [8], which defined it as "logistics facilities where commercial transportation providers (or "carriers") consolidate goods near the final delivery point and serve a limited spatial delivery area in a dense urban environment". Finding and defining a location for micro-hubs is an important and complex task [2, 8]. The rising costs of urban land, lack of adequate infrastructure, changing demand, changing city characteristics [22] and regulatory requirements [8], do not ease the task of being able to find an optimal solution that minimizes operating costs and impact on communities. The most common characteristics addressed in the literature to study this problem were demand (e.g., residential, commercial, and/or employment density), infrastructure (e.g., pedestrian/bicycle infrastructure provision, road classifications, pedestrian zones, and measures to assess traffic), and land use constraints [6, 22, 28]. When the deliveries are made by cargo bikes, the location of the micro-hub should be the closest to the delivery point [22, 29]. Assman et al. [9] recommended locating them in areas of higher commercial density. This need for proximity comes from the capacity limitation of bikes compared to a delivery van, and multiple trips to the micro-hub may be required, so travel time and travel distances are minimized [8]. According to Assman et al. [9], the maximum distance between the micro-hub and the delivery point should not exceed 1000 m. In Rudolph et al. [22] a distance between 500 m and 1200 m is pointed out as the distance range that allows economic feasibility for deliveries made by cargo bikes.

In Faugère et al. [5] and Srivatsa Srinivas et al. [30], the implementation of this type of infrastructure in mobile units was evaluated and, in both studies, they concluded that it can be a viable alternative but under very restricted conditions. Faugère et al. [5] indicated as a condition, the requirement to transport a high volume of orders and a very short maximum transit travel time. In Srivatsa Srinivas et al. [30] the need for a strong analytical engine that can accurately predict demand for a given geographic location and the dynamic optimization of the route and parking location of the mobile warehouse, was the only way to make this alternative viable. The study of stationary micro-hubs is the most widely covered in the literature, but the methods vary among literature papers. When the targets' location points are already known [2, 7, 31, 32], only an evaluation of the performance of each of the locations was done to find the one that best suited the purpose. Naumov et al. [2] developed a mathematical model representative of the network and its behavior and by applying Monte Carlos simulation, evaluated which of the five pre-defined locations allowed minimizing the transportation work. In Kedia et al. [32], the Location-Allocation model, was used to find the locations that minimized the distance that had to be traveled. Bütten et al. [7] uses the Two-Echelon Vehicle Routing Problem 2E-VRP model to find an optimal solution that minimizes costs. In Leyerer et al. [31], the Split Delivery Vehicle Routing Problem with Multiple Products Compartments and Time Windows (SPVRPMPCTW) model is solved, to minimize costs throughout the three stages (LRP, VRP with time window and VRP considering multiple products) that compose model. When there is no pre-knowledge of such locations, other approaches are needed, and possible solutions can be found based on the knowledge of the demand or the geographical characteristics of the cities. Rudolph et al. [22] uses a multi-criteria method to find the most suitable locations and employs the Analytical Hierarchical Process AHP and PROMETHEE algorithms, defining that the main criteria to use are demand, road type and land use. The optimal locations should minimize travel times and travel distances. Song et al. [19], use the LCRS (Longest Common Route Subsequence) algorithm, complemented with a voting system, to find the paths most traveled and where there is a higher concentration of deliveries. This approach allows them to calculate which locations can minimize the time and distance traveled. In the literature we found that, in the approach to this problem, the computational capacity and the time required to explore all possible options, limit the calculation of the optimal points [19, 21, 33, 34]. The implementation costs of micro-hubs and vehicle capacity are often not considered. We can argue that minimizing distances, travel times, and costs are among the most relevant objectives in hubs location.

3 Data Analysis and Modeling

The CRISP-DM methodology, applied in our research, attempts to reduce the cost and increase reliability, repeatability, manageability, and speed of big data mining operations. According to this methodology the life cycle of data mining projects is divided into six parts: business understanding, data understanding, data preparation, modeling, evaluation, and deployment.

3.1 Business Understanding

The data explored was provided by the e-cargo bike urban logistics startup Yoob [35]. As mentioned, the purpose of the study is two-fold: the first, to provide a spatiotemporal characterization of the Yoob e-cargo bike fleet in the parcel collection and delivery processes in Lisbon as well in its outskirts; the second, to propose locations for the new hubs and adjustments to the existing logistics network, in order to strengthen and expand the fleet operations. The company has two types of hubs, the micro-hub, with an area of 36 m^2, a relatively smaller option compared to the values found in SLR, which range between 92 m^2 to 920 m^2 [36]. The functional definition is in line with that found at SLR, with various services being done at the micro hub, namely, consolidation of goods, storage, and recharging of e-cargo bikes. The nano-hubs, which is an innovative concept developed by Yoob, emerged from the adaptation of the pick-up/drop-off concept to last mile delivery logistics, characterized by having relatively small areas ranging between 3 m^2 and 120 m^2, exclusively dedicated as a temporary transition point where the goods remain no longer than 48 h. The type of associated physical infrastructure varies depending on where it is implemented, given it only requires temporary storage capacity for goods [37].

3.2 Data Understanding

The data was extracted from Yoob's database and covered the period of January 1st to April 30th 2022, encompassing 9,175 records and 34 variables. The data does not provide the routes (trajectories) done by the fleet. The geographic information on the route is characterized by latitude and longitude of origin and destination. There are some variables that generated based on mobile devices used by the employees during the entire logistics operation.

In our approach, each record in the data represents a "story", which is geographically composed of two points, one for pickup and the other for delivery. Within each story there are two "sub-stories", where each "sub-story" refers to a geographical location (pickup or delivery) and is always associated to a "route", where the "routes" can be composed of one or more "stories".

3.3 Data Preparation

The first data preparation step was the individual evaluation of all variables. Secondly, the unnecessary variables, outliers and incomplete stories were removed resulting in a dataset with 8,381 records (91,3% of the raw dataset) each one with 26 variables. The third step was to convert our dataset to have a sub-story granularity, by creating two datasets, one referring to the pick-up information and the other referring to drop-off information. These two datasets were merged.

To enrich our dataset, we added extra features:

- ['Elevation_point'] - Elevation of the sub-story geographic location, was obtained by consulting a DEM (Digital Elevation Map) [41].

- ['order route']: Number indicating the order in which the location is visited within the route sequence.
- ['time_enRoute_sec]: Time period in seconds between the ['history.enRoute'] and ['history.arrived'].
- ['time_points_sec']: Time period in seconds between two consecutive points on the same route.

This dataset processing with sub-story granularity resulted in 15,828 records and 27 variables.

To perform the spatial analysis two geographic data frames were generated with the geopandas Python library [42]. In the first the granularity was the route level, and second the granularity was the sub-story level. To be considered valid, a route must have two or more associated sub-stories. Routes that do not meet this requirement were removed. With this procedure we were able to reconstruct 664 routes, representing 95% of the total routes in the original dataset (699 routes), at sub-story level. We have removed 20 records (<0.002%), ending up with a dataset with 15,808 records.

3.4 Modeling

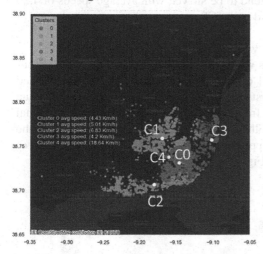

Fig. 1. Clustering the sub-stories with K-Means

In the modeling phase, we applied machine learning techniques, namely K-means, to developed three models to answer our research questions. In the first model we created clusters to identify the behavior of routes in certain geographical areas. In the second model we clustered the routes and evaluated their characteristics, providing answers to our first research question. In the last model we performed a gravity center analysis, with the goal to explore new locations for the implementation of new hubs, answering our second research question. To build the models we used the sklearn [43] library, for pre-processing we used MinMaxScaler [44] and LabelEnconder [45] and to perform cluster and the center of gravity analysis, we used K-Means algorithm [46]. To evaluate the optimal K value in the two first models, we adopted the Knee Elbow method with the knee library [47] and Davies-Bouldin index [48].

First Model – Clustering the Sub-stories with K-Means

In the first model, we identified the behavior of routes in certain geographical areas with cluster analysis. The feature selection was made from the geodataframe data structure with sub-story granularity.

The selected features were ['latitude'], ['longitude'], ['elevation_point'], ['time_points_sec'] and ['distance_to_prev']. Before running the clustering model in our data, we had to scale the data, as it had different measurement units, with Min-MaxScaler. When evaluating the Knee Elbow method and the Davies-Bouldin index through a range from 1 to 30 clusters, we found that the optimal value for K was 5 in knee elbow method, and 4 in the David-Bouldin technique. After testing the model with both values, the knee elbow value was selected as it gave us more information (later confirmed in YOOB briefings). Then we applied the K-Means algorithm with a K value of 5 to our data, and the output is depicted in Fig. 1. Four main clusters (C0 to C3) outstand in the visualization, and a fifth cluster (C4) with dissipated grey dots among the four other main clusters. In this model we can observe the e-cargo bikes' performance according to the geographical area. In Fig. 1, we can see the four well defined clusters and a more disperse cluster (C4) where the e-cargo bikes have a higher average speed of 18.64 km/h, indicating that these are acceleration areas. In the other clusters the average speed is significantly lower. The zones with the second highest average speed were the ones in cluster C2 where e-cargo bikes achieved average speeds of 6.84 km/h, followed by the zones covered by cluster C1 with average speeds of 5.01 km/h. The areas covered by clusters C0 and C3 have a more homogeneous performance. However, in the areas covered by cluster C3 the e-cargo bikes tend to be slower, with average speeds of 4.20 km/h vs 4.43 km/h of the speeds practiced in the C0 areas.

Second Model – Clustering the Routes with K-Means
In the second model the selected features were based on the geodataframe with granularity of the route: ['distancia_total'] and ['distancia_maxima_do_ini']; and were scaled with MinMaxScaler. Much like in the first model, we evaluated the Knee Elbow value and the Davies-Bouldin value in a range from 1 to 30 clusters and selected the optimal value for K (5) provided by the Knee Elbow method, since the optimal value in the David-Bouldin method was far bigger. Applying to our data K-Means with a K value of 5, the output results in five clusters (see Fig. 2, 3, 4, 5, 6, 7, 8 and 9).

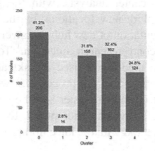

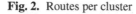

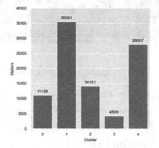

Fig. 2. Routes per cluster   **Fig. 3.** Average total distance per cluster

In Fig. 9, the operation time metric was calculated by subtracting the average total en route time from the total time spent between two locations and dividing the result by twice the number of locations visited, representing the operation time spent at each location. In the presentation of results below, all figures are average numbers.

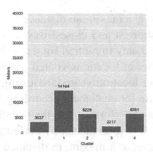

Fig. 4. Average maximum distance from initial location per cluster

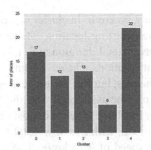

Fig. 5. Average visited locations per cluster

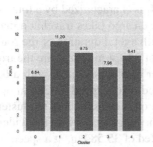

Fig. 6. Average speed per cluster

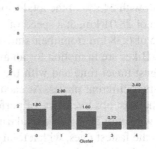

Fig. 7. Average total time in route per cluster

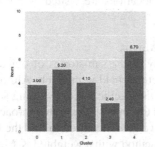

Fig. 8. Average total time between locations per cluster

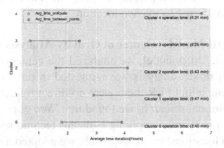

Fig. 9. Average operation time per cluster

The most common performance is the one observed in cluster C0, accounting for 41.2% of the total trips (see Fig. 2). This cluster features a speed of 6.84 km/h, which is the lowest speed of the five clusters, corresponding to a total traveled distance of 11.16 km. Yoob's e-cargo bikes travel at a maximum distance of 3.64 km, from their starting location. The total duration of cluster 0 trips is 3 h and 54 min, and the e-cargo bikes are only in motion for a period of 1h48m. Seventeen different locations are visited, and 3m40s is the shortest operating time per location visited, during trips of cluster C0. The second largest type of performance is observed in cluster C3, which includes 32.4% of the total trips (see Fig. 2). It is characterized by a total distance traveled of 4.31 km, at a speed of 7.96 km/h. In cluster C3, e-cargo bikes travel a maximum distance of 2.22 km from their starting location. These trips have the shortest and closest travel distances. They have a total duration of 2 h 42 m, and bikes are only in motion for 42 m. With six different locations, cluster C3 has the fewest number of locations visited from all five performances, but has the longest operation time per location visited, requiring 8 m 25 s. This may be associated with the high waiting time for customers according to Yoob partners feedback. The third most predominant type of performance is the one observed in cluster C2, with 31.6% of total trips (see Fig. 2). The total distance traveled is 14.15 km at a speed of 9.75 km/h. The e-cargo bikes travel at a maximum distance of 6.23 km from the starting location. The total travel time is 4 h 6 m, with the e-cargo bikes being in motion for 1 h 36 m. Thirteen different locations are visited, and bikers spend 5 m 43 s for each location. The fourth most observed performance type is the one of cluster 4, with 24.8% of the total trips (see Fig. 2). It is characterized by a total traveled distance of 28.01 km, at a speed of 9.41 km/h. The e-cargo bikes travel at a maximum distance of 6.38 km from their starting location, with a total duration of the route, of 6 h 42 m. Bikes are in motion for an average period of 3 h 24 m. These are the trips with the longest travel time and with the largest number of places visited, with a figure of twenty-two different places. At each location visited bikers spend 4m31s in operation time. The least observed type of performance is the one corresponding to cluster 1 (see Fig. 2), with only 2.8% of the total trips. These are the longest trips with the wider range, but also the fastest ones, with a total distance traveled of 35.58 km, at a speed of 11.20 km/h. In this cluster, the e-cargo bikes travel at a maximum distance of 14.16 km, from their starting location. The total travel time of a trip is 5 h 12 m, with the e-bikes being in motion for a period of 2 h 54 m. Twelve different locations are visited, and bikers spend 5 m 47 s in each location.

Third Model – Center of Gravity Analysis with K-Means

In the third model, we analyzed the centers of gravity of the sub-stories of our data. This model analysis was requested in one of the meetings held with Yoob. Although in our initial SLR there were no direct references to this specific topic, by doing some additional research, we found that Wen et al. [49] and Cai et al. [50], both approached this problem by applying K-means techniques with a weighted featured to find the best hub locations. In our approach, we adopted a similar method with a weighted K-Means algorithm.

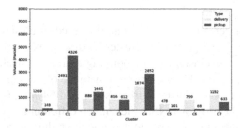

Fig. 10. Volume parcels per proposed new cluster centroid

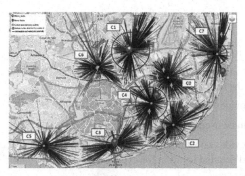

Fig. 11. Center of gravity analysis for eight hubs, using K-Means. Dark lines represent the distances from the hub center to the delivery points

Our model applied the number of locations intended to simulate, and a new variable was considered in the weighting of the cluster. In our model, the number of parcels was considered, as the effort needed to carry out the delivery. As most of the time the pickup parcels were in the hubs or at the collect/delivery locations, we added a penalty value in the delivery parcels, considering these last ones three times bigger in effort than the pickup ones. This forced the algorithm to locate the centroids of the cluster in places where distance and effort would be reduced. The data applied in this model was based on the variables ['latitude'], ['longitude'] and ['parcels'] from the geodataframe with sub-story granularity. A new variable was created designated ['calc_ajusto_de_custo_se_houver'], to include the penalty value. We simulated the center of gravity for 8 hubs, the result is shown in Fig. 10 and the volume associated for each location is depicted in Fig. 11.

3.5 Deployment

The models created were not applied in a real production environment. Software development was developed on a personal computer equipped with Windows 10 (64bits) operating system, Intel(R) Core (TM) i7-11370H 3.30 GHz, with 40 Gb of memory ram. We adopted the Python programming language (v3.10.4) [38], compiled with Visual Studio Code (v1.69.1) [39] on Jupyter Notebooks extension [40]. The developed software material and data sets are available for use by the Yoob company and for further academic research purposes.

4 End-User Evaluation

The end-user evaluation verifies that the findings are consistent with the proposed research objectives and the accuracy of the business requirements.

Table 1. Method assessment questionnaire

Criteria	Objective statement	Eval #1	Eval #2
Utility	It can help business decisions regarding the behavior of the fleet and hub expansion	FA	FA
Understandability	Provides understandable results	FA	FA
Accessibility	Can be used without training	LA	LA
Level of detail	Provides knowledge regarding the mobility of the fleet and detailed location for expansion	FA	FA
Consistency	Gives consistent results	LA	LA
Robustness	Has enough detail to be used in other cases of e-cargo bikes and hub expansion	FA	FA

In the end of the study a questionnaire was sent to the two YOOB partners, with the questions and answers indicated in Table 1. The development of the questionnaire follows the standards defined by the ISO/IEC TS 33061[1] [51], primarily used to assess software development processes. Four levels of the NLPF were employed for evaluation: Not Achieved (NA) - [0–15%]; Partially Achieved (PA) - [15–50%]; Largely Achieved (LA) - [50–85%]; Fully Achieved (FA) - [85–100%]. In this evaluation, we obtained a rating of FA, in the criteria of usefulness, understanding, level of detail and robustness, and LA rating in the criteria of accessibility and consistency. Overall, this indicates that the work done represents an added value for the company, providing useful, detailed, and clear information, appropriate to support decision making, in the context of the e-cargo bike fleet as well as for the expansion of new hubs. The YOOB evaluators consider that this study can be replicated to other case studies with potential for improvement, and implementation readiness. Moreover, the outcomes are aligned with the objectives and requirements proposed for the research presented in this paper.

5 Discussion and Conclusions

We have presented an innovative data science-based study, the first regarding last mile delivery using e-cargo bikes operating in Lisbon, Portugal, as far as the authors are aware. To tackle our research questions, we developed and evaluated three intelligent computing models. Our second model (Clustering the routes with K-Means) in particular, allowed us to answer the first research question, and to characterize the behavior of the e-cargo bike fleet through the traveled distance, time, speed and number of visited locations. Overall, the average of total traveled distance ranges between 4.31 km and 35.50 km, distancing from their start location, between 2.20 km and 14.10 km. 63% of the routes show distance ranges very close or even lower than the values reported by Sheth et al. [25], which considered cargo bikes to have an efficient performance under

---

[1] "ISO - ISO/IEC TS 33061:2021 - Information technology—Process assessment model for software life cycle processes." https://www.iso.org/standard/80362.html.

3.20 km. The average number of different locations visited per route ranges between 6 and 22. The average observed speed varies between 6.84 km/h and 11.20 km/h, a value close to the study by Bütten et al. [7], where these authors looked at several cargo bike projects, and calculated average speeds between 8.00 km/h and 25.00 km/h. The temporal characteristics revealed a time in movement per route from 42 m minutes up to 3 h 24 m, and a total route duration time, ranging between 2 h 42 m and 6 h 42 m. Required transaction time within each route ranged from 3 m 40 s to 8 m 25 s. This higher time may be due to the particularities of certain customers requiring more waiting time. Excluding this last observation, the time metric ranges between 3 m 40 s and 5 m 43 s. This set of characteristics gave us an overview of the needs of each route and the respective performance of the e-cargo bikes in their operation conditions. As for the second research question, the third model (K-Means center gravity analysis), was used as our basis for analysis. The choice of new hubs locations, in the context of an expansion of the e-cargo bikes network, is a complex process due to the high number of constraints that are to be considered in the site search [2, 19, 21, 33, 34]. In the search for new locations the factors considered for the cost function of our model were the distance and the cost associated with each location visited. Then for evaluation of the hub type, the volume associated with each hub of this new structure was analyzed. When simulating an expansion of three more hubs beyond the five that are currently part of YOOB's network, our model suggests that the implementation of these new hubs should be located in the boroughs of Alvalade, Benfica and Algés (Fig. 10). When confronted with the results of this model, the YOOB partners considered that these three new proposed locations are valid options that required further analysis in terms of economic viability. Regarding the 3 remaining computed locations, in the case of C2 (Fig. 10), the choice of the current location of the hub (nr 1), which is within the radius of this cluster, was due to the geographical characteristics of the area, which is on top of a hill, causing the trips to have a downward direction, facilitating the effort required by the biker. In the case of C7 (Fig. 10), the divergence between the location of the hub (nr 4) and the location proposed by our model, raises additional challenges of further changes of location due to the high price of real estate in the area where the centroid calculated by our model is located. Considering the remaining proposed hub locations, the YOOB partners showed complete agreement. By analyzing the volume of parcels associated with each hub in Fig. 11, we can discuss what type of hub is the most adequate for micro-hub or nano-hub requirements. In our study all three new locations are more suitable for nano-hubs. In the already existing nano-hub located in the Saldanha, we observed that due to the high associated volume of parcels it could shift to a micro-hub, and this observation was positively validated by YOOB partners.

Research Limitations
The most significant limitations of our study are related to the dimension, granularity, and structure of the data. The information on the routes was limited to the visited geographical points, lacking information about the order of each visited location, and lacking complete information about the route trajectory (its 3D coordinates) taken from pickup to delivery as well city traffic. Having trajectory and traffic data would allow a deeper and more rigorous analysis of the e-cargo bike fleet route patterns, namely the real trajectories in which route was performed and the actual distances traveled. We collected data in

the period from January to April of 2022, corresponding to the first four months of the company's registered activity (YOOB started operations in Lisbon in the fall of 2021). After data pre-processing, we came up with a dataset comprising 15 828 records and 27 variables, which was considered sufficient for our analysis, but that nevertheless can be limited for long-term trend analysis. The proposed hub locations can be considered the best possible locations with limitations, as many factors were not considered, such as street elevations and, specially, socio-economic factors that need to be taken into account, to tackle costs for the customer and the municipality.

Future Work
The following suggestions are made for upcoming research work:

- Expand the number of observations analyzed to detect long-term trends and produce more insightful results, given that YOOB has the possibility to collect stories and route data on a regular basis.
- Study the shortest and flattest path.
- Perform more detailed cluster analysis, with an increased number of clusters when analyzing route typologies.

Acknowledgements. This work is partially funded by national funds through FCT - Fundação para a Ciência e Tecnologia, I.P., under the project FCT UIDB/04466/2020.

References

1. The future of the last-mile ecosystem transition roadmaps for public-and private-sector players (2020). www.weforum.org
2. Naumov, V.: Substantiation of loading hub location for electric cargo bikes servicing city areas with restricted traffic. Energies **14**(4), 839 (2021). https://doi.org/10.3390/en14040839
3. Page, M.J., et al.: The PRISMA 2020 statement: an updated guideline for reporting systematic reviews. https://doi.org/10.1136/bmj.n71
4. CRISP-DM: a framework for data mining & analysis. https://thinkinsights.net/digital/crisp-dm/. Accessed 20 May 2022
5. Faugère, L., White, C., III., Montreuil, B.: Mobile access hub deployment for urban parcel logistics. Sustainability **12**(17), 7213 (2020). https://doi.org/10.3390/su12177213
6. Urzúa-Morales, J.G., Sepulveda-Rojas, J.P., Alfaro, M., Fuertes, G., Ternero, R., Vargas, M.: Logistic modeling of the last mile: case study Santiago, Chile. Sustainability **12**(2), 648 (2020). https://doi.org/10.3390/su12020648
7. Büttgen, A., Turan, B., Hemmelmayr, V.: Evaluating distribution costs and CO_2-emissions of a two-stage distribution system with cargo bikes: a case study in the city of Innsbruck. Sustainability **13**(24), 13974 (2021). https://doi.org/10.3390/su132413974
8. Katsela, K., Güneş, Ş, Fried, T., Goodchild, A., Browne, M.: Defining urban freight microhubs: a case study analysis. Sustainability **14**(1), 532 (2022). https://doi.org/10.3390/su14010532
9. Assmann, T., Lang, S., Müller, F., Schenk, M.: Impact assessment model for the implementation of cargo bike transshipment points in urban districts. Sustainability **12**(10), 4082 (2020). https://doi.org/10.3390/SU12104082

10. Toro, J.F., Carrion, D., Brovelli, M.A., Percoco, M.: Bikemi bike-sharing service exploratory analysis on mobility patterns. Int. Arch. Photogramm. Remote Sens. Spat. Inf. Sci. **43**, 197–203 (2020). https://doi.org/10.5194/isprs-archives-XLIII-B4-2020-197-2020
11. Guo, X., Xu, Z., Zhang, J., Lu, J., Zhang, H.: An OD flow clustering method based on vector constraints: a case study for Beijing taxi origin-destination data. ISPRS Int. J. Geoinf. **9**(2), 128 (2020). https://doi.org/10.3390/ijgi9020128
12. Ma, X., Liu, C., Wen, H., Wang, Y., Wu, Y.J.: Understanding commuting patterns using transit smart card data. J. Transp. Geogr. **58**, 135–145 (2017). https://doi.org/10.1016/j.jtrangeo.2016.12.001
13. Shen, Y., Zhang, X., Zhao, J.: Understanding the usage of dockless bike sharing in Singapore. Int. J. Sustain. Transp. **12**(9), 686–700 (2018). https://doi.org/10.1080/15568318.2018.1429696
14. Zheng, L., et al.: Spatial–temporal travel pattern mining using massive taxi trajectory data. Phys. A: Stat. Mech. Appl. **501**, 24–41 (2018). https://doi.org/10.1016/j.physa.2018.02.064
15. Huang, Y., Xiao, Z., Wang, D., Jiang, H., Wu, D.: Exploring individual travel patterns across private car trajectory data. IEEE Trans. Intell. Transp. Syst. **21**(12), 5036–5050 (2020). https://doi.org/10.1109/TITS.2019.2948188
16. Wen, R., Yan, W., Zhang, A.N., Chinh, N.Q., Akcan, O.: Spatio-temporal route mining and visualization for busy waterways. In: 2016 IEEE International Conference on Systems, Man, and Cybernetics (SMC), pp. 000849–000854. IEEE (2016). https://doi.org/10.1109/SMC.2016.7844346
17. Amaral, J.C., Cunha, C.B.: An exploratory evaluation of urban street networks for last mile distribution. Cities **107**, 102916 (2020). https://doi.org/10.1016/j.cities.2020.102916
18. Li, F., Shi, W., Zhang, H.: A two-phase clustering approach for urban hotspot detection with spatiotemporal and network constraints. IEEE J. Sel. Top. Appl. Earth Obs. Remote Sens. **14**, 3695–3705 (2021). https://doi.org/10.1109/JSTARS.2021.3068308
19. Song, H.Y., Han, I.: Finding the best location for logistics hub based on actual parcel delivery data. In: Misra, S., et al. (eds.) ICCSA 2019. LNCS, vol. 11619, pp. 603–615. Springer, Cham (2019). https://doi.org/10.1007/978-3-030-24289-3_45
20. Barraza, R., Sepúlveda, J.M., Venegas, J., Monardes, V., Derpich, I.: A model for solving optimal location of hubs: a case study for recovery of tailings dams. In: Dzitac, I., Dzitac, S., Filip, F.G., Kacprzyk, J., Manolescu, M.-J., Oros, H. (eds.) ICCCC 2020. AISC, vol. 1243, pp. 304–312. Springer, Cham (2021). https://doi.org/10.1007/978-3-030-53651-0_26
21. Hwang, J., Lee, J.S., Kho, S., Kim, D.: Hierarchical hub location problem for freight network design. IET Intell. Transp. Syst. **12**(9), 1062–1070 (2018). https://doi.org/10.1049/iet-its.2018.5289
22. Rudolph, C., Nsamzinshuti, A., Bonsu, S., Ndiaye, A.B., Rigo, N.: Localization of relevant urban micro-consolidation centers for last-mile cargo bike delivery based on real demand data and city characteristics. Transp. Res. Rec. **2676**(1), 365–375 (2022). https://doi.org/10.1177/03611981211036351
23. Atluri, G., Karpatne, A., Kumar, V.: Spatio-temporal data mining: a survey of problems and methods. ACM Comput. Surv. **51**(4), 1–41 (2018). https://doi.org/10.1145/3161602
24. Conway, A., Cheng, J., Kamga, C., Wan, D.: Cargo cycles for local delivery in New York city: performance and impacts. Res. Transp. Bus. Manag. **24**, 90–100 (2017). https://doi.org/10.1016/j.rtbm.2017.07.001
25. Sheth, M., Butrina, P., Goodchild, A., McCormack, E.: Measuring delivery route cost trade-offs between electric-assist cargo bicycles and delivery trucks in dense urban areas. Eur. Transp. Res. Rev. **11**(1), 1–12 (2019). https://doi.org/10.1186/s12544-019-0349-5
26. Caggiani, L., Colovic, A., Prencipe, L.P., Ottomanelli, M.: A green logistics solution for last-mile deliveries considering e-vans and e-cargo bikes. Transp. Res. Procedia **52**, 75–82 (2021). https://doi.org/10.1016/j.trpro.2021.01.010

27. Arrieta-Prieto, M., Ismael, A., Rivera-Gonzalez, C., Mitchell, J.E.: Location of urban micro-consolidation centers to reduce the social cost of last-mile deliveries of cargo: a heuristic approach. Networks **79**(3), 292–313 (2022). https://doi.org/10.1002/net.22076
28. Golini, R., Guerlain, C., Lagorio, A., Pinto, R.: An assessment framework to support collective decision making on urban freight transport. Transport **33**(4), 890–901 (2018). https://doi.org/10.3846/transport.2018.6591
29. Özbekler, T.M., Karaman Akgül, A.: Last mile logistics in the framework of smart cities: a typology of city logistics schemes. Int. Arch. Photogramm. Remote Sens. Spat. Inf. Sci. **44**, 335–337 (2020). https://doi.org/10.5194/isprs-archives-XLIV-4-W3-2020-335-2020
30. Srinivas, S.S., Marathe, R.R.: Moving towards "mobile warehouse": last-mile logistics during COVID-19 and beyond. Transp. Res. Interdiscip. Perspect. **10**, 100339 (2021). https://doi.org/10.1016/j.trip.2021.100339
31. Leyerer, M., Sonneberg, M.-O., Heumann, M., Breitner, M.H.: Shortening the last mile in urban areas: optimizing a smart logistics concept for e-grocery operations. Smart Cities **3**(3), 585–603 (2020). https://doi.org/10.3390/smartcities3030031
32. Kedia, A., Kusumastuti, D., Nicholson, A.: Locating collection and delivery points for goods' last-mile travel: a case study in New Zealand. Transp. Res. Procedia **46**, 85–92 (2020). https://doi.org/10.1016/j.trpro.2020.03.167
33. Ghaffarinasab, N.: A tabu search heuristic for the bi-objective star hub location problem. Int. J. Manag. Sci. Eng. Manag. **15**(3), 213–225 (2020). https://doi.org/10.1080/17509653.2019.1709992
34. Huang, Z., Huang, W., Guo, F.: Integrated sustainable planning of micro-hub network with mixed routing strategy. Comput. Ind. Eng. **149**, 106872 (2020). https://doi.org/10.1016/j.cie.2020.106872
35. https://yoob.pt/
36. Clarke, S., Leonardi, J.: Agile Gnewt Cargo: parcels deliveries with electric vehicles in central London multi-carrier central London micro-consolidation and final delivery via low carbon vehicles (2017). www.london.gov.uk
37. Abranches, R., Ogando, M.: YOOB interview
38. www.Python.org. https://www.python.org/. Accessed 13 July 2022
39. Visual Studio Code. https://code.visualstudio.com/. Accessed 13 July 2022
40. Project Jupyter. https://jupyter.org/. Accessed 13 July 2022
41. EU-DEM v1.1 — Copernicus Land Monitoring Service. https://land.copernicus.eu/imagery-in-situ/eu-dem/eu-dem-v1.1?tab=metadata. Accessed 14 July 2022
42. GeoPandas 0.11.0 — GeoPandas 0.11.0+0.g1977b50.dirty documentation. https://geopandas.org/en/stable/. Accessed 13 July 2022
43. Scikit-learn: machine learning in Python — scikit-learn 1.1.1 documentation. https://scikit-learn.org/stable/. Accessed 13 July 2022
44. Sklearn.preprocessing.MinMaxScaler — scikit-learn 1.1.1 documentation. https://scikit-learn.org/stable/modules/generated/sklearn.preprocessing.MinMaxScaler.html. Accessed 18 July 2022
45. Sklearn.preprocessing.LabelEncoder — scikit-learn 1.1.1 documentation. https://scikit-learn.org/stable/modules/generated/sklearn.preprocessing.LabelEncoder.html. Accessed 18 July 2022
46. Sklearn.cluster.KMeans — scikit-learn 1.1.1 documentation. https://scikit-learn.org/stable/modules/generated/sklearn.cluster.KMeans.html. Accessed 18 July 2022
47. Welcome to kneed's documentation! — kneed 0.6.0 documentation. https://kneed.readthedocs.io/en/stable/. Accessed 13 July 2022
48. Sklearn.metrics.davies_bouldin_score — scikit-learn 1.1.1 documentation. https://scikit-learn.org/stable/modules/generated/sklearn.metrics.davies_bouldin_score.html. Accessed 18 July 2022

49. Wen, R., Yan, W., Zhang, A.N.: Weighted clustering of spatial pattern for optimal logistics hub deployment. In: 2016 IEEE International Conference on Big Data (Big Data), pp. 3792–3797. IEEE (2016). https://doi.org/10.1109/BigData.2016.7841050

50. Cai, C., Luo, Y., Cui, Y., Chen, F.: Solving multiple distribution center location allocation problem using K-means algorithm and center of gravity method take Jinjiang district of Chengdu as an example. In: IOP Conference Series: Earth and Environmental Science, vol. 587, No. 1, p. 012120. IOP Publishing (2020). https://doi.org/10.1088/1755-1315/587/1/012120

Analyzing Urban Mobility Based on Smartphone Data: The Lisbon Case Study

Daniel Leal[1], Vitória Albuquerque[2] , Miguel Sales Dias[1](✉) ,
and João Carlos Ferreira[1,3]

[1] Instituto Universitário de Lisboa (ISCTE-IUL), ISTAR, 1649-026 Lisbon, Portugal
{drllo,miguel.dias}@iscte-iul.pt
[2] NOVA Information Management School (NOVA IMS), Universidade Nova de Lisboa,
Campus de Campolide, 1070-312 Lisbon, Portugal
[3] INOV INESC Inovação—Instituto de Novas Tecnologias, 1000-029 Lisbon, Portugal

Abstract. Our paper addresses the mobility patterns in Lisbon in the vicinity of historical and transportation points of interest, with a case study conducted in the parish of Santa Maria Maior, a vibrant touristic neighborhood. We propose a data science-based approach to analyze such patterns. Our dataset includes five months of georeferenced mobile phone data, collected during late 2021 and early 2022, provided by the municipality of Lisbon. We performed a systematic literature review, using the PRISMA methodology and adopted the CRISP-DM methodology, to perform data curation, statistical and clustering analysis, and visualization, following the recommendations of the literature. For clustering we used the DBSCAN algorithm. We found eight clusters in Santa Maria Maior, with outstanding clusters along 28-E tram and Lisbon Cruise Terminal, where mobility is high, particularly for non-roaming travelers. This paper contributes to the digital transformation of Lisbon into a smart city, by improving improved understanding of urban mobility patterns.

Keywords: smartphone data · urban mobility · visualisation · point of interest · DBSCAN · PRISMA · CRISP-DM

1 Introduction

1.1 Motivation and Topic Relevance

The analysis of available Internet of Things (IoT) data in urban settings by relevant stakeholders, shows that city decision-makers can alleviate urbanization's pressures by providing a new experience for citizens, making their day-to-day life more comfortable and secure. In smart cities, IoT refers to the use of smart computing and networking technology and linked devices for real-time data collection. Rising urbanization, increased demand for efficient infrastructure in metropolitan areas, as well as for energy-efficient resources, traffic management, waste management, public safety, and security, which in turn, are development factors for the total market. Connected internet technologies and

A. L. Martins et al. (Eds.): INTSYS 2022, LNICST 486, pp. 40–54, 2023.
https://doi.org/10.1007/978-3-031-30855-0_3

devices can be used to alleviate problems, improve the quality of residents' life, and minimize resource consumption in smart cities.

In urban settings, it has become increasingly crucial to determine the location of mobile phone users in the Global System for Mobile (GSM) networks. The location of a mobile phone can be determined using the network architecture of the telecom service provider. It is possible to collect raw radio data of a handset using the subscriber identity module (SIM) in GSM and Universal Mobile Telecommunications System (UMTS) devices. The precision of any localization system is critical to the success of the technology in the long run, and it is determined by the density of cellular base stations, with urban areas obtaining the best potential accuracy due to the increased number of cell towers, as well as the use of the most up-to-date timing methods and technologies. Numerous factors can affect the accuracy of location data, including its source, which may include Global Position System (GPS) signals, Wi-Fi, or cell tower triangulation.

Rush hours and traffic jams have become part of our daily routines over the years, as well as the research drive to reduce this phenomenon. As result, it is becoming increasingly vital to revolutionize traffic management in urban areas using data and a variety of computing methods to help cities to understand what is happening and provide new mobility strategies.

The availability of Vodafone Portugal [1] mobile phone data provided by Câmara Municipal de Lisboa (CML), opened an opportunity and interest to study this data in the scope of urban mobility in the city of Lisbon, especially to understand how, when and where people travel in the city. Considering this data, the aim of our research is to understand mobility patterns in Lisbon, by performing analysis and visualization of mobility phenomena during a given time period.

The results of this study will provide knowledge to the policy and decision makers at CML, enabling better mobility patterns understanding, as well as the implementation of sustainable urban mobility and tourism strategies for the city.

1.2 Research Question and Objective

This research theme was proposed by Isctc in partnership with CML's Center for Management and Urban Intelligence by the LxDataLab [2] and also in partnership with Vodafone Portugal.

Our research question can be stated in the following way: "what are the mobility patterns of smartphone users in the city of Lisbon related to points of interest, namely, historical places and public transportation?".

This research question led us to our research objective that, in short, aims to understand the mobility patterns in Lisbon by analysing mobile phone data, in the vicinity of the mentioned points of interest. We propose to perform analysis and visualization of mobile Vodafone data and open-source mapping data to identify mobility patterns in Lisbon, using data mining and visualization. Our data mining approach, adopts the CRISP-DM methodology [3, 4], and for the modelling, we will use statistical analysis and cluster analysis, this last one with the Density-Based Spatial Clustering of Applications with Noise (DBSCAN) method, following literature recommendations.

1.3 Structure

This paper is organized in four sections. In Sect. 1, we introduce the theme of the paper, the topic context, research questions and goals, methodology, and structure. Section 2 introduces the results of our systematic literature review and bibliometric analysis using the Preferred Reporting Items for Systematic Reviews and Meta-Analyses (PRISMA) [5] with findings on the latest state-of-the-art methodologies applied to urban mobility behavior patterns, based on the analysis of mobile phone data. In Sect. 3, we use a data science approach to perform data mining, namely, adopting statistical analysis, DBSCAN clustering and visualization. In Sect. 4, we discuss our results and research limitations, present our conclusions, and propose future lines of research work.

2 Literature Review

2.1 Methodology

PRISMA [5] was applied with the purpose of identifying, evaluating, and critically appraising research, to provide an answer to a well-formulated query related to our research question. This methodology is a set of elements for systematic reviews and meta-analyses that is scientific proof.

2.2 Results

In this study we used the following keywords to query academic repositories (Scopus and Web of Science): "data mining" and "machine learning" and "smartphone" and "data". It returned the most relevant papers, that were screened for eligibility and full text reading, resulting in a total of 12 papers that were included in our bibliometric analysis.

Based on the articles resulting from the PRISMA survey, we analyzed their methods and applications. We observed a trend in the application of DBSCAN method [6–9]. Other methods include visualization and analysis of mobility patterns with and without point of interest (POI) [10–15], k-means clustering algorithm [16], Dynamic Time Warping (DTW) [12], and analytic methods such as Point Density and Kernel Density Estimation [17].

We identified the use of the DBSCAN method in "Vehicular traffic flow intensity detection and prediction through mobile data usage" [6] where its application is made in an artificial neural network trained with the traffic levels of the network nodes in a time series to predict the traffic of the nodes. In paper "A cluster-Based Approach Using Smartphone Data for Bike-Sharing Docking Stations Identification: Lisbon Case Study" [16] for the identification of soft mobility hotspots at specific bike share docking stations using k-means clustering algorithm. Moreover, "Spatio-Temporal Mining To Identify Potential Traffic Congestion Based On Transportation Mode" [7] for the identification of potential traffic congestion using DBSCAN clustering algorithm; "Understanding individual mobility pattern and portrait depiction based on mobile phone data" [8] studied the application for individual mobility pattern analysis and portrayed the depiction in various Chinese cities. Also, "Clustering Large-Scale Origin-Destination Pairs: A Case

Study for Public Transit in Beijing" [9]. Study applied as well, DBSCAN to determine the bus passengers in Beijing mobility patterns.

We also identified visualizations and statistical analysis methods in the articles "Applying Big Data Analytics to Monitor Tourist Flow for the Scenic Area Operation Management" [10] in which these methods are applied to the identification of tourist movement in Beijing. "Understanding Human Mobility Flows from Aggregated Mobile Phone Data" [11] used these methods to identify the population behavior in Milan". Extracting Dynamic Urban Mobility Patterns Phone Data" [12] also used these methods to identify urban mobility patterns. The research "Ensemble-spotting: Ranking urban vibrancy via POI embedding with multi-view spatial graphs" [13] study identified mobility patterns with POIs to the discover the association between vibrant communities and geographical items. The research "Using bundling to visualize multivariate urban mobility structure patterns in the São Paulo Metropolitan Area" [14] identified spatial grouping and some visualization using the application of bundling approach to support multi-attribute trail datasets in the São Paulo metropolitan area.

The identification of urban mobility patterns in the city of Shanghai used an analytical approach with Point Density and Kernel Density Estimation in "Role of big data in development of smart city by studying the density of citizens in Shanghai" [17] also to be considered.

3 Data Mining

The data mining CRISP-DM methodology [3, 4] is implemented throughout this research.

3.1 Business Understanding

LxDataLab [2] is supported by CML and was established to respond to the need to build analytical solutions for the city of Lisbon, capable of enhancing urban planning, and improve resilience, security, mobility, operational, and emergency management in the city, using innovative data analysis and machine learning techniques.

LxDataLab launched yearly challenges to the academia and research communities to understand different city domains: environment, energy, citizen, economy, governance, mobility, and quality of life.

This study addresses challenge 70 theme on "Mobility in the city of Lisbon based on mobile phone data". This challenge in the urban mobility domain, in collaboration with a mobile service operator (Vodafone), aims to understand how people handling a mobile phone move in the city, which is fully in line with our research objectives.

This paper tackles this challenge by analyzing the georeferenced data collected by Vodafone during a five-month period, from September 2021 to January 2022 and answering to our research question. In essence, the study aims to build an analytical research model centered on the CML smart city framework, looking at the mobility patterns of smartphone users (nationals or roaming users), looking particularly at points of interest in the city, namely historic places and public transportation, helping decision makers of CML in the area of urban mobility.

3.2 Data Understanding

Five datasets were provided for each month, namely, September, October, November, December 2020, and January 2021. The data was compiled into 3,743 200-by-200 square meters (a grid of quadrants or quads).

According to Vodafone's metadata, there were no records reported with values less than 10 devices, and data was gathered every five minutes. Each monthly dataset provides the number of devices present in a certain quad every 5 min (along with a time marker), or more than 5 min for roaming and non-roaming, city enters and exits, terminal exits from the quad, top ten roaming nations and top ten applications, and downstream and upstream rates.

We have seventeen million records in the September dataset (17,233,318), thirty-two million records in the October dataset (32,627,308), twenty-one million records in the November dataset (21,619,292), thirty-three million records in the December dataset (33,121,657), and thirty-three million records in the January dataset (33,344,624). This resulted in a cumulative total of roughly 137 million records spread across five months.

An additional dataset with geoinformation, known as Vodafone grid, was provided by CML, and combined with the monthly datasets. This dataset complements the monthly datasets by containing information regarding the parish, street name, neighborhood or zone, position, and geometric information of the squares. It should be noted that two columns are shown for Lisbon parishes (freguesia and freguesias), which differ due to parish renaming and merging since November 8, 2012 [18]. As such we used the updated parishes information, set up after 2012.

3.3 Data Preparation

We included in our data type information, three ordinal qualitative variables - extract_year_2, extract_month_3, and extract_day_4 - and three continuous variables – Grid_ID, Datetime, and C3 or C.

Some of the datasets (September, November, December, and January) contain 44 nulls in column C3/C4, 30 nulls in column extract_year_2, and 43 nulls in column extract_day_4. We eliminated their entries due to the small quantity of nulls in the datasets.

After cleaning, we retained the following number of records: sixteen million records in the September dataset (16,166,066), thirty million records in the October dataset (30,604,296), twenty million records in the November dataset (20,142,789), thirteen million records in the December dataset (13,048,266), and thirty-one million records in the January dataset thirty-one million (31,277,197). This resulted in a total 111 million records to be used in this research, meaning that nearly 26 million records were deleted. The listing of the column "nome" values was visually analyzed to remove highways from the datasets, as these locations are prone to congestion, leading us to misinterpretation of the data and misconception of our objective. Therefore, the following road routes and were removed from the "name" column: "A5", "Eixo Norte-Sul", "CRIL", "2ª Circular", and "A2", given that they correspond to is arriving, leaving or crossing the city.

A Python script was developed to group the data for a given month by parish and add up each parish's number of devices. The result of this analysis determined which Lisbon parish was going to be selected to be our case study. Additionally, we analyzed and visualized the number of stopped devices, the number of historical Points-of-Interest - POIs, the number of bus stop POIs, the number of metro station POIs, and the number of train station POIs, in the parishes of Lisbon, using choropleth maps. These POIs are related with tourism and sightseeing themes, arising from the combination of transportation and historical landmarks, that were chosen for this analysis to understand how people move in the city and how this behavior is related with the mentioned POIs, and to narrow our data modeling study to an outstanding parish.

POIs data was collected from the OSMnx library [19] via category-specific queries. We created two queries (due to museums' inclusion in the tourism category) for the historical POIs. For the train transportation POIs, a search for train stations was conducted, but the results also contained metro POIs, which were subsequently merged. Finally, for collecting bus stops and metro stations, a direct and simple search was sufficient.

In December (see Fig. 1), the non-roaming map shows that the interior and north parishes of Lisbon are more likely to have more devices. Avenidas Novas and Alvalade, for example, have more than 310 million devices, probably due to the traffic, workplaces, universities and cultural places location. On the other hand, the roaming map shows that the inner core of Lisbon, from Avenidas Novas to Santa Maria Maior, has more devices. Santa Maria Maior parish has more than 26 million devices, followed by Misericórdia, Santa António, Avenidas Novas, and Olivais, with more than 13 million. Estrela and Arroios have more than 7 million, and the remaining parishes have fewer than 7 million devices.

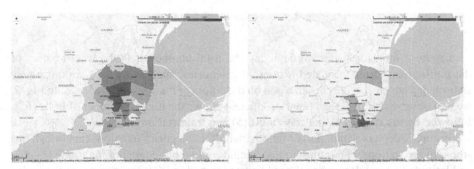

Fig. 1. Average number of devices (millions) per Lisbon parish in December: non-roaming (left) and roaming (right). Dark green areas have a higher number of smartphone devices.

Santa Maria Maior is the parish with the higher number of historical POIs, and we decided this criterion to analyze further this parish as a case study in our paper. In this scenario, we recognized that Santa Maria Maior has not the higher number of observed devices but, still holds many data observations (between 31 million and 101 million).

3.4   Modeling

In this section, we present the data model results regarding the Santa Maria Maior parish, by analyzing mobile phone data and POIs data, showing insights on people's mobility patterns in this parish. We analyzed all the months of the datasets although, for the purpose of this paper, we are only presenting the month of December.

3.4.1 Statistical Analysis Model

For our statistical analysis, we started by analyzing POIs data, followed by mobile phone data and a combined analysis of both. Finally, we applied the DBSCAN clustering algorithm to the datasets, given that it is a technique adopted by the literature to similar problems, as shown in our literature survey.

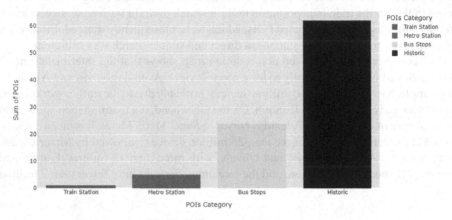

Fig. 2. POIs category histogram.

Figure 2 shows a histogram depicting the total number of POIs, where colors of the public transportation-related histogram categories, such as metro station, railway station, and bus stop, were chosen based on the colors of their respective logos. In Fig. 2, we can observe that historical points of interest shows the highest number of POIs (62), followed by bus stops (24), metro stations (5) and train stations (1).

Figure 3, depicts Santa Maria Maior parish POI categories locations (historical, bus stops, metro stations, and train stations), including two bar charts, of longitude (x-axis) and latitude (y-axis). Regarding the public transportation POIs, we can notice the multimodality nature of the system, particularly in Rossio, in the Santa Justa area, where there are 9 bus stops, 1 metro station, and 1 train station. This bridges mobility connections both within and outside this parish. The presence of bus stops and historic points of interest across the parish of Santa Maria Maior is noticable. We can observe the maximum concentration of POIs at the latitude between 38.710 and 38.714 with slightly over 40 points covered in total, with the distribution of POIs becoming increasingly smaller as one proceeds away from these locations. These correspond to stops and historical locations, and metro station serving the areas of Santo Estêvão, São Miguel, Alfama, Santiago, Sacramento, Chiado, and Castelo. The highest concentration in longitude is between −9.1425 and −9.1400, with about 20 points covered, and these POIs are largely bus stops and historical places, followed by metro stations and the train station, that spread in the areas of Santa Justa, Sacramento, Chiado, Mártires, and São Nicolau.

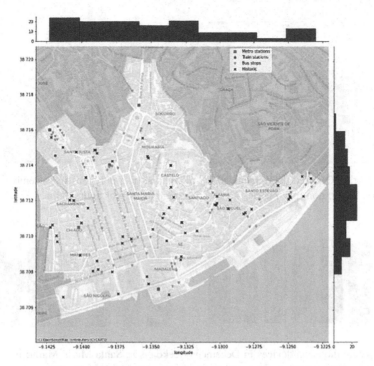

Fig. 3. POIs location distribution in Santa Maria Maior.

In our our data model and for each month, we associated the number of devices present in a given square polygon (of the 200 m × 200 m grid of the data resolution), with the various POIs categories considered for this work, with the following technique: if a given POI point is inside a given square polygon, that POI will receive the number of devices collected for that polygon. Thus, we can conclude that x number of devices remained stationary for more than five minutes in a specific POI. The limitation of our approach is that different POIs, regardless of category, have the same number of devices associated, if they belong to the same polygon.

In Fig. 4, we can notice that, for both non-roaming and roaming data, it is highly concentrated in the Chiado area. We can observe also some orphan POIs, i.e., points that will not be considered since they were located beyond the data polygons associated with the parish in study.

Figure 5, depicts two plot bars with average number of non-roaming and roaming devices, for the seven days of the week.

Observing the non-roaming plot bar, the weekly behavior on the number of devices tended to be very similar from Monday to Tuesday, with almost 350 thousand devices, rising on Wednesday with over 350 thousand devices, dropping to a maximum minimum of around 325 thousand devices on Thursday, and starting to rise until Saturday, when it reaches its highest value, around 375 thousand devices, and then dropping on Sunday. We observed that all weekdays have values close to 350 thousand devices, except for Wednesday, which has slightly more than 350 thousand devices.

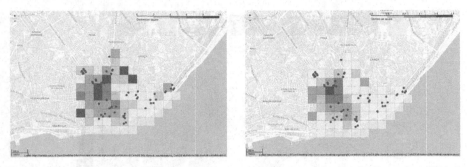

Fig. 4. Historic POIs (red dots), included in smartphone data polygons in December 2021, in Santa Maria Maior: non-roaming (left) and roaming (right) (Color figure online).

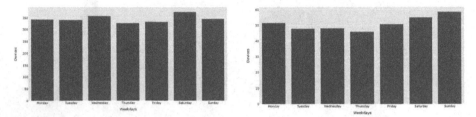

Fig. 5. Average thousand devices in December weekdays in Santa Maria Maior: non-roaming (left) and roaming (right).

The graph for the roaming showed that the weekly behavior tended to decrease from Monday with just over 50 thousand devices, followed by Tuesday and Wednesday with under 50 thousand devices, Wednesday with close to 45 thousand devices, Friday with just over 50 thousand devices, Saturday with close to 55 thousand devices, and Sunday with nearly 60 thousand devices.

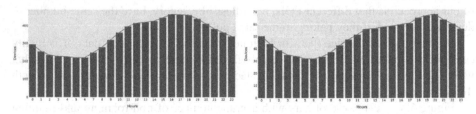

Fig. 6. Average thousand devices in December daily hours in Santa Maria Maior: non-roaming (left) and roaming (right).

In Fig. 6, we show two bar plots with the average number of non-roaming and roaming devices, in December's daily hours. For non-roaming data we verify that the minimum device peak is at 6 a.m. with slightly more than 200 thousand devices, and the maximum device peak is at 4 p.m. with around 450 thousand devices, showing that it took 10 h to reach the maximum value. The common commute pattern considers the morning peak between 8 a.m. to 9 a.m. and at the afternoon peak between 5 p.m. or 6 p.m., which explains the observed behavior. For roaming data, we notice that the minimum device peak occurs at 6 a.m. with a little more than 30 thousand devices, and the maximum device peak occurs at 8 p.m. with nearly 70 devices, requiring 14 h to achieve the maximum figure. Roaming mobile phone data shows a later appearance than non-roaming devices.

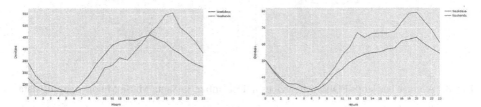

Fig. 7. Average thousand devices in December weekdays (blue line) and weekends (red line), per hours of the day, in Santa Maria Maior: non-roaming (left) and roaming (right) (Color figure online).

In Fig. 7, we compare the average number of devices per hour of the day during the week (blue line) and on weekends (red line), using two-line plots for non-roaming (left) and roaming (right).

In the non-roaming graph, the contrast in the number of devices between the two categories outstood, with fewer devices on weekends. Following a pattern quite like that depicted in Fig. 6, the number of devices in Santa Maria Maior begins to increase at 6 a.m. in the morning for the working days of the week and weekends scenarios and continues to rise until 4 pm for the working days the week and 5 pm for the weekends, when the values begin to decrease. We confirmed that during the weekends, the devices only have higher values between 4 p.m. until 5 a.m. Moreover, Santa Maria Maior has more devices on working days during the day and on weekends during the night.

The roaming graph, with the two-line plots showed almost identical despite the difference during the day, as in the weekend showed highest values than the weekdays. The weekday values began to increase at 5 a.m. and continued to rise until 8 p.m., at which point they begin to fall until 5 a.m. On the other hand, the weekdays started increasing at 6 a.m., peaking at 12 p.m., declining until 1 p.m., and rising again until 8 p.m., decreasing till 5 a.m. In this scenario, there are already more data on weekends than during the week.

Results and conclusions from graps' visualization are in line with expectations since Santa Maria Maior is one of most popular and touristics parishes in Lisbon.

Looking in more detail on POIs category analysis, we created visualizations using an ascending horizontal bar chart, with month by month average device figures, in each POI (see Fig. 8). The subway and train POIs were grouped together. As mentioned, if two POIs are paired with the same quadrant, they will have the same number of devices.

In the non-roaming case Praça da Figueira had most of the devices, nearly 35 million, Martim Moniz, with over 25 million devices and Praça do Comércio, with nearly 25 million devices in December (the month with the highest number of devices). These

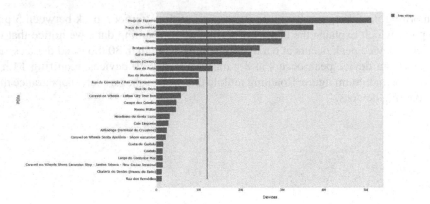

Fig. 8. Average bus stops POIs with devices in December, in Santa Maria Maior: roaming data.

areas of Santa Maria Maior correspond to high concentration areas of bus stops. The bus stops in the areas of Jardim do Tabaco, Rua dos Remédios and Chafariz de Dentro have the fewest number of devices, around 1 million each.

In the roaming graph (see Fig. 8), the top 3 areas were the same, with the order shift of 2nd and 3rd place: Praça da Figueira with more than 5 million devices, Praça do Comércio with just over 3.5 million, and Martim Moniz with just over 3 million. Again, the bus stop areas with the lowest number of devices were Jardim do Tabaco, Chafariz de Dentro, and Rua dos Remédios, with a total less than half a million.

When comparing the graphs between non-roaming and roaming, non-roaming shows an average of around 8 million, and roaming an average of approximately 1 million (Fig. 9).

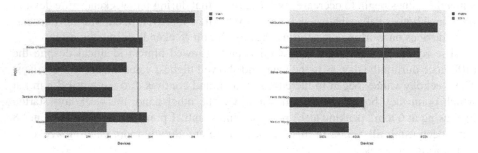

Fig. 9. Average train and metro stations POIs with devices in December, in Santa Maria Maior: non-roaming (left) and roaming (right).

In the non-roaming case the railway station with the most devices in December was Restauradores, together with the homonymous metro station, which has slightly more than 7 million devices, while the fewest devices were observed in the Rossio train station, with almost 2 million devices. These POIs contain an average devices of nearly 4.5 million.

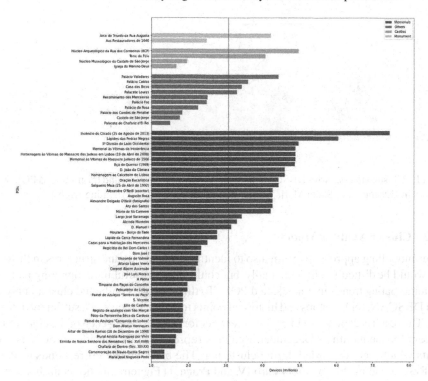

Fig. 10. Average historic POIs with devices in December, in Santa Maria Maior: non-roaming (left) and roaming (right).

In the roaming graph (see Fig. 10), between Rossio and Martim Moniz, Restauradores metro station had the highest number of devices with approximately 900,000 devices, followed by Rossio, with nearly 800,000 devices, Baixa-Chiado, Rossio, and Terreiro do Paco with values below 500,000 devices, and Martim Moniz with just under 400,000 devices. Comparing non-roaming and roaming, the non-roaming case has an average of around 4.5 million devices and the roaming case has an average of approximately 500,000.

Therefore, we modified our modelling approach and instead of having all our original groups—castle, memorial, monument, etc.—we created four groups: castle, memorial, monument + museum and others with the remaining groups (see Fig. 10).

In Fig. 10, we show that memorials had the highest number of historic POIs (44), followed by castles (10), others (4), and monuments (2), where other comprise churches, city walls, and archaeological sites. In both non-roaming and roaming cases, the memorial type not only has the largest number of POIs (more than half of POIs, but also showed the bigger presence of devices, with more than 2.5 million non-roaming, and 3 million roaming. The historical site with the most devices is the memorial of the Incêndio do Chiado (5.5 million non-roaming, and 7.5 million roaming), and the memorial of Maria José Nogueira Pinto and Comemoração do Navio-Escola Sagres are the sites with the fewest with less than 1.5 million devices (non-roaming and roaming).

Fig. 11. Cluster analysis with DBSCAN of historic, bus stops, metro, and train stations POIs with devices in December, in Santa Maria Maior: non-roaming (left) and roaming (right).

3.4.2 Cluster Analysis Model

In our modelling approach we aim also to identify correlations and structures in the data that would be difficult to find manually, but could also be useful in recognizing patterns and anticipating trends in our selected POIs. To this aim, we conducted cluster analyses with DBSCAN, for bus stops and historical points together, to achieve a sufficient data set size. The result is depicted in Fig. 11 where the color dots represent each of the eight found clusters for the month of December. Red dots represent POIs considered outliers, i.e., points which were discarded during clustering. The black cluster corresponds to Praça dos Restauradores, Praça Dom Pedro IV, and Praça da Figueira, in the Santa Justa area. The pink cluster regards Praça Martim Moniz, in the Mouraria neighborhood. Chiado and Sacramento correspond, respectively. To the dark orange and deep pink clusters The longest cluster is colored purple and extends from Mártires to Castelo/Santiago. The yellow cluster is located in the Madalena neighborhood. The brown cluster corresponds to the neighborhood of Sé. The orange cluster includes the areas of Alfama and São Miguel. The blue cluster is located between São Miguel and Santo Estêvão. And close to the São Vicente parish, Santo Estêvão neighborhood, the green cluster evolves around the Lisbon Military Museum.

We highlight two of the found clusters: the purple and the blue. The purple cluster follows the route of the well-known electric tram 28E | Martim Moniz – Prazeres across the Baixa area, whereas the blue cluster is located in the Lisbon Cruise Terminal area bordering the green cluster in the Museu Militar. In Fig. 11 we can observe that, in these clusters, non-roaming mobility is higher.

3.5 Discussion

The literature review led to the collection of academic papers that determined the method-ologies applied in this paper. Our study addressed the understanding of how travelers handling a mobile phone (nationals or roaming users), move in the city of Lisbon, partic-ularly in the vicinity of POIs in the city, namely historic places and public transportation, with a special focus in the Santa Maria Maior parish. We analyzing georeferenced data collected by Vodafone during a five-month period, from September 2021 to January

2022 and open-source mapping data of the City [19] (OSMnx). We used statistical analysis and clustering analysis with DBSCAN, to investigate such travel phenomena. The development of various combinations between categories of POIs with DBSCAN [6–9] led us to conclude that the optimal result was eight clusters, of which two clusters, the purple cluster and the blue cluster, stood out due to their proximity to 28E tram route and Lisbon Cruise Terminal.

This research produced an innovative study taking the perspective of public transportation rather than shared transportation [16], with a focus case in the parish of Santa Maria Maior. This was chosen due to the large number of observed devices for non-roaming and roaming travelers, as well as the large number of POIs.

3.6 Research Limitations

We can highlight a few limitations, regarding the mobile phone data quality. The month of September data only begins on the 15th, making it an incomplete month. Additionally, the monthly datasets were encoded incorrectly, resulting in certain damaged values and improper formatting of the datetime and polygon objects. The data lacks also information on the nationalities of the roaming devices. The identification of the time they spend in a specific square polygon could result in an interesting analysis of trajectory patterns. The data corresponds to a pandemic-restricted season, which does not represent a usual mobility period. The inclusion of anonymous device identification could also allow a more extensive study to better understand the trajectories of travelers.

3.7 Future Work

Future work could cross-reference mobile phone data with public transportation cards (Viva/Navegante) data, in order to understand the entries and exits in transportation modalities. The availability the roaming nationality variable, would enable to comprehend distinct behavioral patterns from different nationalities. With a higher processing capacity, it would be possible to analyze all monthly data in a single dataset and generate more dynamic graphs, including the analysis of daily peaks, during the day, afternoon, or night, taking into account the full dataset.

Acknowledgements. This work is partially funded by national funds through FCT - Fundação para a Ciência e Tecnologia, I.P., under the project FCT UIDB/04466/2020.

References

1. Mobilidade na cidade de Lisboa com base em dados de telemóveis – LxDataLab. https://lisboainteligente.cm-lisboa.pt/lxdatalab/desafios/mobilidade-na-cidade-de-lisboa-com-base-em-dados-de-telemoveis/. Accessed 30 Aug 2022
2. LxDataLab - Lisboa Inteligente. https://lisboainteligente.cm-lisboa.pt/lxi-iniciativas/lxdatalab/. Accessed 03 Sep 2022
3. CRISP-DM - a framework for data mining & analysis. https://thinkinsights.net/data-literacy/crisp-dm/. Accessed 21 Oct 2022

4. Schröer, C., Kruse, F., Gómez, J.M.: A systematic literature review on applying CRISP-DM process model. Procedia Comput. Sci. **181**, 526–534 (2021). https://doi.org/10.1016/J.PROCS.2021.01.199

5. Page, M.J., et al.: The PRISMA 2020 statement: an updated guideline for reporting systematic reviews. BMJ, **372** (2021). https://doi.org/10.1136/BMJ.N71

6. Saliba, M., Abela, C., Layfield, C.: Vehicular traffic flow intensity detection and prediction through mobile data usage. In: CEUR Workshop Proceedings, vol. 2259, pp. 66–77 (2018)

7. Irrevaldy, Saptawati, G.A.P.: Spatio-temporal mining to identify potential traff congestion based on transportation mode. In: Proceedings of 2017 International Conference on Data and Software Engineering, ICoDSE, pp. 1–6 (2017). https://doi.org/10.1109/ICODSE.2017.8285857

8. Li, C., Hu, J., Dai, Z., Fan, Z., Wu, Z.: Understanding individual mobility pattern and portrait depiction based on mobile phone data. ISPRS Int. J. Geoinf. **9**(11), 666 (2020). https://doi.org/10.3390/ijgi9110666

9. Li, M., Jin, B., Tang, H., Zhang, F.: Clustering large-scale origin-destination pairs: a case study for public transit in Beijing. In: Proceedings - 2018 IEEE SmartWorld, Ubiquitous Intelligence and Computing, Advanced and Trusted Computing, Scalable Computing and Communications, Cloud and Big Data Computing, Internet of People and Smart City Innovations, SmartWorld/UIC/ATC/ScalCom/CBDCo, pp. 705–712, (2018). https://doi.org/10.1109/SmartWorld.2018.00137

10. Qin, S., Man, J., Wang, X., Li, C., Dong, H., Ge, X.: Applying big data analytics to monitor tourist flow for the scenic area operation management. Discrete Dyn. Nat. Soc. **2019**, 1–11 (2019). https://doi.org/10.1155/2019/8239047

11. Balzotti, C., Bragagnini, A., Briani, M., Cristiani, E.: Understanding human mobility flows from aggregated mobile phone data. IFAC-PapersOnLine **51**(9), 25–30 (2018). https://doi.org/10.1016/j.ifacol.2018.07.005

12. Yuan, Y., Raubal, M.: Extracting dynamic urban mobility patterns from mobile phone data. In: Xiao, N., Kwan, M.-P., Goodchild, M.F., Shekhar, S. (eds.) GIScience 2012. LNCS, vol. 7478, pp. 354–367. Springer, Heidelberg (2012). https://doi.org/10.1007/978-3-642-33024-7_26

13. Wang, P., Zhang, J., Liu, G., Fuu, Y., Aggarwal, C.: Ensemble-spotting: ranking urban vibrancy via POI embedding with multi-view spatial graphs. In: SIAM International Conference on Data Mining, SDM 2018, pp. 351–359 (2018). https://doi.org/10.1137/1.9781611975321.40

14. Martins, T.G., Lago, N., Santana, E.F.Z., Telea, A., Kon, F., de Souza, H.A.: Using bundling to visualize multivariate urban mobility structure patterns in the São Paulo metropolitan area. J. Internet Serv. Appl. **12**(1), 1–32 (2021). https://doi.org/10.1186/s13174-021-00136-9

15. Senaratne, H., et al.: Urban mobility analysis with mobile network data: a visual analytics approach. IEEE Trans. Intell. Transp. Syst. **19**(5), 1537–1546 (2018). https://doi.org/10.1109/TITS.2017.2727281

16. Fontes, T., Arantes, M., Figueiredo, P.V., Novais, P.: A cluster-based approach using smartphone data for bike-sharing docking stations identification: lisbon case study. Smart Cities **5**(1), 251–275 (2022). https://doi.org/10.3390/smartcities5010016

17. Haidery, S.A., Ullah, H., Khan, N.U., Fatima, K., Rizvi, S.S., Kwon, S.J.: Role of big data in the development of smart city by analyzing the density of residents in shanghai. Electronics **9**(5), 837 (2020). https://doi.org/10.3390/electronics9050837

18. Diário da República, 1.ª série — N.º 216 — 8 de novembro de 2012 (2012). https://files.dre.pt/1s/2012/11/21600/0645406460.pdf. Accessed 09 Sep 2022

19. OSMnx 1.2.2 — OSMnx 1.2.2 documentation. https://osmnx.readthedocs.io/en/stable/. Accessed 09 Sep 2022

Traceability, Optimization
and Cooperative Vehicles Platooning

Development of a Hardware in the Loop Ad-Hoc Testbed for Cooperative Vehicles Platooning

Enio Vasconcelos Filho[1](✉) ⓘ, Bruno Mendes[1], Pedro M. Santos[1] ⓘ,
Ricardo Severino[2] ⓘ, and Eduardo Tovar[1] ⓘ

[1] CISTER Research Centre, ISEP, Rua Alfredo Allen 535, 4200-135 Porto, Portugal
{enpvf,1180752,emt}@isep.ipp.pt
[2] PORTIC Porto Research, Technology & Innovation Center, P.PORTO, Rua
Arquitecto Lobão Vital, 172, 4200-375 Porto, Portugal
sev@portic.ipp.pt

Abstract. Cooperative Cyber-Physical Devices (Co-CPS) are reaching into the most diverse areas and pose new integration challenges. For cooperative autonomous machines, safety and reliability must be guaranteed without human presence. Among these, Cooperative Vehicular Platooning (Co-VP) applications offer an exciting promise, as they allow to improve road occupation, reduce accidents, and provide fuel savings. The high complexity and safety-critical characteristics of these applications requires them to be validated, to ensure their reliability before being applied in real scenarios, notably regarding their underlying communication transactions.

This paper presents an architecture for validating a Co-VP system via Hardware-In-the-Loop (HIL) integration of IEEE 802.11 communications and co-simulation support of a 3D simulator. We present it in a scenario of communication according to the ETSI ITS model and information exchange frequencies between the vehicles. Through these scenarios that mimic realistic conditions of Co-VP applications, we observe the impact of such variations on the number of messages received, network delay, and lateral and longitudinal platoon errors.

Keywords: Cooperative Vehicular Platooning · Vehicular Networks · Safety · Hardware in The Loop

1 Introduction

The advance of communication technologies has expanded the ability of devices to cooperate in an unprecedented way [1,2]. Cooperative Cyber-Physical Devices (Co-CPS) have emerged from these advances, being applied to diverse industrial [3], residential [4], logistics [5], and automotive [6] applications. Among these, one prominent application is Cooperative Vehicular Platooning (Co-VP) [7]. Co-VP enables fuel savings [8], reduced traffic flows [9], and contribute to decreasing

A. L. Martins et al. (Eds.): INTSYS 2022, LNICST 486, pp. 57–72, 2023.
https://doi.org/10.1007/978-3-031-30855-0_4

the number of accidents [10]. In a Co-VP application, platoon members receive information from neighbors, other vehicles (V2X), or the infrastructure (V2I). An overview of the connectivity that can enable Co-VP is illustrated in Fig. 1. Co-VP is highly affected by the network conditions since the vehicle controller and platoon safety rely on information received from the environment [11].

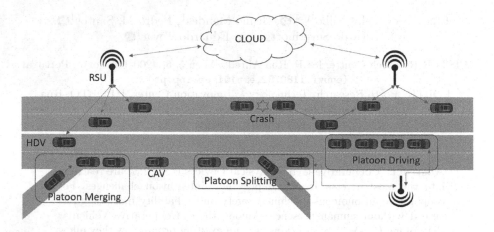

Fig. 1. Co-VP general View

Due to the variety of agents involved, the vehicle speed and the need of real-time response, system failures could result in damages and even loss of lives. Thus, they are classified as safety-critical systems [12] and thorough validation before implementing these systems is required [13]. In this context, simulators are essential to validate Co-VP systems, given their flexibility, scalability, and low-cost [14]. Nevertheless, this cannot replace system validation at the real hardware platforms, since simulators cannot encompass all real-world dynamics and the imperfections produced by process characteristics or hardware constraints [15]. However, given the cost and complexity of Co-CPS and Co-VP applications, along with the safety risks, safety limits are complex and expensive to validate in such configurations.

An intermediate model between full simulation and the real system is the Hardware in the Loop (HIL) [16]. Typically used in automotive environments, HIL provides a well-defined condition for the Device Under Test (DUT), commonly used to test complex physical systems and processes. Compared to field testing, it is a cheaper solution and presents results that are easier to replicate [17]. In addition, the HIL-based approach allows experimentation and analysis of a specific component in the Co-VP study, such as On Board Units (OBUs) and Road Side Units (RSUs). These tests can be realized over additional safety-critical scenarios, enabling the analysis of the vehicle response while ensuring a risk-free environment.

In this paper, we present an implementation of HIL aimed at validating the communication infrastructure of Co-VP systems, using as a base the CopaDrive

Table 1. Acronyms Table

Acronym	Meaning	Acronym	Meaning
BSP	Basic Service Profile	OBU	On Board unit
CAM	Cooperative Awareness Messages	PF	Predecessor-Follower
Co-CPS	Cooperative CPS	ROS	Robot Operating System
Co-VP	Cooperative Vehicular Platooning	RSU	Road Side Unit
CPS	Cyber-Physical Systems	TRC	Transmission Rate Control
DUT	Device Under Test	V2I	Vehicle to Infrastructure
ETSI	European Telecommunications Standards Institute	V2V	Vehicle to Vehicle
HIL	Hardware in The Loop	VANET	Vehicular Ad Hoc Network
IFT	Information Flow Topology	WAVE	Wireless Access in Vehicular Environment

model shown in [14]. So, we integrated the CopaDrive and Wi-Fi communication devices (IEEE 802.11), using the Robot Operating System (ROS) as an interface. The contributions of this work can be divided into three aspects:

- To present a HIL architecture integrating a 3D simulator and a real communications model to validate the communications infrastructure and its impact on the vehicles' platooning performance.
- Present a hybrid communications model between the application layer of ETSI ITS-G5 [18] and the physical layers of IEEE 802.11. We validate this communication model and the delays between messages using control boards used in real vehicles.
- Analysis of the Co-VP use case using different maximum communication frequencies and the message triggers defined in ITS-G5, analyzing the lateral and longitudinal platooning errors.

The organization of the rest of this paper is as follows. In Sect. 2, we present related work describing HIL implementations. The architecture of the developed HIL is explained in Sect. 3, including the equipment and technologies used. Next, we present the proposed scenarios and the evaluation tests. Final remarks are drawn Sect. 5. An acronyms list is presented in Table 1 to the reader's convenience.

2 Background

The flexibility of HIL in enabling the interaction between physical test vehicles and virtual vehicles from traffic simulation models has been studied before [19], showing it increases validation scalability and reduces costs. Another advantage of HIL is to evaluate safety-critical systems and resources that usually operate in highly variable environments in a controlled and limited environment. It also allows for parallel development of different system components on the fly [20]. The general HIL architecture for Co-VP scenarios is presented in Fig. 2, where a bidirectional information flow between the Cyber-Physical physical and virtual subsystems is shown.

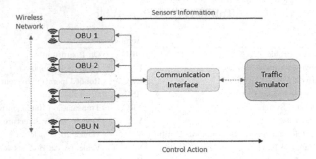

Fig. 2. HIL General Architecture

Just a few works address the HIL application in Co-VP environments. For instance, the work presented in [21] enables Co-VP performance evaluation based on stability and collision risk analysis. Furthermore, extensive simulation using real-world vehicle parameters can examine longitudinal controller specifications and network characteristics, observing platooning performance limits caused by network constraints and control system settings. Extending the network constraint analyses, the impact of Transmission Rate Control (TRC) on a Co-VP scenario based on industrial V2X nodes operating on ETSI ITS-G5 channels is the main focus of [22]. It evaluates the longitudinal distance of simulated vehicles in congested scenarios by changing the message frequency based on a simulation of four vehicle OBUs with data logging over Matlab Software.

Otherwise, the authors of [23] implemented a HIL test platform using the Carsim/Simulink vehicle simulator integrated with real DSRC modems. This HIL allowed a realistic evaluation of the parameter selection method of a Co-VP model based on a feedforward controller within a stable column boundary. In addition, this platform also evaluates the impact of dropout and communication delay on the longitudinal column stability of the Co-VP. Finally, an LTE C-V2X [24] HIL implementation was presented in [25]. Although this work is still under development, the authors have already presented an interesting platform based on the CARLA simulator, integrated with Simulation of Urban MObility (SUMO) and direct communication between the simulated vehicles via C-V2X Mode 4 modules. This platform implements a Software-Defined-Radio (SDR) based on three radio devices that mimic three real vehicles. In future HIL implementation developments, various Co-VP controller models can be evaluated based on the SUMO simulator.

2.1   Cooperative Vehicular Platooning

The interest in platooning applications is increasing in industrial and academic environments due to its advantages for traffic and drivers. Co-VP applications increase road efficiency in traffic, reducing vehicle distances, lowering energy consumption, and reducing CO_2 emissions. On drivers side, it reduces the travels time and a reduction in travel time due to reduced traffic congestion [26,27].

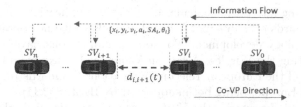

Fig. 3. Co-VP Predecessor-Follower Information Flow Topology (PF-IFT) [31]

In this work, we assume a platoon of $n + 1$ vehicles under a V2X communication environment using a Predecessor-Follower Information Flow Topology (PF-IFT) [28], as presented in Fig. 3. Each vehicle has sensors to measure its global position, speed, acceleration, and heading. The vehicles in the platoon are referred to as car_i (where $i \in \{0 \leq i \leq n, i \in \mathbb{N}\}$), with car_1 being the platoon leader. Each car_i can be both a local leader of car_{i+1} and a follower of car_{i-1}. Each follower decides their behavior based solely on the messages received from the local leader, transmitted upon activation of kinematic triggers based on the ETSI ITS-G5 standard. Each car_i sends a message $m_{i,i+1}(t)$ containing its current global position $(x_i(t), y_i(t))$, speed $(v_i(t))$, acceleration $a_i(t)$, steering angle $\alpha_i(t)$ and heading $\theta_i(t)$ to SV_{i+1}. The platoon members control model is based on the integrated lateral and longitudinal Look Ahead Controller, as presented in [29, 30].

2.2   Vehicular Communications

Communication between vehicles and infrastructure is increasingly necessary, thus opening up the possibility of creating effective C-ITS, allowing road users and traffic managers to share information and use it to coordinate and co-decide on their actions. This information flow is built upon an IEEE 802.11n network on a Vehicular AdHoc Network (VANET). So a VANET is a subclass of a mobile AdHoc network, which does not depend on fixed infrastructure, allowing the network nodes (mostly vehicles) to move freely. The VANET has two main goals: continuous connectivity for mobile users while on the road and efficient wireless connection between vehicles without access to any fixed infrastructure [32].

Regarding vehicle communications, several studies have been performed in VANETs, including comparisons between different technologies [33]. Among the most studied and promising ones are IEEE 802.16e [34], LTE C-V2X [35], and IEEE 802.11p [32]. Despite the great discussion of which will prevail in the future, an in-depth comparison of each of them will not be analyzed within this project's scope. It is a fact that the IEEE 802.11p is the most used, tested, and accepted nowadays for vehicular communications [36,37]. As a complement, 5G with all its features [38] network slicing, a greater number of connected devices, lower latency, and greater speed in transmissions that can be up to ten times faster than 4G [39] become all communications faster and more secure.

The increasing interest in vehicular cooperative applications induced the definition of standards over different VANET models to define conditions and use cases for technology development. So, some organizations have worked in this direction, creating the Wireless Access in Vehicular Environments (WAVE) [40] in the U.S.A and the European Telecommunications Standards Institute (ETSI) ITS-G5 [41] in Europe, being both supported by IEEE 802.11p.

In an embedded scenario, the V2V communication is ensured by the OBU, present in each vehicle. This module will be responsible for transmitting messages between vehicles and sending and receiving data from the neighbors. Looking forward to speeding up message transmissions, the general V2V communication model defines a broadcast message containing the vehicle information to be used by neighbors. In addition, the ETSI ITS-G5 standard and WAVE define the transmission of basic messages, called Cooperative Awareness Messages (CAM) and Basic Safety Messages (BSM), respectively, enabling collective perception. The CAMs can be transmitted periodically, at a pre-defined time interval, or event-triggered when a kinematic threshold is crossed, e.g., when speed or heading angle strikes a given value [31].

3   HIL Simulation Architecture

An HIL architecture allows to simulate a complex scenario (e.g., vehicular platooning) while integrating real-world components for validation within the architecture. Conceptually, the single entity *vehicle* is actually composed of two subsystems: the communication subsystem, in the form of On-board Units (OBU) that provide ad-hoc communication between vehicles, and the physical vehicle itself. In the presented HIL architecture, the first subsystem is accurately replicated by actual OBUs (one per each vehicle in the scenario), whereas the vehicles and the world in which they exist are simulated using ROS nodes and Gazebo, a simulator of vehicle dynamics and control. The HIL architecture and implementation presented in this paper is based on the version of Copadrive described in [14]; a more detailed representation of it can be found in Fig. 4.

3.1   Platooning Application

We consider three vehicles in which the first, Car_1, is the global leader of the Co-VP application, acting autonomously to follow a line in the track. The followers are respectively Car_2 and Car_3, but this configuration can easily be extended to more vehicles. The vehicle speed and position controller model is based on the integrated system presented in [29]. Thus, it is possible to validate the lateral and longitudinal errors between the vehicles during their movement. This controller is based on a double PID controller, responsible for the vehicle's speed and steering angle.

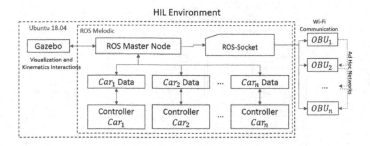

Fig. 4. HIL implementation View

3.2   Communication via Wireless Media

In this implementation, we are using Jetsons TX2 [42] equipped with Wi-fi interfaces as OBUs. The wireless link is meant to provided solely communication between the local leader and its follower. To share data between OBUs, each Jetson contains two processes, a ROS Server and ROS Client, shown in Fig. 5. The ROS Server provides vehicle information (received from the ROS Master) to the ROS Clients present at other OBUs through the wireless medium. Upon reception of a message, the ROS Clients transmit that information to its respective ROS Server.

3.3   OBU-Simulation Connection

Each Jetson has access to all necessary ROS topics through a Master-Slave connection setup between the Master (deployed at the machine running the simulation) and each Slave (the Jetsons). This connection model allows a ROS full-duplex communication, so each Jetson can publish and subscribe to the necessary topics. To this end, we set up a socket connection in stream mode using TCP/IP.

The ROS Server at each vehicle has access to the vehicle information by subscribing to the topic $car_i/carINFO$ published, after which it builds messages in CAM format. Whenever required, the data is serialized [43] and sent to the bonded clients. On the ROS Client side, the data has to be deserialized to reconstruct the CAM, which is immediately published in the topic $car_i/RXNetwork\_wi\_fi$, where the leader vehicle subscribes to the $car_1/carINFO$ topic and forward the data to the other two vehicles, which will respectively publish in the $car2/RXNetwork\_wi\_fi$ and $car3/RXNetwork\_wi\_fi$ topics.

As all OBUs can monitor ROS topics, all vehicles have access to their neighbor's information. However, by design, the follower only uses local leader information.

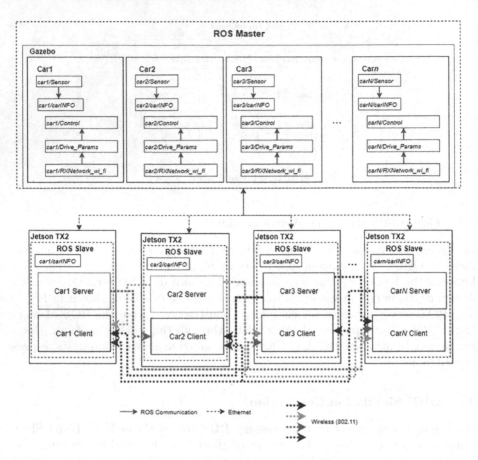

Fig. 5. System Architecture

4   System Evaluation

To evaluate the capability of the proposed HIL system, we define a realistic scenario that allows the comparison between different messaging profiles. The ETSI ITS-G5 [41] standard presents a set of rules for triggering CAM messages, defined in [31] as Basic Service Profile (BSP), based on the variation of speed, distance, and heading of the vehicle between two measurements, presented as follows:

- Maximum time (T_{max}) interval between CAM generations: 1 s;
- Minimum time (T_{min}) interval between CAM generations: 0.1 s;
- Heading difference: the absolute difference between the current and last heading provided in a CAM; a CAM is triggered if heading difference > 4°;
- Position difference: a CAM is triggered
  if position difference > 4 m;

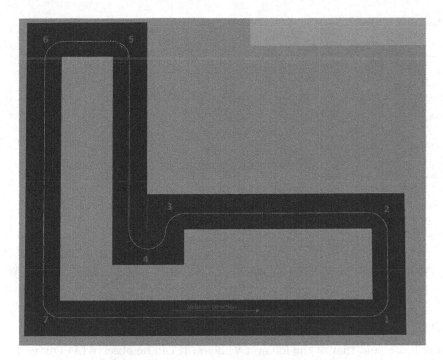

Fig. 6. HIL's evaluation circuit scenario

- Speed difference: a CAM is triggered
  if speed difference > 0.5 m/s;

The circuit used during the validation intends to imitate a possible city scenario with five 90° turns and a 180°, as presented in Fig. 6. In each scenario, the maximum message firing frequency was changed between 10 Hz, 7.5 Hz, 5 Hz, 2 Hz, and 1 Hz. Under these conditions, the kinematic triggers of message sending and the proposed time limit were evaluated. We also compare the HIL results in each scenario with the one presented in a fully simulated scenario, with no message delays. Thus, it can be observed how the different communication conditions affect the control of the vehicles in the proposed scenario.

Regarding the actual OBU equipment, whereas in [14] commercial ETSI ITS-compliant OBUs were used, in the present implementation these have been replaced by Jetsons TX2 [42] equipped with WiFi communication. This does not affect, however, the validity of the proposed HIL approach.

4.1 Scenario Results

Figure 7 demonstrates the trajectory traveled by the platoon leader and vehicles 2 and 3 in each simulation in scenario A. The analysis of the trajectory traveled by the vehicles using the BSP shows that the profiles with lower maximum messaging frequency have a more significant discrepancy between the trajectory

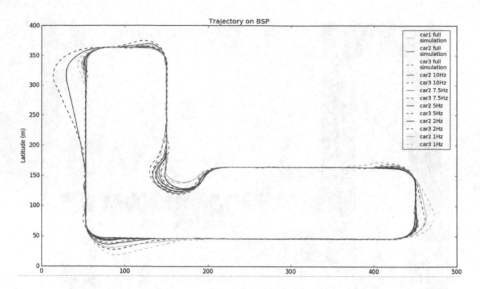

Fig. 7. Performed Trajectory on BSP

of the leader and that of the follower vehicles. It can be observed in curves 1, 2, and 7 and curves 5, 6, and 7, respectively, at a maximum frequency of 1 Hz and 2 Hz. The analysis of Fig. 7 further illustrates that the trajectory error of car_3 is greater than that of car_2 at almost all frequency variations. However, as the communication frequency increases, this difference is reduced and inexists for frequencies beyond 7.5 Hz. In other words, even motion triggers are not enough to guarantee that the trajectory is the same among all vehicles since increasing the sending frequency improves this adjustment.

Finally, the joint analysis of the tests demonstrates the impact of the delay between messages on the vehicle control system. This impact is illustrated by comparing the simulated follower's trajectory, with near zero inter-message delays, and in the HIL implemented models. In the entire simulation scenario, the followers can perform the same trajectory as the leader, while this capacity is reduced as we reduce the communication frequency.

The conclusions obtained from the vehicle's trajectory are corroborated by analyzing the error of the longitudinal distance between them during the trip. The desired distance between the vehicles is defined in [29] as a constant time-headway policy (CTHP) that uses the vehicle's current speed to define the safety distance. Thus, the distance error is calculated as the difference between the current and the desired distance. This error is presented in Fig. 8 as the error of the longitudinal PID controller. This figure illustrates how the maximum values of the longitudinal error increase with decreasing maximum messaging frequency. The distance error varies along the route, being corrected on the straight lines, but suffers a high impact with the circuit curves.

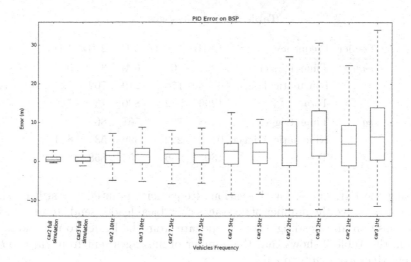

Fig. 8. PID Error on BSP

Another analysis of the performance of the Co-VP system is performed concerning the follower's lateral error compared to the leader. As observed in Fig. 7, the curves performed by the followers that move over a lower messaging frequency exhibit a higher error. This observation is reinforced in Fig. 9, which indicates the fit of the heading of the leader and the followers at different frequencies for curve 7. This figure illustrates that the HIL simulations with higher sending frequencies present less oscillation and quick stabilization, returning to the correct trajectory. However, this oscillation is more significant in the lower frequency cases and prevents the system from stabilizing quickly.

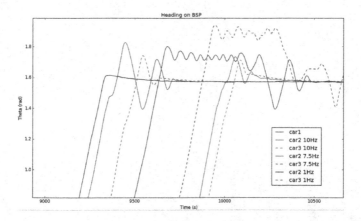

Fig. 9. BSP Heading Comparison

Table 2. Sent Messages

Sender	Frequency	10 Hz	7.5 Hz	5 Hz	2 Hz	1 Hz
car_1	Time Trigger	1296	762	620	34	0
	Kinematic Trigger	0	170	210	702	728
	Total	1296	932	830	736	728
car_2	Time Trigger	1303	734	561	805	0
	Kinematic Trigger	0	222	396	53	804
	Total	1303	956	957	858	804

Using the HIL model for the various frequencies pointed out still makes it possible to observe the number of messages each local leader sends to its follower. As the position and heading errors propagate from the leader to the end of the platoon, the Table 2 shows that the number of messages sent from car_2 to car_3 is higher than from car_1 to car_2.

Finally, we also evaluate the delay between messages sent from car_1 to car_2 and from car_2 to car_3 at each given frequency. This analysis studies the time between messages sent by the ROS server allocated respectively on cars 1 and 2 to the client version of ROS on cars 2 and 3. As this HIL implementation includes OBUs using Wi-Fi as the communication medium, capturing this information is essential for different studies and modeling Co-VP systems. This delay is shown in Fig. 10. This figure illustrates that above the frequency of 5 Hz, the difference between the delays is minimal. This difference is reflected in the car's movements on the track and their trajectory. At lower frequencies, this delay increases, implying larger trajectory, distance, and heading errors.

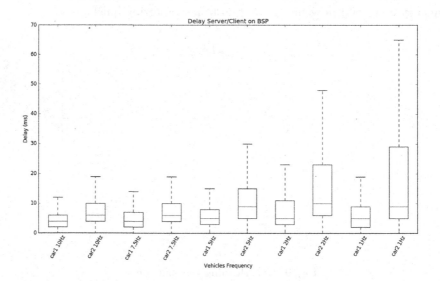

Fig. 10. Delay During the BSP Tests

5   Conclusion and Future Works

This paper presents a HIL architecture for the evaluation of Co-VP systems. The architecture brings together actual radio equipment – 802.11 (WiFi)-capable On-Board Units – and a software simulation of the physical dynamics and control of vehicles – based on ROS and Gazebo. This allows us to analyze the impacts of communication in the performance of Co-VP applications in a realistic fashion, as message exchanges are carried out by actual hardware. To showcase the presented HIL implementation, we deployed a simulated platoon using control algorithms already experimentally validated in realistic circuit, and quantified application performance (lateral and longitudinal errors) and communication performance (delays between messages) while varying the message-sending frequencies and triggers across the ranges defined in ETSI ITS standards family. Thus, we firmly believe this tool can contribute to different studies on Co-VP systems, both in the control and communications areas, due to the implemented client-server structure for communication between the devices.

We hope to scale the system to more vehicles and study the impact of other communication models on the platoon, ensuring its safety conditions and minimizing the errors found.

Acknowledgements. This work was partially supported by National Funds through FCT/MCTES (Portuguese Foundation for Science and Technology), within the CIS-TER Research Unit (UIDP/UIDB/04234/2020); by the FCT and the Portuguese National Innovation Agency (ANI), under the CMU Portugal partnership, through the European Regional Development Fund (ERDF) of the Operational Competitiveness Programme and Internationalization (COMPETE 2020), under the PT2020 Partnership Agreement, within project FLOYD (grant nr. 45912); and by FCT and the EU ECSEL JU under the H2020 Framework Programme, within project ECSEL/0010/2019, JU grant nr. 876019 (ADACORSA). The JU receives support from the European Union's Horizon 2020 research and innovation program and Germany, Netherlands, Austria, France, Sweden, Cyprus, Greece, Lithuania, Portugal, Italy, Finland, and Turkey. The ECSEL JU and the European Commission are not responsible for the content on this paper or any use that may be made of the information it contains.

References

1. Cheng, X., Huang, Z., Chen, S.: Vehicular communication channel measurement, modelling, and application for beyond 5G and 6G. IET Commun. **14**, 3303–3311 (2020)
2. Rahim, A., Malik, P.K., Sankar Ponnapalli, V.A.: State of the art: a review on vehicular communications, impact of 5G, fractal antennas for future communication. In: Singh, P.K., Pawłowski, W., Tanwar, S., Kumar, N., Rodrigues, J.J.P.C., Obaidat, M.S. (eds.) Proceedings of First International Conference on Computing, Communications, and Cyber-Security (IC4S 2019). LNNS, vol. 121, pp. 3–15. Springer, Singapore (2020). https://doi.org/10.1007/978-981-15-3369-3_1

3. Pivoto, D.G., de Almeida, L.F., da Rosa Righi, R., Rodrigues, J.J., Lugli, A.B., Alberti, A.M.: Cyber-physical systems architectures for industrial internet of things applications in industry 4.0: a literature review. J. Manuf. Syst. **58**, 176–192 (2021)
4. Mazumder, S.K., et al.: A review of current research trends in power-electronic innovations in cyber-physical systems. IEEE J. Emerg. Sel. Top. Power Electron. **9**, 5146–5163 (2021)
5. Kong, X.T., Kang, K., Zhong, R.Y., Luo, H., Xu, S.X.: Cyber physical system-enabled on-demand logistics trading. Int. J. Prod. Econ. **233**, 108005 (2021)
6. Son, Y.H., Park, K.T., Lee, D., Jeon, S.W., Do Noh, S.: Digital twin-based cyber-physical system for automotive body production lines. Int. J. Adv. Manuf. Technol. **115**, 291–310 (2021)
7. Balador, A., Bazzi, A., Hernandez-Jayo, U., de la Iglesia, I., Ahmadvand, H.: A survey on vehicular communication for cooperative truck platooning application. Veh. Commun. **35**, 100460 (2022)
8. Earnhardt, C., Groelke, B., Borek, J., Pelletier, E., Brennan, S., Vermillion, C.: Cooperative exchange-based platooning using predicted fuel-optimal operation of heavy-duty vehicles. IEEE Trans. Intell. Transp. Syst. **23**, 17312–17324 (2022)
9. Li, K., Wang, J., Zheng, Y.: Cooperative formation of autonomous vehicles in mixed traffic flow: beyond platooning. IEEE Trans. Intell. Transp. Syst. **23**, 15951–15966 (2022)
10. Vasconcelos Filho, E., Severino, R., Koubaa, A., Tovar, E.: A real time QoS monitor architecture proposal for cooperative vehicular platooning. In: Book of Abstracts of the Symposium on Transport Systems and Mobility, (Porto, Portugal), p. 4. FEUP (2021)
11. Xiao, S., Ge, X., Han, Q.L., Zhang, Y.: Secure distributed adaptive platooning control of automated vehicles over vehicular ad-hoc networks under denial-of-service attacks. IEEE Trans. Cybern. **52**, 1–13 (2021)
12. Knight, J.: Safety critical systems: challenges and directions. In: Proceedings of the 24th International Conference on Software Engineering. ICSE 2002, pp. 547–550 (2002)
13. Wolschke, C., Sangchoolie, B., Simon, J., Marksteiner, S., Braun, T., Hamazaryan, H.: SaSeVAL: a safety/security-aware approach for validation of safety-critical systems. In: 2021 51st Annual IEEE/IFIP International Conference on Dependable Systems and Networks Workshops (DSN-W), (Taipei, Taiwan), pp. 27–34. IEEE (2021)
14. Filho, E.V., Severino, R., Rodrigues, J., Gonçalves, B., Koubaa, A., Tovar, E.: CopaDrive: an integrated ROS cooperative driving test and validation framework. In: Koubaa, A. (ed.) Robot Operating System (ROS). SCI, vol. 962, pp. 121–174. Springer, Cham (2021). https://doi.org/10.1007/978-3-030-75472-3_4
15. Drechsler, M.F., Sharma, V., Reway, F., Schütz, C., Huber, W.: Dynamic vehicle-in-the-loop: a novel method for testing automated driving functions. SAE Int. J. Connected Autom. Veh. **5**, 12–05-04-0029 (2022)
16. Shao, Y., Zulkefli, M.A.M., Sun, Z., Huang, P.: Evaluating connected and autonomous vehicles using a hardware-in-the-loop testbed and a living lab. Transp. Res. Part C Emerg. Technol. **102**, 121–135 (2019)
17. Obermaier, C., Riebl, R., Facchi, C.: Fully reactive hardware-in-the-loop simulation for VANET devices. In: 2018 21st International Conference on Intelligent Transportation Systems (ITSC), (Maui, Hawaii, USA), pp. 3755–3760, IEEE (2018)
18. European Telecommunications Standards Institute. ETSI EN 302 637–2 V1.4.0 Intelligent Transport Systems (ITS); Vehicular Communications; Basic Set of

Applications; Part 2: Specification of Cooperative Awareness Basic Service, Technical report V1.4.0, ETSI (2018)

19. Ma, J., Zhou, F., Huang, Z., James, R.: Hardware-in-the-loop testing of connected and automated vehicle applications: a use case for cooperative adaptive cruise control. In: 2018 21st International Conference on Intelligent Transportation Systems (ITSC), (Maui, Hawaii, USA), pp. 2878–2883. IEEE (2018). ISSN: 2153–0017

20. Joshi, A.: A novel approach for validating adaptive cruise control (ACC) using two hardware-in-the-loop (HIL) simulation benches. SAE Technical Paper 2019–01-1038, SAE International, Warrendale, PA (2019). ISSN: 0148–7191, 2688–3627

21. Plöger, D., Krüger, L., Timm-Giel, A.: analysis of communication demands of networked control systems for autonomous platooning. In: 2018 IEEE 19th International Symposium on A World of Wireless, Mobile and Multimedia Networks (WoWMoM), (Chania, Greece), pp. 14–19. IEEE (2018)

22. Zhu, S., Goswami, D., Li, H.: Evaluation platform of platoon control algorithms in complex communication scenarios. In: 2019 IEEE 89th Vehicular Technology Conference (VTC2019-Spring), (Kuala Lumpur, Malaysia), pp. 1–5. IEEE (2019)

23. Ma,F.: Distributed control of cooperative vehicular platoon with nonideal communication condition. In: IEEE Transactions on Vehicular Technology, vol. 69, pp. 8207–8220 (2020)

24. Dahlman, E., Parkvall, S., Skold, J.: 4G: LTE/LTE-Advanced for Mobile Broadband, 2nd edn. Elsevier, Amsterdam (2014)

25. Zhang, W., Fu, S., Cao, Z., Jiang, Z., Zhang, S., Xu, S.: An SDR-in-the-loop Carla simulator for C-V2X-based autonomous driving. In :IEEE INFOCOM 2020 - IEEE Conference on Computer Communications Workshops (INFOCOM WKSHPS), (Online), pp. 1270–1271. IEEE (2020)

26. U.S. Department Of Transportation. How an Automated Car Platoon Works | Volpe National Transportation Systems Center (2017)

27. Bichiou, Y., Rakha, H., Abdelghaffar, H.M.: A cooperative platooning controller for connected vehicles. In: Proceedings of the 7th International Conference on Vehicle Technology and Intelligent Transport Systems, (Online Streaming, – Select a Country –), pp. 378–385. SCITEPRESS - Science and Technology Publications (2021)

28. Li, Z.: System and method for operating a follower vehicle in a vehicle platoon (2018)

29. Vasconcelos Filho, E., Severino, R., Koubaa, A., Tovar, E.: An integrated lateral and longitudinal look ahead controller for cooperative vehicular platooning. In: Martins, A.L., Ferreira, J.C., Kocian, A., Costa, V. (eds.) INTSYS 2020. LNICST, vol. 364, pp. 142–159. Springer, Cham (2021). https://doi.org/10.1007/978-3-030-71454-3_9

30. Filho, E.V.: Towards a cooperative robotic platooning testbed. In: IEEE International Conference on Autonomous Robot Systems and Competitions (ICARSC), 2020, (Ponta Delgada, Portugal), pp. 332–337. IEEE (2020)

31. Filho, E.V., Santos, P.M., Severino, R., Koubaa, A., Tovar, E.: Improving the performance of cooperative platooning with restricted message trigger thresholds. IEEE Access **10**, 45562–45575 (2022)

32. Sharef, B.T., Alsaqour, R.A., Ismail, M.: Vehicular communication ad hoc routing protocols: a survey. J. Netw. Comput. Appl. **40**, 363–396 (2014)

33. Hussain, R., Lee, J., Zeadally, S.: Trust in VANET: a survey of current solutions and future research opportunities. IEEE Trans. Intell. Transp. Syst. **22**, 2553–2571 (2021)

34. Benkirane, S., Benaziz, M.: Performance evaluation of IEEE 802.11p and IEEE 802.16e for vehicular ad hoc networks using simulation tools. In: 2018 IEEE 5th International Congress on Information Science and Technology (CiSt), pp. 573–577 (2018). ISSN: 2327–1884

35. Sehla, K., Nguyen, T.M.T., Pujolle, G., Velloso, P.B.: resource allocation modes in C-V2X: from LTE-V2X to 5G–V2X. IEEE Int. Things J. **9**, 8291–8314 (2022)

36. Filippi, A., Moerman, K., Martinez, V., Turley, A., Haran, O., Toledano, R.: IEEE802. 11p ahead of LTE-V2V for safety applications. NXP Autotalks **1**(1), 19 (2017)

37. Festag, A.: Standards for vehicular communication-from IEEE 802.11p to 5G. Elektrotechnik und Informationstechnik **132**, 409–416 (2015)

38. Intel. Benefits of 5G Technology and Advantages of 5G Networks (2021)

39. Beutnagel, W.: 5G - How the automotive industry benefits from the new mobile communications standard (2020)

40. Eichler, S.: Performance evaluation of the IEEE 802.11p WAVE communication standard. In: 2007 IEEE 66th Vehicular Technology Conference, (Baltimore, MD, USA), pp. 2199–2203. IEEE (2007)

41. European Telecommunications Standards Institute. ETSI TR 102 638 V1.1.1 - Intelligent Transport Systems (ITS); Vehicular Communications; Basic Set of Applications; Definitions, Technical report TR 102 638, European Telecommunications Standards Institute (2009)

42. JetsonHacks. NVIDIA Jetson TX2 J21 Header Pinout (2020). https://www.jetsonhacks.com/nvidia-jetson-tx2-j21-header-pinout/

43. Agrawal, A.: Python pickling: what it is and how to use it securely | Synopsys (2014)

Optimal Control Based Trajectory Planning Under Uncertainty

Shangyuan Zhang[1,2]($\boxtimes$) (iD), Makhlouf Hadji[2] (iD), and Abdel Lisser[1] (iD)

[1] CentraleSupelec, L2S, Université Paris Saclay, 3 Rue Curie Joliot,
91190 Gif-sur-Yvette, France
abdel.lisser@l2s.centralesupelec.fr
[2] Institut de Recherche Technologique SystemX, 8 Avenue de la Vauve,
91120 Palaiseau, France
{shangyuan.zhang,makhlouf.hadji}@irt-systemx.fr

Abstract. In this paper, we propose a constrained optimal control approach as a reference trajectory generator for a driving scenario with uncertainty. With a given scenario, this generator can produce a reference trajectory in order to make validations for autonomous vehicle's decision-making problems. The constrained optimal control problem guarantees obtaining a collision-free trajectory with safety and comfort based on the design of the objective function and the constraints of the vehicle. The uncertainty of environmental information provided by sensors is taken into account, and a stochastic optimization problem is proposed to limit the risk of violating safety requirements. Numerical experiments show that the stochastic model can better ensure the robustness of the obtained solutions.

Keywords: Autonomous vehicle · Trajectory planning · Stochastic optimization · Optimal control · Chance constraint

1 Introduction

Autonomous vehicles have been an active research area of both academia and industry in recent years as a way to achieve a safer and more effective mode of transportation. Various challenges are faced in different subtasks, and trajectory planning is one of them. An autonomous vehicle's decision-making module has to determine a collision-free and feasible trajectory that takes the vehicle from its current position to its destination in a dynamic and unpredictable driving environment.

Because of the complexity of the autonomous vehicle's system and the possible failure of coherence among the modules, the algorithm's performance may not be initially envisioned, and malfunctions may sometimes occur. It is, therefore, essential to validate the reliability and safety of autonomous vehicles prior to their commercialization. Furthermore, there is no practical way to conduct a

A. L. Martins et al. (Eds.): INTSYS 2022, LNICST 486, pp. 73–88, 2023.
https://doi.org/10.1007/978-3-031-30855-0_5

complete on-road vehicle-level test that covers all driving scenarios. A promising solution is to make the assessment through driving scenarios in simulations to reduce costs and effort. Thus, to evaluate the performance of the decision-making module of an autonomous vehicle, a reference generator is used to generate a reference trajectory and compare the original trajectory with this reference trajectory in order to make an assessment.

In addition, uncertainties arising from sensor noise, measurement fluctuations, and weather conditions must be taken into account to achieve maximum practical performance. These factors have a huge impact on safety assessment. The reliability of trajectory generators depends on their ability to model uncertainty effectively and ensure that the generated trajectory is robust and promising.

The main contribution of this paper is to propose a numerical optimal control method to formulate the reference generation problem under various driving scenarios. The model considers factors like safety, comfort, and effectiveness, as well as features such as adaptive cruise control and lane-keeping assist. In addition, we also address uncertainty and employ a chance constraint to assess safety.

The remainder of this paper is organized as follows: In Sect. 2, state-of-art trajectory planning techniques are discussed. Section 3 describes the formulation of our reference generation model and the stochastic component. Section 4 presents the numerical experiments and compares the performance of different approaches. Conclusions and future perspectives are provided in Sect. 5.

2   Related Work

There has been an increasing amount of trajectory planning techniques derived from robotics and adapted to the application of autonomous vehicle decision-making. A variety of approaches has been developed in order to meet different needs across a wide range of driving scenarios.

One widely applied approach is the sampling-based method, including the Rapidly-exploring Random Tree (RRT) [1] and its variants [2–4]. RRT explores the configuration space with a random search for connections in order to obtain a feasible trajectory. It's widely used in online path planning problems. In [5], improvement has been made by removing the steering function in RRT while providing asymptotic near-optimality for kinodynamic planning. Despite the fact that sampling in a semi-structured space allows for fast planning, there is no guarantee for the optimality and continuity of the results.

There is also interest in graph search-based algorithms at different planning levels. The A* algorithm uses heuristics to perform the process of online trajectory planning efficiently with a fast node search. While it is useful for searching areas known to the vehicle a priori, it is slow and memory-intensive for large areas. Its extensions like AD* [6], ARA* [7] and AIT* [8] aim to find a suboptimal solution quickly by executing an A* with inflated heuristics and then refine the solution incrementally. Typically, a heuristic rule for this type of algorithm is not straightforward to find in complex driving environments, and the trajectory is not always smooth.

In order to generate a smooth trajectory that respects the precise constraints, optimization methods have demonstrated their effectiveness. In [9], The optimal control solutions are presented and analyzed for various maneuvers for models of different complexities. Another example is [10], in which numerical optimal control and homotopy methods are combined for motion planning in nonconvex environments, the problem is formulated as Sequential Quadratic Programming (SQP), and the obstacles are categorized according to their topological properties. The optimization methods typically encode constraints and objectives in continuous optimal control, transform them into a nonlinear optimization problem, and then develop efficient and reliable algorithms to solve it.

3 Problem Formulation

3.1 Driving Scenario

In this section, we break down all the elements of the input to our reference generator model. The driving scenario could be understood as such: a driving scenario is the precise description of all the components in the environment and the trajectory information of all other traffic actors, including vehicles, pedestrians, etc., over a period of time (typically $\leq$ 30s). It could be a simulator or a real-life driving scenario, and the information could be retrieved and stored properly to reproduce it.

The necessary information on the road and other moving objects should be available in a typical driving scenario as follows:

- The trajectory of the ith vehicle at time t: this is represented and noted by $X_i(t), Y_i(t)$.
- The ith center lane of the road is noticed by $C_i(x)$.
- The boundary of the road noted by $B_i(x)$.
- Regulations and code of the road, including maximal speed, which is indicated by v_{max}.

In order to produce the reference trajectory, we also need our ego vehicle's planning information as follows:

- The initial state of the ego vehicle: z_0.
- Predefined way-point as an indicator of the expected maneuver (lane change, overtaking, steady driving, etc.).
- The measure of the optimality that based on an evaluation function.
- Constraints of the vehicle: cinematic and dynamic constraints and consideration of passenger's comfort.

Our reference generator needs to take that information as input and output the reference trajectory for the ego car given the driving scenario.

3.2 Optimal Control Problem

The objective of our work is to develop a reference trajectory generator with various functionalities in a driving scenario. With a scenario as input, this reference path generator should output a list of commands to execute to create a reference trajectory for further evaluation. The reference trajectory must maintain a safe distance from the leading vehicle and drive in the middle of the lane, taking into account all relevant vehicle constraints. This problem can be well-defined under the optimal control framework.

In an optimal control problem, the optimal control input $u(t)$ is determined to minimize an objective function $\ell(\cdot)$ while respecting the system dynamics $f(\cdot)$ and proposed constraints. The problem is formulated as follows:

$$
\begin{aligned}
\min_{z(\cdot),u(\cdot)} \quad & \int_{t_0}^{t_n} \ell(z(t),\,u(t))dt \\
\text{s.t.} \quad & \dot{z}(t) = f(z(t),u(t)), \\
& c(z(t),u(t)) \leq 0, \\
& z(t_0) = z_{\text{init}}, \quad z(t_n) = z_{\text{term}}, \\
& z(t) \in \mathcal{Z}, \quad u(t) \in \mathcal{U}.
\end{aligned}
\tag{1}
$$

where t_0 and t_n are start time and end time, z_{init} and z_{term} are inital and terminal states, $c(\cdot)$ is the inequality constraint function, $\mathcal{Z}$ and $\mathcal{U}$ are feasible sets of states and control inputs.

Various methods are available for solving this continuous optimal control problem, which can be classified into direct and indirect methods. Through indirect methods, the original problem is first transformed into a boundary value problem and then solved numerically, while direct methods solve the nonlinear optimization problem through the discretization of the integral form.

For a given period of time, the whole duration is equally divided in N phase $[t_0, t_1, ...t_i, ...\ t_n]$ where $t_{i+1} = t_i + dt$, $\forall i \in \{0,1,...\ n-1\}$, and dt is the duration of one frame during which the state and control inputs are constant.

$$
\begin{aligned}
\min_{u,z} \quad & \sum_{k=1}^{k=n} \ell(z_k, u_k) \\
\text{s.t.} \quad & z_{k+1} = z_k + f(z_k, u_k)dt, \\
& c(z_k, u_k) \leq 0, \\
& z_0 = z_{\text{init}}, \quad z_n = z_{\text{term}}, \\
& z_k \in \mathcal{Z}, \quad u_k \in \mathcal{U}, \\
& k = 0, 1, \cdots n.
\end{aligned}
\tag{2}
$$

Once this nonlinear optimization problem is solved, we can re-establish the reference trajectory using the initial state of the vehicle and the result commands.

3.3 An Example of Our Module

In the sequel, we provide an explicit example of the modeling of a reference trajectory generator.

We chose the unicycle kinematic model as the vehicle model for trajectory planning. The state of the ego vehicle at time k is given by:

$$z_k = [x_k, y_k, \theta_k, v_k]^T,$$

where x is the longitudinal position, y is the lateral position, θ is the heading angle, and v is the speed.

The control input at time k is given by

$$u_k = [a_k, \omega_k],$$

where a_k is the linear acceleration and ω_k is the angular velocity.

And the ego vehicle's control-state relationship is :

$$z_{k+1} = z_k + f(z_k, u_k)dt, \tag{3}$$

where $f(z_k, u_k) = [v_k \cos\theta_k, v_k \sin\theta_k, \omega_k, a_k]^T$.

We can formulate the reference trajectory generation as an optimal control problem in discrete form, which gives the following nonlinear optimization problem (NLP).

$$\min_{\mathbf{u,z}} \sum_{k=1}^{k=n} \{ w_g D_k^2(x_k, y_k) + w_v(v_r - v_k)^2 + w_a a_k^2$$
$$+ w_\omega \omega_k^2 + w_j(a_k - a_{k-1})^2 + w_h H(\theta_k)^2$$
$$+ w_p P(x_k^{tgt}, y_k^{tgt}, x_k, y_k) \} \tag{4}$$

$$\text{s.t.} \quad z_{k+1} = z_k + f(z_k, u_k)dt, \tag{4a}$$
$$L(x_k, y_k) <= 0, \tag{4b}$$
$$|v_k| \leq v_{max}, \tag{4c}$$
$$|\omega_k| \leq \omega_{max}, \tag{4d}$$
$$|a_k| \leq a_{max}, \tag{4e}$$
$$|a_k - a_{k-1}| \leq j_{max}, \tag{4f}$$
$$K(x_k^{tgt}, y_k^{tgt}, x_k, y_k) \geq d_{min}$$
$$k = 0, 1, \cdots n. \tag{4g}$$

where $\mathbf{u}$ and $\mathbf{z}$ are vectors, including all the discrete control inputs and states during the scenario.

The objective function (4) consists of several different terms to regulate the behavior of the ego vehicle. $D_k^2(x_k, y_k)$ is the distance to the waypoint at time

k. Minimizing their sums allows the vehicle to travel at the desired speed while staying at the center line. $(v_r - v_k)^2$ regulates the vehicle's actual speed to the desired speed. a_k^2 and ω_k^2 penalize the large control input, and minimizing the jerk term $(a_k - a_{k-1})^2$ improves the comfort of passengers in the vehicle. $H(\theta_k)^2$ drives the vehicle to align its heading with the curvature of the center lane. The potential field function $P(d_k)$ is based on the headway distance d_k to the leading vehicle. This term is used to regulate the headway distance in order to achieve ACC functionality. The weights w are chosen according to needs. They represent the importance of each factor and the trade-off among comfort, security, and effectiveness.

Constraint (4a) comes from the vehicle's kinematic model. Constraint (4b) guarantees the vehicle to drive within the road range. By interpolating polynomials, we can represent the boundaries of roads and restrict the reach of ego vehicles. Constraints (4c, 4d, 4e, 4f) present the speed limit, the actuator limits of the vehicle, and the range of jerk. The safety and comfort of passengers are ensured by those terms. Constraint (4f) is the collision avoidance constraint. The minimum distance between the ego vehicle and the heading vehicle should exceed a threshold d_{min}.

3.4   Stochastic Model

The model above assumed that the ego vehicle could obtain exact environmental information. In real-life scenarios, sophisticated sensors in ego vehicles do not always provide accurate information in complex driving scenarios. The inability to handle the involved uncertainty may lead to a security failure for autonomous vehicles. In our paper, a chance-constraint stochastic optimization model [11] is proposed to solve problems with uncertainty in order to achieve better performance.

In our stochastic model, the leading car's position at time k, (x_k^{tgt}, y_k^{tgt}), contains random noises following normal distributions due to sensor inaccuracy. Hence, we consider $x_k^{tgt} \sim N(\mu_{xk}, \sigma_{xk}^2)$ and $y_k^{tgt} \sim N(\mu_{yk}, \sigma_{yk}^2)$. Adding the random variable in the optimization problem, we need to treat the objective function and the constraints independently.

In objective function (4), the uncertainty part lies in the term $P(x_k^{tgt}, y_k^{tgt}, x_k, y_k)$, so we can replace x_k^{tgt} and y_k^{tgt} with μ_{xk} and μ_{yk} to get the approximate expectation.

The constraint (4g) is the only constraint involving uncertainty.

$$|x_k^{tgt} - x_k| + |y_k^{tgt} - y_k| \geq d_{min}$$

Applying triangle inequality to the left side, we have

$$|x_k^{tgt} - x_k| + |y_k^{tgt} - y_k| \geq |x_k^{tgt} - x_k + y_k^{tgt} - y_k|$$

Thus the constraint (4g) can be replaced by a more strict constraint

$$|x_k^{tgt} - x_k + y_k^{tgt} - y_k| \geq d_{min}$$

Based on the property of normal distribution, we have $r = x_k^{tgt} + y_k^{tgt}$ following normal distribution $N(\mu_{xk} + \mu_{yk}, \sigma_{xk}^2 + \sigma_{yk}^2)$ with a given a threshold α. The chance constraint can be transformed as follows:

$$\mathbb{P}(|x_k^{tgt} - x_k + y_k^{tgt} - y_k| \geq d_{min}) \geq \alpha, \; \forall k$$
$$=\mathbb{P}(|x_k^{tgt} - x_k + y_k^{tgt} - y_k| \leq d_{min}) \leq 1 - \alpha,$$
$$=\mathbb{P}(\frac{-d_{min} - \mu_{xk} - \mu_{yk} + x_k + y_k}{\sqrt{\sigma_{xk}^2 + \sigma_{yk}^2}}$$
$$\leq \frac{x_k^{tgt} + y_k^{tgt} - \mu_{xk} - \mu_{yk}}{\sqrt{\sigma_{xk}^2 + \sigma_{yk}^2}} \leq \frac{d_{min} - \mu_{xk} - \mu_{yk} + x_k + y_k)}{\sqrt{\sigma_{xk}^2 + \sigma_{yk}^2}}) \quad \leq 1 - \alpha \quad (5)$$
$$=F_N(\frac{x_k + y_k + d_{min} - \mu_{xk} - \mu_{yk}}{\sqrt{\sigma_{xk}^2 + \sigma_{yk}^2}})$$
$$- F_N(\frac{x_k + y_k - d_{min} - \mu_{xk} - \mu_{yk}}{\sqrt{\sigma_{xk}^2 + \sigma_{yk}^2}}) \leq 1 - \alpha.$$

This is equivalent to

$$\mathbb{P}(x_k^{tgt} - x_k + y_k^{tgt} - y_k \leq d_{min}) \geq \beta_1$$
$$\mathbb{P}(x_k^{tgt} - x_k + y_k^{tgt} - y_k \geq -d_{min}) \geq \beta_2$$
$$1 \leq \beta_1 + \beta_2 \leq 2 - \alpha \quad (6)$$
$$\beta_1, \beta_2 \in [0, 1].$$

A sufficient condition is to consider $\beta_1 = \beta_2 = 1 - \alpha/2$. Then the above constraints can be transformed to

$$\mathbb{P}(x_k^{tgt} - x_k + y_k^{tgt} - y_k \leq d_{min}) \geq 1 - \alpha/2, \; \forall k$$
$$=\mathbb{P}(\frac{x_k^{tgt} + y_k^{tgt} - \mu_{xk} - \mu_{yk}}{\sqrt{\sigma_{xk}^2 + \sigma_{yk}^2}} \leq \frac{d_{min} + x_k + y_k - \mu_{xk} - \mu_{yk}}{\sqrt{\sigma_{xk}^2 + \sigma_{yk}^2}})$$
$$\geq 1 - \alpha/2 \quad (7)$$
$$=\frac{d_{min} + x_k + y_k - \mu_{xk} - \mu_{yk}}{\sqrt{\sigma_{xk}^2 + \sigma_{yk}^2}} \geq F_N^{-1}(1 - \alpha/2)$$
$$=x_k + y_k \geq \mu_{xk} + \mu_{yk} - d_{min} + \sqrt{\sigma_{xk}^2 + \sigma_{yk}^2} \cdot F_N^{-1}(1 - \alpha/2).$$

In a similar way, we have:

$$\mathbb{P}(x_k^{tgt} - x_k + y_k^{tgt} - y_k \geq -d_{min}) \geq 1 - \alpha/2, \; \forall k$$

$$=\mathbb{P}(\frac{x_k^{tgt} + y_k^{tgt} - \mu_{xk} - \mu_{yk}}{\sqrt{\sigma_{xk}^2 + \sigma_{yk}^2}} \leq \frac{-d_{min} + x_k + y_k - \mu_{xk} - \mu_{yk}}{\sqrt{\sigma_{xk}^2 + \sigma_{yk}^2}})$$

$$\leq \alpha/2 \qquad\qquad\qquad\qquad\qquad\qquad\qquad (8)$$

$$=\frac{-d_{min} + x_k + y_k - \mu_{xk} - \mu_{yk}}{\sqrt{\sigma_{xk}^2 + \sigma_{yk}^2}} \leq F_N^{-1}(\alpha/2)$$

$$=x_k + y_k \leq \mu_{xk} + \mu_{yk} + d_{min} + \sqrt{\sigma_{xk}^2 + \sigma_{yk}^2} \cdot F_N^{-1}(\alpha/2),$$

where F_N is the cumulative distribution function of standard normal distribution.

Using the last constraint instead of the previous one (4g), we can get a new optimization problem to generate a reference trajectory considering sensor uncertainties.

4 Numerical Experiments

In this section, numerical tests are conducted to prove the efficiency of the reference trajectory generation model under various driving scenarios. Our driving scenarios are generated with SCANeR Studio [12], which is a commercial driving simulation software that helps develop and validate ADAS. The modules in SCANeR Studio for vehicle dynamics, environment building, and sensor modeling offer us the flexibility to define road states and conditions based on our requirements. The driving data in SCANeR Studio could be exported for further analysis. We solve nonlinear programming models with the help of the Python package GEKKO [13], which has an active set sequential quadratic programming solver for our constrained nonlinear optimization problem.

Following are descriptions of our experimental set-up, examples of results, and a comparison of the performance of our deterministic and stochastic models.

4.1 Experimentation Set-Up

Our model consists of driving-related parameters, such as the maximum speed and the minimum inter-vehicle distance, etc. Those parameters should be adjusted to reflect real-world regulations and traffic rules. In response to changing scenarios, they should be adjusted as well. For example, the reference speed, and the maximum speed in highway scenarios must be higher than those in urban driving scenarios.

Our experiment is based on an urban driving scenario. Parameters like the reference velocity, minimal distance and maximum velocity should be inferior to those in highway driving. The table below lists the values of parameters during the numerical experiments:

Table 1. Parameters' values during the simulation.

Parameter	meaning	Value
v_r	reference velocity	$12 \; m/s$
dt	time step	$0.05 \; s$
d_{min}	minimum distance	$5 \; m$
v_{max}	maximum velocity	$40 \; m/s$
ω_{max}	maximum angular velocity	$\pi/6 \; s^{-1}$
j_{max}	maximum jerk	$0.6 \; m/s^2$

Another set of parameters is weights in the objective function, representing the importance of corresponding terms to optimize. In order to achieve the best performance of the model, the weights should be fine-tuned from an engineering perspective.

The stochastic model takes into account the uncertainty of the sensors, which results in errors in the position of the leading vehicle. Thus the detected leading vehicle's position is equal to the real leading vehicle's position plus a random noise with a normal distribution $N(0, 1)$.

4.2 Examples of Solutions

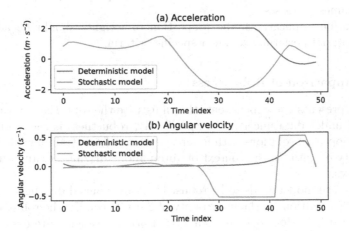

Fig. 1. Result of an example scenario.

The following result has been obtained in a driving scenario generated in SCANeR, using the deterministic and stochastic models with the previously indicated parameters.

In Fig. 1, we show the generated acceleration and angular velocity profile during the scenarios to get the optimal reference trajectory.

Table 2. Comparison under different configurations.

$w_g : w_v : w_a : w_\omega : w_j : w_h : w_p$	5:1:1:1:1:1:1			1:5:1:1:1:1:1			1:1:5:1:1:1:1			1:1:1:5:1:1:1		
N	20	40	60	20	40	60	20	40	60	20	40	60
Average CPU time(s)	0.36	0.68	2.38	1.34	5.93	3.52	1.18	12.48	3.39	0.73	1.05	2.66
Average acceleration	1.62	1.84	1.88	0.57	0.74	0.72	0.34	1.24	1.47	1.05	1.53	1.59
Average angular velocity	0	0	0.09	0	0	0.04	0	0	-0.07	0	0	0.08
Average velocity	14.80	15.82	16.82	14.36	15.32	16.19	14.13	15.54	16.63	14.61	15.74	16.73
Average distance	20.72	19.80	18.50	20.82	19.94	18.52	20.92	19.88	18.49	20.76	19.81	18.50
$w_g : w_v : w_a : w_\omega : w_j : w_h : w_p$	1:1:1:1:5:1:1			1:1:1:1:1:5:1			1:1:1:1:1:1:5			1:1:1:1:1:1:1		
N	20	40	60	20	40	60	20	40	60	20	40	60
Average CPU time(s)	1.24	2.56	3.92	0.55	4.07	3.82	0.82	3.51	3.54	0.95	3.06	3.25
Average acceleration	1.04	1.53	1.59	1.03	1.55	1.61	1.05	1.53	1.60	1.05	1.53	1.60
Average angular velocity	0	0	0.08	0	0	0.08	0	0	0.08	0	0	0.08
Average velocity	14.61	15.74	16.73	14.56	15.74	16.74	14.61	15.74	16.73	14.61	15.74	16.73
Average distance	20.76	19.81	18.50	20.78	19.82	18.50	20.76	19.81	18.50	20.76	19.81	18.50

4.3   Effects of Different Configurations

In Table 2, we considered various values of the objective weights proportion and the number of sampling times N to analyze its impact on the results and calculation.

We can observe that the average CPU time is always constant, and when the weight w_a, w_v is high, the acceleration is low, and high weight w_ω leads to low angular velocity. The average CPU time increases proportionally as the number of time frames increases.

In real-life applications, the proportion of weights should be adjusted to achieve optimal performance under specific criteria.

4.4   Comparison of Robustness

This part presents two experiments that illustrate the robustness of the stochastic model under data uncertainty. Specifically, robustness is the ability to produce near-optimal solutions with fewer violations of constraints while facing the uncertainty of data. In the context of autonomous driving, it can be illustrated in two ways.

Firstly, the model needs to be robust to an unchanged driving scenario with numerous realizations of the uncertainty of data. Secondly, the robustness needs to be proved in various driving scenarios. Two experiments are designed based on these two aspects.

Our first experiment fixes the driving scenario and generates 100 realizations of its random variables X_{tgt}, Y_{tgt}. Next, we run the deterministic model and stochastic model over 100 instances and compare the number of the violated constraints.

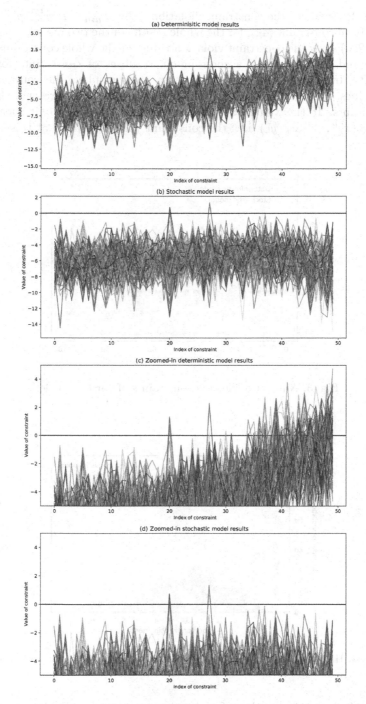

Fig. 2. Constraint function values of all instances for deterministic and stochastic models.

Figure 2 visualizes the constraint violation value $d_{min} - K(x_k^{tgt}, y_k^{tgt}, x_k, y_k)$, adapted from constraint (4g), for the whole results of the two models. Figure 2(a) and Fig. 2(b) show the constraint violation value for the whole constraints, whilst Fig. 2(c) and Fig. 2(d) show a zoom-in on a subset of constraints for better readability. In Fig. 2, each curve in its own color displays the constraint violation values of a driving scenario result, and the x-axis represents the index of constraints. If the value at constraint index i exceeds 0, it means that $d_{min} > K(x_k^{tgt}, y_k^{tgt}, x_k, y_k)$, i.e., the constraint (4g) is violated at this sampling time.

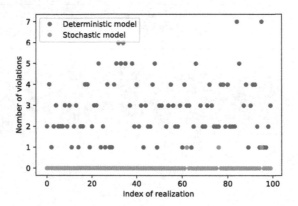

Fig. 3. Number of violated constraints of our two models.

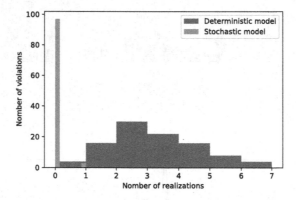

Fig. 4. Histogram of the number of violated constraints of our two models.

Figure 3 shows the number of violated constraints for simulations with 100 realizations. The blue dots represent the number of violated constraints for our

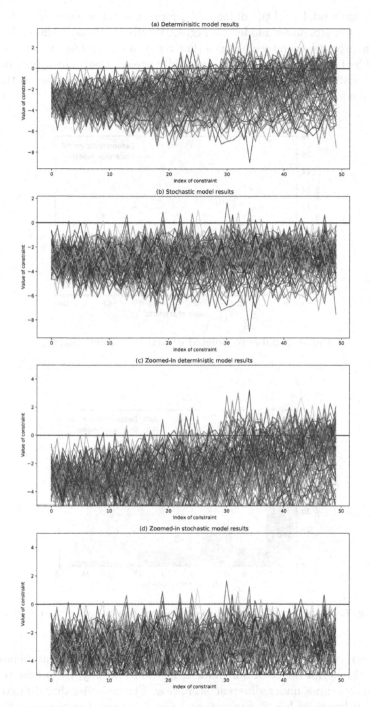

Fig. 5. Constraint function values of all instances for deterministic and stochastic models.

deterministic model, and the orange dots represent the number of violated constraints in the stochastic model. In Fig. 4, the distribution of the violated constraints is presented, and we observe that most of the stochastic models results are feasible, i.e., no constraints are violated; there are only three instances with a single constraint violation. Conversely, the constraint violations in the deterministic model are typically around two and three.

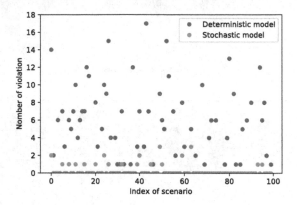

Fig. 6. Number of violated constraints of two models.

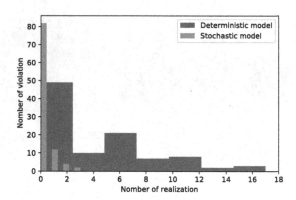

Fig. 7. Histogram of the number of violated constraints of two models.

Similarly, we conduct our second experiment with 100 different scenarios and compare the performance of our models, in the same way, to further prove our model's robustness under different scenarios. Figure 5 visualize the constraint violation value as in Fig. 2. Figure 6 and Fig. 7 present the number of violated constraints and their distribution, respectively. As a result of the diversity of scenarios, the number of violated constraints is more divergent compared with the precedent experiment. Meanwhile, the stochastic model still yields fewer constraint violations than the deterministic model.

We can conclude from the two experiments above that the stochastic model produces more robust solutions both in terms of stability and diversity.

5   Conclusions and Future Work

In this paper, an optimal control based reference trajectory generator has been proposed and implemented. With a scenario and prior waypoints, this generator can find an optimal collision-free trajectory for further validation. Stochastic programming has been used to address the uncertainty of autonomous vehicles. We also thoroughly analyse the performance of the deterministic model and the stochastic model under different configurations. Based on the comparison, it appears the stochastic model can produce more robust solutions than the deterministic model when uncertainty is present.

Future work includes the development of an increasingly sophisticated vehicle model and modeling of uncertainty involving dependent random variables. Another extension is to solve online autonomous driving planning problems with an adapted similar optimization-based framework.

Acknowledgement. This work was supported by the French government under the "France 2030" program, as part of the SystemX Technological Research Institute.

References

1. LaValle, S.M., Kuffner, J.J., Jr.: Randomized kinodynamic planning. Int. J. Robot. Res. **20**(5), 378–400 (2001)
2. Gammell, J.D., Srinivasa, S.S., Barfoot, T.D.: Informed RRT: Optimal sampling-based path planning focused via direct sampling of an admissible ellipsoidal heuristic. In: 2014 IEEE/RSJ International Conference on Intelligent Robots and Systems, pp. 2997–3004. IEEE (2014)
3. Perez, A., Platt, R., Konidaris, G., Kaelbling, L., Lozano-Perez, T.: LQR-RRT: optimal sampling-based motion planning with automatically derived extension heuristics. In: 2012 IEEE International Conference on Robotics and Automation, pp. 2537–2542. IEEE (2012)
4. Chen, J.: R2-RRT: reliability-based robust mission planning of off-road autonomous ground vehicle under uncertain terrain environment. IEEE Trans. Autom. Sci. Eng. **19**(2), 1030–1046 (2021)
5. Li, Y., Littlefield, Z., Bekris, K.E.: Sparse methods for efficient asymptotically optimal kinodynamic planning. In: Akin, H.L., Amato, N.M., Isler, V., van der Stappen, A.F. (eds.) Algorithmic Foundations of Robotics XI. STAR, vol. 107, pp. 263–282. Springer, Cham (2015). https://doi.org/10.1007/978-3-319-16595-0_16
6. Likhachev, M., Ferguson, D.I., Gordon, G.J., Stentz, A., Thrun, S.: Anytime dynamic A*: an anytime, replanning algorithm. In: ICAPS, vol. 5, pp. 262–271 (2005)

7. Likhachev, M., Gordon, G.J., Thrun, S.: ARA*: anytime A* with provable bounds on sub-optimality. In: Advances in Neural Information Processing Systems, vol. 16 (2003)
8. Strub, M.P., Gammell, J.D.: AIT* and EIT*: asymmetric bidirectional sampling-based path planning. arXiv preprint arXiv:2111.01877 (2021)
9. Berntorp, K., Olofsson, B., Lundahl, K., Nielsen, L.: Models and methodology for optimal trajectory generation in safety-critical road-vehicle manoeuvres. Veh. Syst. Dyn. **52**(10), 1304–1332 (2014)
10. Bergman, K., Axehill, D.: Combining homotopy methods and numerical optimal control to solve motion planning problems. In: 2018 IEEE Intelligent Vehicles Symposium (IV), pp. 347–354. IEEE (2018)
11. Prékopa, A.: Stochastic Programming, vol. 324. Springer Science & Business Media (2013)
12. That, T.N., Casas, J.: An integrated framework combining a traffic simulator and a driving simulator. Procedia Soc. Behav. Sci. **20**, 648–655 (2011)
13. Beal, L., Hill, D., Martin, R., Hedengren, J.: Gekko optimization suite. Processes **6**(8), 106 (2018)

Traceable Distribution of Fish Products: State of the Art of Blockchain Technology Applications to Fish Supply Chains

Ulpan Tokkozhina[1,2,3](✉) iD, Ana Lucia Martins[1,2,3] iD, Joao C. Ferreira[2,3,4,5] iD, and Augusto Casaca[3] iD

[1] Business Research Unit (BRU-IUL), Lisbon, Portugal
ulpan_tokkozhina@iscte-iul.pt
[2] Instituto Universitário de Lisboa (ISCTE-IUL), 1649-026 Lisbon, Portugal
[3] Inov Inesc Inovação/Inesc-ID, 1000-029 Lisbon, Portugal
[4] Information Sciences and Technologies and Architecture Research Centre (ISTAR-IUL), Lisbon, Portugal
[5] Logistics, Molde University College, NO-6410 Molde, Norway

Abstract. Fish products traceability is a sensitive issue for supply chains (SCs) involved in the capturing processes and successful distribution of these commodities. Full transparency and traceability of fish products' locomotion has a potential to stop the flow of illegally or unethically caught/processed fish. Blockchain technology (BCT) is considered to become a crucial part of the fish traceability solution, providing an end-to-end visibility, thus creating value for all stakeholders, including final consumers. In this study, we are aiming to explore the current state of the BCT implementations to the fish distribution SCs This study applies a systematic literature review (SLR) approach of academic literature to reveal the status quo of BCT adoption in the fish and seafood SC cases, revealing the opportunities it holds in improving the levels of traceability, as well as the challenges that were identified in extant literature that need to be addressed throughout the development of the fish industry applications.

Keywords: blockchain · supply chain management · fish distribution

1 Introduction

Fish and seafood industry is one of the biggest worldwide, representing 12% of livelihoods across the globe, generating wealth to 1 out of every 10 people in the world [1]. In the last 50 years worldwide fish consumption grew almost in double – full market size figures surmounted $500 billion USD [2]. Marine ecosystems are facing with high levels of pressure, where illegal, unreported, or unregulated (IUU) fishing activities are posing threat to the overall sustainability of ecosystems, thus seriously affecting the global economies and creating risks of consumer contamination cases. [3] estimated that, on a global scale, IUU fishing holds around 30% of the total global fisheries catch, resulting

A. L. Martins et al. (Eds.): INTSYS 2022, LNICST 486, pp. 89–100, 2023.
https://doi.org/10.1007/978-3-031-30855-0_6

into around 10 to 23.5 billion US$ annual losses worldwide (around 11 to 26 million tons of fish products).

Seafood and fish products traceability is becoming critical for supply chains (SCs) involved in these commodities. Therefore, experts see full traceability and transparency of SCs as the only way to stop the flow of illegally or unethically caught/processed fish. Blockchain technology (BCT) has potential to become a significant part of the solution, providing end-to-end transparency and traceability, thus creating value for all stakeholders, including final consumers. In order to understand why BCT has a potential to address IUU fishing problem, it is essential to understand the features of the technology itself. Blockchain technology is based on a decentralized peer-to-peer architecture and is also defined as an encrypted digital ledger [4]. It is able to create a continuous, visible and unalterable sharable record of transactions and movements around SC in an immutable manner [5]. Like this, BCT is a set of chain blocks, that altogether represent a tamper-proof, permanent sequence of data and transactions that can be verified anytime in the future. This network is built based on the consensus algorithm, achieved by various voting mechanisms, where the chain can be extended with a next block, only when the majority of participants agree with it [6].

In this study, we are aiming to explore the current state of the BCT implications to the fish SCs and the existing scholar investigations in the field. This study will shed light on the traceability and transparency achievement with BCT implementation, other significant advantages and improvements that BCT can bring to fish and seafood SCs, as well as the current challenges in the field. The next sections are built as following: Sect. 2 will bring a general understanding of BCT and its potential in SC practices, Sect. 3 will disclose the methodology selected for the study, Sect. 4 will generate a discussion of extant literature systematization and Sect. 5 will provide conclusions of the study and future paths for the research.

2 Blockchain Technology Features and Implications to Supply Chain Management

The global supply chain is an industry that is running the global economy and brings to consumers everything that is needed: food, transportation means, clothing and generally anything that might be needed for everyday life activities. Like this, one of the most emergent, promising technologies that holds the potential to transform and improve SC activities is Blockchain [7].

The distributed nature of BCT, the immutability of its records, and the ability to operate in a decentralized logic through smart contracts use make BCT-based networks significantly different from those previously developed and based on the Internet (e.g. Industry 4.0 sectors and supply chains) [8]. Smart contracts are essentially pre-defined self-executing codes, that are preventing risk of corruptions or tampers within the execution of a given contract [9]. Smart contract feature is one of the main novelties of BCT-based networks, and it is expected to play a crucial role in managing partnership efficiency – due to the information immutability, and automation it may result in transparency and improvement of SC collaboration [10]. BCT is assumed to become a "next holy grail for the enterprise", as it holds huge potential for SC improvement in all of its aspects, such as manufacturing, production, orders placing, transportation, delivery and consumption [11].

By its nature, BCT is bringing transparency throughout the whole supply network, in this way providing reliability in information about products' origins and confidence in its provenance [12]. BCT-based distributed ledgers provide a single version of truth through consensus protocols [13], therefore enhancing the performance of SC, and eliminating the need in establishing trust relationships among players, since every participant will be a holder of all information flow existing around the network [9]. Transparency of records and transactions about products and processes empowers suppliers to be engaged with further activities and decisions, like strategies development, joint knowledge creation and innovation support [14].

Scholars were already proposing BCT applications to various sections and fields that would improve life and experiences of populations, including smart cities applications to parking spaces gamifications [15], construction engineering [9], agriculture [16], automobile trade [17], wine counterfeiting reduction [18] and many other fields. BCT applications are actively discussed to bring improvements to the SCs related to perishable commodities, as all data regarding movement, storage conditions and temperature can be successfully traced and assured for safety purposes. In this light, fish SCs were used as a potential field of application of BCT [19, 20], as the sensitivity and potential food risk for consumers make fish SCs justified for transparent technology integration. In the next sections, BCT-based academic solutions for fish and seafood SCs will be discussed closely, exploring important scholarly articles in the field.

3   Methodology

In order to address the aims of this study, a systematic literature review (SLR) was chosen as a suitable methodology, which enables clarity and academic integrity to follow a pre-defined route for choosing and analyzing the most relevant extant literature in the field. For the SLR, this study followed the Preferred Reporting Items for Systematic Reviews and Meta-Analysis (PRISMA) checklist, that allows a structured and transparent process of literature selection, that can be reproduced by other scholars. The graphical representation of the literature selection process can be found in a flow diagram (Fig. 1).

Three academic databases were used for the query: Web of Knowledge (WoS), ProQuest, and Scopus. These databases were chosen as being trusted global databases for academic queries and for the capacity to provide publications from top international multidisciplinary journals. The keywords for the search were 'blockchain' and 'fish', with an advanced search function to extract studies with both keywords found in the abstract. The search was further limited only to peer-reviewed articles written in English. All publications available up to beginning of April 2022 were included, without any limitations per year.

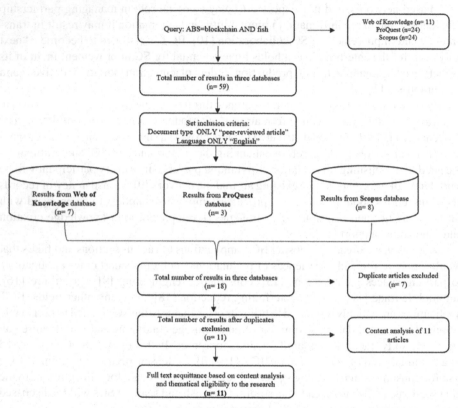

Fig. 1. Literature selection process

As can be seen in Fig. 1, the initial number of studies identified in three databases upon abstract keyword inclusion criteria was 59. It is important to note, that among these documents, the types include conference proceedings, newspaper articles, erratum etc. This highlights the interest in the topic not only in the scientific field, but a general public interest in fish traceability solutions. In order to focus more on academic studies, we further used the filter to exclude it to peer-reviewed articles only. Total number of peer-reviewed articles resulted in 18 studies, after excluding the duplicates, final result revealed 11 unique articles. All of the 11 articles were thoroughly screened through full-text for their suitability and soundness to the purpose of this study. As a result, all 11 articles were kept for final inclusion to this SLR, as they serve the aim of the study and bring different aspects to further discussion.

Figure 2 represents the ratio of the 11 selected articles based on the year of publication, which reveals that the highest level of academic interest in fish traceability solutions was witnessed in 2020. It can be further assumed, that the worldwide pandemic situation awakens an increased interest to the provenance and safety assurance of products, including perishable commodities, such as fish products.

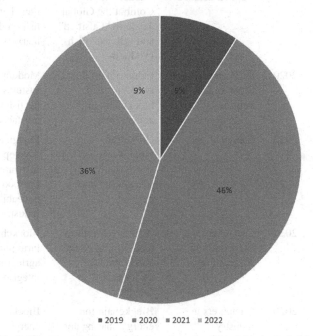

Fig. 2. Publications ratio per year based on the 11 articles included in SLR

Table 1 shows the full list of articles, that were selected for this SLR. Table 1 reflects the multidisciplinary nature of the topic the journals, where articles were published include different spectrum of fields: technological, business, and environmental studies. The primary focus of the selected articles, as can be seen from Table 1 is the development and proposition of traceability and monitoring solutions for fish products supply chains. This focus signifies the interest of consumers in fish products processing and transportation transparency, that will ensure food safety. In the next section, the discussion of issues addressed by selected studies will be performed, including views on transparency solutions, other improvements that BCT is able to bring to fish supply chains, and the current challenges in the field.

Table 1. Full list of 11 articles included in systematic literature review

Author(s)	Year	Journal	Title	Issues discussed
Korneyko and Podvolotskaya	2019	Journal of Engineering and Applied Sciences	Assessment of the Blockchain Capabilities to Combat the Global Trade in "Falsified" and "Illegal" Fish Products	Review of literature on blockchain-based solutions to combat illegal and falsified fish products in markets
Altoukhov, A	2020	Earth and Environmental Science	Industrial product platforms and blockchain in aquaculture	Modern automation systems integration for fishes and crustaceans farming
Grecuccio et al	2020	Energies	Combining blockchain and IoT: Food-chain traceability and beyond	Design and development of a software framework for food supply chains traceability under Industry 4.0 context
Hang et al	2020	Computers and Electronics in Agriculture	A secure fish farm platform based on blockchain for agriculture data integrity	Blockchain-based fish farm platform for agricultural data integrity assurance
Petri et al	2020	Computers in Industry	Blockchain for energy sharing and trading in distributed prosumer communities	Blockchain-based energy framework proposition based on real fish processing industrial site
Probst, W	2020	ICES Journal of Marine Science	How emerging data technologies can increase trust and transparency in fisheries	Digital data technologies impact on commercial fisheries
Low et al	2021	Chemical Engineering Transactions	Development of Traceability System for Seafood Supply Chains in Malaysia	Food management tool development for seafood supply chains traceability

(*continued*)

Table 1. (*continued*)

Author(s)	Year	Journal	Title	Issues discussed
Rahman et al	2021	Foods	Traceability of Sustainability and Safety in Fishery Supply Chain Management Systems Using Radio Frequency Identification Technology	Traceability systems for food safety, sustainability and product quality assurance of fish supply chains
Sengupta et al	2021	Information Systems Frontiers	Disruptive Technologies for Achieving Supply Chain Resilience in COVID-19 Era: An Implementation Case Study of Satellite Imagery and Blockchain Technologies in Fish Supply Chain	Fish supply chain challenges in developing countries and disruptive technologies integrating solutions
Tsolakis et al	2021	Journal of Business Research	Supply network design to address United Nations Sustainable Development Goals: A case study of blockchain implementation in Thai fish industry	Design of a blockchain-based fish supply chain for Sustainable Development Goal achievement
Feng et al	2022	Computers and Electronics in Agriculture	Modeling and evaluation of quality monitoring based on wireless sensor and blockchain technology for live fish waterless transportation	Waterless fish transportation and intelligent monitoring solutions

4 Discussion

Some of the brightest innovative features of BCT are: improved transparency and further traceability of information, as well as increased trust between stakeholders [21]. Fast-moving SCs, such as those dealing with perishable items, that require a cold chain storage were named among the most crucial industries for BCT penetration [5]. In this context, fish product SCs represent a perfect example of disruptive technology integration for the traceability and trust improvement purposes. In the following subsections the transparency solutions, further advantages and challenges of BCT-based networks for fish SCs will be discussed; the discussion is based upon the set of studies selected for the SLR.

4.1 Traceability and Transparency of Blockchain-Based Fish Supply Chains

At this stage of globalization and international long SCs, global traceability systems are required to bring together all the processes and shared data across seafood industry stakeholders; and BCT is specifically interesting for seafood trade applications, as such networks can guarantee unaltered and veridical real-time data [22]. Like this, [22] believe that final consumers would not question the accuracy of data, as the immutability feature of BCT allows to rely on authenticity of available data. However, not only final consumers might value high transparency of data, such controlling agents as non-governmental organizations (NGOs) and management authorities are generally interested in traceable information availability for sensitive commodities [23]. In his study, [23] highlights the application of various disruptive technologies for different levels of fish SCs. Like this, he claims, that data mining and artificial intelligence (AI) seem to be useful for stages of monitoring and controlling fishing vessels, as they help accumulating knowledge on catches and following compliance to rules and standards at the sea; BCT and smart contracts, on their turn, are useful for information transparency assurance across the given supply chain.

A motivation for BCT-based application architecture for [24] was the detection of trust absence towards fish quality from consumers, as upstream activities information, such as catchment source, storage conditions and packaging processes are generally not available for the final consumer. The proposition is to build a BCT-based app, which can scan the QR code on fish and seafood products and bring transparency to information such as satellite-based fish zone data, hyper local weather data, and GPS and IoT based vessel communication; like this, quality and safety measures in the fresh fish and seafood SCs can be improved [24]. Among other applications of BCT-technologies to fish SCs, an innovative waterless transportation monitoring system based on flexible wireless sensor for live sea bass was suggested [25]. This application showed the ability to reach dynamic and continuous monitoring and tracing of transportation parameters, and with the use of BCT ensure security and reliability of shared data.

A seafood traceability system for inputting data was proposed by [22], which is designed to deal with complex SCs, bringing to a unified network all players, starting from aquafarms, all the way to final consumers. As complex SCs have a higher risk of food contamination and poisoning, the proposed system simplifies the tracking and tracing information kept on blockchain all the way back to the potential affected batch of products [22]. An interoperable solution, involving a combination of blockchain with multiple technologies, such as Internet of Things (IoT), wireless sensor networks (WSN), and radio frequency identification (RFID) also enables building a traceability system for sustainable and safe fisheries SCs [26]. Besides having a potential to improve aquaculture and seafood traceability, such technologically advanced SCs may resolve potential issues of managing customer requests and responding quickly to unexpected changes in orders [26, 27] explain BCT-based networks by drawing analogy with Enterprise Resource Planning (ERP) software, where registered batches of products, and any information related to the product's lifecycle can be stored in an immutable manner, being available to all network players simultaneously. The potential of BCT-based solutions in bringing transparency and traceability to products SCs is obvious, and fish SCs are identified as a suitable application case, due to perishability and short lifecycle of the product. Transparent information and traceability possibilities can bring value-added aspect not only to final consumers, but to every stakeholder of such SC, as it assures the safe concerns and decreases the risk of fish and seafood contamination cases.

4.2 Blockchain Driven Improvements for Fish Supply Chains

Apart from bringing a previously unattainable level of transparency to supply networks, BCT has other significant inherited features, that are able to improve SC processes. BCT-based solutions make it perfect to apply in use cases, where trust of network participants lacks due to lengthy and poor communication across network, e.g. SCs of imported seafood products that are flowing through multiple responsible controlling authorities when crossing borders [23]. The trust-improving factor will drive social and economic benefits to fishermen as well, as it will highlight consumer trust towards sellers, create a better management of fish SCs and develop more resilience across SCs to cope with emergency situations [24].

BCT is maintained to be as well the technology, that can help in identifying anomalies throughout the production and consumption processes, e.g. a frozen fish fillet can be traced back and checked for saturated water and chemicals additives, that could be illegally used to increase fillet's weight [28]. Another improvement, that BCT can bring to fish SCs is flexibility and the speed of information updating for players; it can as well result in reduction of costs by creating digital certification for products involved [29]. The BCT-based platform proposed in one of the selected studies, can provide fish farmers with benefits of secure, tamper-proof storage of big agriculture data, and automate transactions via smart contract usage; therefore, reducing levels of errors or data manipulation [30]. Moreover, when combined with other technologies, such as IoT, BCT is claimed to bring even more advantages to food SCs, by overall improvement of business processes and increasing customer satisfaction, e.g. when applied to cold-chain use cases [27].

4.3 Current Challenges of Blockchain-Based Solutions for Fish Supply Chains

When talking about advantages, that BCT-based networks are able to bring to the fish SCs, it is important to keep in mind the infancy of this technology applications to business practices. Hence, there are still some challenges and considerations that need to be kept in mind when developing an implementation plan to a real use case.

When designing BCT-based solutions, one thing that should be primarily evaluated and considered is the existing data structuring type and technology specifications in each given case; for instance, when applied to Thai government system, the challenge remained in the data inaccuracy and initial incorrect number of registered vessels, making the traceability in this case incomplete [31]. Thus, each specific case of a specific country cannot be fully generalized, as there can be nuances that are only characteristic to that specific SC and existing regulations and flaws. [24] further support, that cultural differences and contextual conditions may result in a degree of complexities for different regions – depending on the existing infrastructure, it requires the willingness of stakeholders in the BCT adoption process.

The real-life implementation of anti-counterfeit BCT is still challenging due to general limitations such as the heterogeneity of participation in global SCs, the high cost of technology implementation and support, and the potential risk of software vulnerability, caused by uncertain legally recognized status in many countries across the globe [28]. As from the scientific side, there are already some propositions of models and systems that are existing, the practical implementation is still at a lower level of progress. For instance, the system proposed by [22] should be further implemented in a real use case to validate the system and check the food hazards sensitivity. Trustworthiness of smart meters, proposed by [32] should as well be further evaluated through usage of trust and reputation techniques to check the level of reliability of smart devices and their associated risks. Overall, in-depth research for the technical aspects of BCT deployment is required, such concerns as storage capability, speed of transactions, and its overall performance and behavior, when used in a combination with other technology, such as IoT [25].

5   Conclusions and Future Research

In general, the application of BCT to a specific SC of fish distribution opens many frontiers for industry improvement. Fish industry represents a network of stakeholders that are involved in a fast-moving SC, where the product under distribution is perishable and sensitive to storage conditions. Thus, BCT implementation would allow a real-time data visibility for upstream players to manage the fluctuations in demand, as well as would bring more trust for downstream players (final consumers), as information about the origins would be open and easily accessible. It would also serve a purpose of social and economic benefit creation for fishermen, as it would exlude data manipulation in further SC stages and would build trust for the product, potentially leading to a higher rates of consumption of fish products. However, it is important to keep in mind the introductory stages of BCT applications in businesses, so challenges like heterogenity of participation in technology adoption and concerns regarding high costs of technology implementation and its further support may still arise at this stage.

The focus, therefore should be on both academic and practical exploration of BCT potential to bring improvements to fish SCs. We hope that this study helped gaining a status quo of BCT adoption in the fish and seafood SC cases, revealing the opportunities it holds in improving the levels of traceability and transparency to all network players, including the final consumers. The challenges identified in the selected set of articles were revealed, and need to be addressed by further scholar and industry applications.

Acknowledgement. This work was supported by EEA Grants Blue Growth Programme (Call #5), Project PT-INNOVATION-0069 – Fish2Fork.

References

1. Our Ocean. http://ourocean2016.org/sustainable-fisheries. Accessed 05 Oct 2022
2. Holland, J.: UN: the world is producing and consuming more seafood, but overfishing remains rife. (2020). https://www.seafoodsource.com/news/supply-trade/un-the-world-is-producing-and-consuming-more-seafood-but-overfishing-remains-rife. Accessed 05 Oct 2022
3. Food and agriculture organization of the united nation. (2018). https://www.fao.org/fao-stories/article/en/c/1136937/. Accessed 05 Oct 2022
4. O'Leary, D.E.: Configuring blockchain architectures for transaction information in blockchain consortiums: the case of accounting and supply chain systems. Intell. Syst. Acc. Finan. Manag. **24**(4), 138–147 (2017)
5. Wang, Y., Singgih, M., Wang, J., Rit, M.: Making sense of blockchain technology: how will it transform supply chains? Int. J. Prod. Econ. **211**, 221–236 (2019)
6. Li, D., Du, R., Fu, Y., Au, M.H.: Meta-key: a secure data-sharing protocol under blockchain-based decentralized storage architecture. IEEE Networking Lett. **1**(1), 30–33 (2019)
7. Nayak, G., Dhaigude, A.S.: A conceptual model of sustainable supply chain management in small and medium enterprises using blockchain technology. Cogent Econ. Finance **7**(1), 1667184 (2019)
8. Rejeb, A., Keogh, J.G., Treiblmaier, H.: Leveraging the internet of things and blockchain technology in supply chain management. Future Internet **11**(7), 161 (2019)
9. Wang, J., Wu, P., Wang, X., Shou, W.: The outlook of blockchain technology for construction engineering management. Front. Eng. Manag. 67–75 (2017)
10. Kim, J.S., Shin, N.: The impact of blockchain technology application on supply chain partnership and performance. Sustainability **11**(21), 6181 (2019)
11. Sachdev, D.: Enabling data democracy in supply chain using blockchain and Iot. J. Manag. **6**(1), 66–83 (2019)
12. Montecchi, M., Kirk, P., Michael, E.: It's real, trust me! Establishing supply chain provenance using blockchain. Bus. Horiz. **62**(3), 283–293 (2019)
13. Schuetz, S., Venkatesh, V.: Blockchain, adoption, and financial inclusion in India: research opportunities. Int. J. Inf. Manage. **52**, 101936 (2020)
14. Huang, Y., Han, W., Macbeth, D.K.: The complexity of collaboration in supply chain networks. Supply Chain Manag. **25**(3), 393–410 (2020)
15. Ferreira, J.C., Martins, A.L., Gonçalves, F., Maia, R.: A blockchain and gamification approach for smart parking. In: Ferreira, J.C., Martins, A.L., Monteiro, V. (eds.) INTSYS 2018. LNICSSITE, vol. 267, pp. 3–14. Springer, Cham (2019). https://doi.org/10.1007/978-3-030-14757-0_1
16. Kamble, S.S., Gunasekaran, A., Sharma, R.: Modeling the blockchain enabled traceability in agriculture supply chain. Int. J. Inf. Manage. **52**, 101967 (2020)
17. Ada, N., et al.: Blockchain technology for enhancing traceability and efficiency in automobile supply chain—a case study. Sustainability **13**(24), 13667 (2021)
18. Tokkozhina, U., Ferreira, J.C., Martins, A.L.: Wine traceability and counterfeit reduction: blockchain-based application for a wine supply Chain. In: Martins, A.L., Ferreira, J.C., Kocian, A. (eds) International Conference on Intelligent Transport Systems, pp. 59–70, Springer, Cham (2021) https://doi.org/10.1007/978-3-030-97603-3_5
19. Tokkozhina, U., Martins, A.L., Ferreira, J.C.: Adopting blockchain in supply chain – an approach for a pilot. In: Martins, A.L., Ferreira, J.C., Kocian, A., Costa, V. (eds.) INTSYS 2020. LNICSSITE, vol. 364, pp. 125–141. Springer, Cham (2021). https://doi.org/10.1007/978-3-030-71454-3_8

20. Ferreira, J.C., Martins, A.L., Tokkozhina, U., Helgheim, B.I.: Fish control process and traceability for value creation using blockchain technology. In: International Conference on Innovations in Bio-Inspired Computing and Applications, pp. 761–773, Springer, Cham (2021). https://doi.org/10.1007/978-3-030-96299-9_72
21. Köhler, S., Pizzol, M.: Technology assessment of blockchain-based technologies in the food supply chain. J. Clean. Prod. **269**, 122193 (2020)
22. Low, X.Y., Yunus, N.A., Muhamad, I.I.: Development of traceability system for seafood supply Chains in Malaysia. Chem. Eng. Trans. **89**, 427–432 (2021)
23. Probst, W.N.: How emerging data technologies can increase trust and transparency in fisheries. ICES J. Mar. Sci. **77**(4), 1286–1294 (2020)
24. Sengupta, T., Narayanamurthy, G., Moser, R., Pereira, V., Bhattacharjee, D.: Disruptive technologies for achieving supply chain resilience in COVID-19 era: an implementation case study of satellite imagery and blockchain technologies in fish supply Chain. Inf. Syst. Front. **24**, 1–17 (2021). https://doi.org/10.1007/s10796-021-10228-3
25. Feng, H., Zhang, M., Gecevska, V., Chen, B., Saeed, R., Zhang, X.: Modeling and evaluation of quality monitoring based on wireless sensor and blockchain technology for live fish waterless transportation. Comput. Electron. Agric. **193**, 106642 (2022)
26. Rahman, L.F., Alam, L., Marufuzzaman, M., Sumaila, U.R.: Traceability of sustainability and safety in fishery supply chain management systems using radio frequency identification technology. Foods **10**(10), 2265 (2021)
27. Grecuccio, J., Giusto, E., Fiori, F., Rebaudengo, M.: Combining blockchain and IoT: Food-chain traceability and beyond. Energies **13**(15), 3820 (2020)
28. Korneyko, O., Podvolotskaya, A., Street, S.: Assessment of the blockchain capabilities to combat the global trade in "Falsified" and "Illegal" fish products. J. Eng. Appl. Sci. **14**(10), 3310–3315 (2019)
29. Altoukhov, A.: Industrial product platforms and blockchain in aquaculture. In: IOP Conference Series: Earth and Environmental Science, vol. 421, no. 4, pp. 1–6 (2020)
30. Hang, L., Ullah, I., Kim, D.H.: A secure fish farm platform based on blockchain for agriculture data integrity. Comput. Electron. Agric. **170**, 105251 (2020)
31. Tsolakis, N., Niedenzu, D., Simonetto, M., Dora, M., Kumar, M.: Supply network design to address United Nations Sustainable Development Goals: a case study of blockchain implementation in Thai fish industry. J. Bus. Res. **131**, 495–519 (2021)
32. Petri, I., Masoud, B., Yacine, R., Omer, F.: Blockchain for energy sharing and trading in distributed prosumer communities. Comput. Ind. **123**, 103282 (2020)

Transportation Modes and AI

Train Rides Through Europe – Which Changes Do the Passengers Need?

Markus Linnartz[✉] and Nicola Fricke

Karlsruhe University of Applied Sciences, Moltkestr. 30, 76133 Karlsruhe, Germany
{markus.linnartz,nicola.fricke}@h-ka.de

Abstract. In view of climate change, the expansion of European rail transport is important. Compared to air travel, comparatively few people travel by train on trans-European routes. This paper summarizes findings from a focus-group study which was conducted to explore problems and requirements of European train travelling. During the focus group discussion, five participants aged 24–61 years were asked about their experiences with European train travel and the problems they face today. Additionally, they discussed which changes and potential measures could increase their train usage in the future. Results from the study show that the participants would like to travel by train through Europe, but some obstacles prevent them from doing so. They mentioned the high ticket prices, the lack of an integrated European booking platform and the lack of comfort at stations and on the trains. They also criticize long in-vehicle travel times, long transfer times, missing information, and overcrowded trains. Their stated requirements for using rail for inner-European journeys more often include a unified and consistent ticketing system, faster travel times, coordinated connections, and accessibility to rural areas, rather than just big cities. For longer journeys, participants prefer comfortable stations and trains where they can work, better information, consistently-available contact persons and the possibility to drop-off their luggage.

Keywords: European rail transport · international travel · travel behavior · European green mobility

1 Introduction

Rail transport is one of the most environmentally-friendly means of transport and is therefore seen as a transport mode that will be used more often in the future [1, 2]. Especially in view of climate change, the railway system should be increasingly supported in the upcoming years. This has become a consensus in the European Union [1]. In reality, however, the passenger volume of airports in the European Union (EU) has increased from 750 million to over one billion in the last 10 years [3]. On the contrary, cross-border rail travel still comes with a lot of problems and does not have much to offer compared to low-cost airlines and the private car on longer journeys [4, 5]. However, many short distance flights and car journeys within the EU could be replaced by train [6]. In order for people to consider train rides instead of car rides, the conditions for using

A. L. Martins et al. (Eds.): INTSYS 2022, LNICST 486, pp. 103–113, 2023.
https://doi.org/10.1007/978-3-031-30855-0_7

trains have to improve. Therefore, according to the EU Commission and many national governments and in view of climate change, rail travel should become more attractive on longer routes in Europe, so that emissions from short-haul flights and private cars can be reduced [7]. The EU is also pursuing this goal and has, for example, declared 2021 the "Year of Rail" and held several events and conferences [8]. The aim was to find possibilities to strengthen the railroads in Europe and thus achieve the self-established goals of doubling rail transport from the European Green Deal and Fit for 55 programs [1, 8].The overall goal is to make rail travel in Europe more attractive so that users will prefer the train over other means of transport. In the following section, research on travel mode choice and train travel in general is summarized. Afterwards, the study method is explained and results are provided. In the final section, the results are discussed in the context of the findings from literature.

2 Influencing Factors of Travel Mode Choice

Theoretically, there is great potential for trans-European train travel [6]. Studies show that the availability of good railway services allows people to switch modes from plane to train trips [9, 10]. However, this potential is reduced by the unavailability of direct train connections, expensive prices, complicated ticket booking, high travel times and the respective advantages of driving by car or flying [4, 9, 11]. Furthermore, other factors such as comfort at the stations and in trains, the accessibility to the train station, the frequency and reliability of trains, safety, and the positive perception of stimuli like appearance or smell [12–14] are also influencing the choice of mode of transport. All these factors and advantages of the train are in competition with the advantages of the plane, which is faster; the car, which is more flexible; and the bus, which is cheaper [15].

In addition, however, there are additional psychological factors like habits, personal attitudes towards transport modes, environmental awareness, social influence, culture and morals [15–18]. All these factors may differ in how they influence the travel mode choice of potential users. For example, one factor which is usually rated negatively, is the longer travel time on a train compared to a car drive. This factor can be positively framed in such a way that it is possible to use the free time to read and work [15, 19]. Of course, this option of working/reading should then be supported by e.g. the cabin-design (e.g. through quiet areas, technological equipment). Depending on who are potential target users, different barriers have to be addressed [19].

There has been research about ticketing to counteract some disadvantages of train rides in Europe [20]. They found that various national railway providers do not cooperate and are not interested in relinquishing sovereignty over their network. Nevertheless, new private railway companies are entering the market creating competition, but making ticketing for international travel even more complicated [20, 21]. One study shows that booking multiple tickets on international journeys with the different rail operators is often the only option [20]. This makes the journey more expensive and if the connecting train is missed due to a delay, a new ticket must be bought as there is no transfer guarantee [11, 20]. In her qualitative study, she concludes that a check-in/check-out system, where customers can use any train in Europe would make the train much more attractive [20]. With that system, the passengers do not have to buy a ticket; they just have to put a smartcard on a reader when entering the first station (check in) and leaving the last station (check out) and a standardized price will be automatically deducted from their bank account [20].

General problems with national rail services, such as the high prices and frequent transfers are well known [4, 9, 11]. However, other, previously unknown problems may exist which are particularly prevalent on trans-European railway journeys and have not yet been considered in the literature. Furthermore, the requirements of the passengers on these journeys must also be considered from a user perspective. With the knowledge of the problems from the user's perspective, it is possible to see urgent need for change and whether the measures which are planned in relation to the European Green Deal, can contribute to the benefit of the passengers. The following study explores possible problems and requirements for trans-European rail transport in detail and from the user's point of view.

3 Study Design

3.1 Method

For the purpose of exploring the topic of trans-European railway network a focus-group method was selected in order to detect new ideas and possible barriers for using trains on European journeys [22]. One advantage of performing a focus group is that new creative ideas can be generated collaboratively, which may have remained hidden in individual interviews [23]. Through group dynamics, ideas can be further discussed, extended, and directly evaluated by several potential users. While it is true that focus group studies cannot be representative as they are a qualitative method with few participants, they provide the potential for insights into topics that are under-researched so that they can be further investigated in future research.

The focus group discussion took place online and in German. The participants were guided through the different topics, which are described in Sect. 3.3, with a Power-Point presentation that included questions and images. For one question Mural (a digital bulletin board) was used to brainstorm ideas. Amberscript software was used for transcription of the material and MaxQDA for coding the transcripts.

3.2 Participants

Five participants were recruited for the focus group. As shown in Table 1, three of the participants were aged 24–26. Of these, one uses the car as the main mode of transport, one uses the bicycle and one uses public transport. All of them often use the train for shorter journeys, and two out of three also use it for longer journeys through Europe. Two of them have an academic degree and work now in a full-time job. One is still studying. In addition, there was also a participant in her 60 s who has a higher position in a larger business group and a participant in her 40 s who has a larger family with children. Both of them use the car as their main mode of transport and do not travel at all or only very rarely by train.

Table 1. Participants

Participant 1	Age: 24 I Cologne, Germany I Full-time Job I male Main mode of transport: Car and public transport
Participant 2	Age: 25 I Ulm, Germany I Student I female Main mode of transport: Public transport
Participant 3	Age: 26 I Stuttgart, Germanyl Full-time job I female Main mode of transport: Public transport
Participant 4	Age: 45 I Esslingen, Germany I Part-time job I female I two kids Main mode of transport: Car
Participant 5	Age: 61 I Nuremberg, Germany I Full-Time Job I female Main mode of transport: Car

3.3 Procedure of the Focus Group Discussion

As mentioned above, the focus group was conducted using a PowerPoint to give structure to the discussion. The following steps were taken during the discussion:

1. Welcome and introduction of the participants.
2. First general discussion on past experiences with longer train journeys including international trips.
3. Discussion of problems and possible barriers for travelling by train in Europe.
4. Collection of ideas with online tool Mural on how deficits could be eliminated. Ideas were sorted into three categories: "Before the journey", "During the journey," and "After the journey".
5. Collection of needed changes in the railway system, using the example of their way from home to their favorite holiday destination in Europe.
6. Opinions on three ideas for modern train travel in Europe were discussed. The three ideas included modern sleeping cars in the night-trains of the ÖBB, a universal European booking system with low prices and a check-in/check-out system like in the Netherlands.
7. Final comments about future travelling by train were discussed.

4 Results

The results of the study can be sorted into two categories. First, the barriers that, according to the participants, exist in today's trans-European rail transport, and their needs and expectations for using the European rail transport mode more often in the future.

4.1 Barriers

There are many factors identified by participants that currently prevent them from travelling by train and which can be divided into three categories: Station, Information, and Services.

Station. One important point that was mentioned is the comfort of the train station in many (not all) European countries. Participants compared the atmosphere and the feel-good factor with airports, which have more shops, relaxing zones, and comfort to offer. On the contrary, it was mentioned that at many railway stations there are almost no opportunities to pass the time with only few warm places to sit, especially in the winter. One participant said: "And especially in the winter, it is very unpleasant if you had to wait for half an hour on the platform and would like to read" (translated from German). The presence of strange people and the resulting feeling of insecurity was also mentioned.

Information. This category addresses the absence or lack of various types of information. It was mentioned that people are forced to wait on the cold platform because that is the only place where information about the train is available: "There was a storm, which means that everything took forever. And then you couldn't actually leave the […] platform because you were always dependent on the information on the platform about what to do next, even if it was raining through the roof and it was totally cold." (translated form German). In addition, the information reported was often contradictory across various information channels or simply not available. Regarding stations in non-German-speaking regions, the information is sometimes only available in the national language. Also, stations in other countries have a different structure, which leads to confusion when the track cannot be found. Moreover, the person to contact in case of difficulties is not clear when you buy tickets from several railway companies. Changing between two stations, such as in Paris, was also viewed negatively if the effort is not explicitly known.

Service. It was also criticized by participants that in some countries, trains can be overbooked and therefore a few people have to stand in the long distance trains for hours. This leads to overcrowded trains and even for passengers with reservations it turns into awkward and stressful situations to squeeze through the crowds, especially with children and big suitcases. It is even more difficult, when the train arrives in another order than indicated. Additionally, concerning suitcases, it is also noted that it is particularly stressful on longer journeys with a lot of luggage and several changes. This is especially the case when going skiing or on other activity-based holidays, when you need lots of luggage. It is also noted that arriving in the touristic areas like mountains or coasts by train becomes a problem because it is difficult to get around in these rural areas and driving from home by car is more pleasant. The participants also mentioned that it is difficult to book trans-European tickets in general. One of the participants said that to get to Spain from Germany, it is necessary to buy three tickets: one for the German operator, one for the French operator, and one for the Spanish operator. This leads to more expensive tickets and no guarantee of connecting trains. In addition, the connections are not coordinated, and the transfer times are too long and make the time advantage of the flight even greater. Together with the low-cost plane tickets, the train seems unattractive for the passengers. All these barriers mentioned above are summarized in the following Table 2.

Table 2. Barriers

Station	Insecure und uncomfortable feeling
	Cold and uncomfortable waiting areas at the platforms
	Gate areas in Airports are more attractive
Information	Only in the local language and on the platforms
	Complicated to find the correct platform
	Incorrect wagon-order indicators on the platform
	Assistance only from the specific train operator
Services	Overcrowded trains
	Different operators → More than one ticket → No connection guarantee
	Expensive tickets
	No coordinated connections → Long transfer and travel times

4.2 Needs and Requirements

The needs and requirements from the participants can be sorted into basic requirements which are necessary for them to travel with the train through Europe, and additional requirements which make the train ride a journey that is comfortable and feels good.

Basic Requirements. The basic requirements are mainly related to the points of services and accessibility and are necessary for the participants to use the train on European routes at all. A European booking platform, with which one ticket can be bought for directly getting to the destination, allowing easier enforcement of passenger rights in the event of a delay was mentioned. In addition, the connections should be better coordinated. For the younger price-conscious participants, the rail prices for the entire journey should be cheaper or more competitive with air fares, especially with low-cost airlines, so that they consider travelling by rail. On the other hand, participants who have already been working for a few years state that they would like to travel more flexibly and not be tied to specific times. Regarding the travel time during the day, one participant mentioned 8–9 h as the limit for train journeys, other participants are more open if the comfort of travelling by train is increased in the future. For long distance routes, diverse night train connections should be available, where you arrive at your destination well-rested with sufficient comfort, privacy, and silence. A high density of accessibility to the railway system, especially in rural areas, is also noted. Not only the large cities should be easily accessible; there should also be good public transport connections to destinations in rural regions so that the train is more attractive than the car. In addition, there should be car-sharing and rental car providers at all larger stations, so that people who need the car at their destinations can rent one directly after arrival.

Additional Requirements. The additional requirements will make the train ride more attractive and comfortable so that the journey is pleasant, and people enjoy travelling by train trough Europe, even on longer journeys. The participants would like to have a significant improvement in the condition of the stations. They mentioned an extra area where only passengers with a valid ticket have access and where a variety of opportunities to spend time and eat are available, as is the case at airport transfer areas. The participants would like to have warm places to sit and work in silence, shops, and sufficient food options. People without a ticket should not have access to these spaces, so that the passengers feel safer. In this passenger-only area, all information on all connections should be given via display boards and loudspeaker announcements, exactly as on the platform. Nevertheless, there should also be enough comfortable waiting areas on the platform, including warm ones in the winter.

The same can be transferred to the in-train design. Opportunities inside the train should also be created so that working on the move is possible without any problems. There should also be a good choice of food aboard for longer journeys. In addition, the space for sitting should be sufficiently large and comfortable, the Wi-Fi should work permanently, and only as many tickets as seats inside the train should be sold. There should be enough quiet compartments for participants who need to rest. A board entertainment system was also desired. In order to simplify the boarding process, everyone should be assigned a seat and so everyone can be directly at the right carriage of the train, e.g., with the help of electronic carriage position indicators. There should also be enough staff available at boarding to simplify the process and to answer questions at any time. As far as luggage is concerned, participants would like to be able to either drop off larger luggage at the station and pick it up again at the destination station without having to lug it along every time they change trains, or to have it delivered directly to their accommodation at their destination. At the same time, more storage space for luggage should be available, especially on night trains.

In summary, participants would be willing to choose the train as their means of transport more often in case of the changes mentioned. The required changes are summarized in Table 3. One participant described appropriately as follows: "I mean, I would leave from Cologne [...] to Paris and it takes about three and a half hours. If you have an on-board restaurant there, you have your seat, that's comfortable. You could maybe have a nice dinner there, then watch a series in your seat, then arrive in Paris and at the same station there would be a night train to Spain [...] You'd leave at 6 p.m. in Cologne, then travel from Paris to Spain by night train at 10 p.m., and then I would perhaps be in Spain in the morning. I would think that would be much more pleasant than flying because my holiday would kind of already start when I leave Cologne. If it all works out. If everything is coordinated and I'm well rested the next morning at my holiday destination and don't have to get on a plane in the evening than I would take the train." (Translated from German).

5   Discussion

The barriers people reported in this study concerning today's trans-European train network are similar compared to the literature which focused on national and international rail services [4, 6, 11, 24]. These are mainly factors related to comfort, time, price, and availability which keep many passengers from travelling by train today.

Table 3. Basic and Additional Requirements

Basic Requirements	Services	European-ticket-booking platform
		Coordinated international services
		English-speaking assistance/information everywhere
		Competitive price and flexible booking
		Less travel time (max. 8–9 h)
		Comfortable night trains (for longer journeys)
	Accessibility	Accessibility in rural areas
		Car-sharing/Car-rental at train stations
Additional Requirements	Stations	Access only for passengers
		Comfortable and warm seating and working areas
		Shopping, eating and entertainment
		Electronic carriage position indicator at platforms
	Trains	Comfortable seating
		One seat for each passenger
		Good food at restaurants
		Working possibilities (quiet area with Wi-Fi)
		Board entertainment system
		Enough storage space
	Services	Luggage drop off

Additionally, slight differences to findings from the literature are recognized with regard to the requirements. For example, the participants of this study would like to have one European booking platform through which all railway companies are obliged to sell tickets with which is similar to findings from another study [11]. The big advantage of the booking system would be that train connections can be easily compared and booked simply as is the case with well-known air travel sites. In contrast to the private train sites, the booking fee could be saved, no extreme price would be charged, and the guarantee of a connection would be granted. Van Overhagen on the contrary, concludes a different result [20]. As described earlier in Sect. 2, her study supports a "check-in/check-out" system for passengers. This type of system was not preferred by participants in this study. This may be due to the fact that she conducted her study in the Netherlands, where the check-in/check-out system has been a standard for a long time.

The introduction of a European timetable is also being discussed in the political arena, i.e. connections with short transfer times that are coordinated throughout Europe. The expansion of night trains is now being promoted jointly by several European railway companies [25]. The ÖBB (Austrian Railway) is therefore ordering new night trains, which will be available in the near future.

The requirements concerning the comfort of the equipment is comparable to the results of Lee et al. [24]. According to the participants, it is not only the comfort on the trains that is prioritized, but also at the station before and after the journey, and when changing trains. With a good internet connection on the train and at the stations, the train could also be an option for business trips longer than 4 h. The shopping and dining options mentioned would also add to the enjoyment of train travel for private journeys, as Lee et al. has already mentioned [24].

6 Conclusion and Further Work

The willingness to travel by train on longer European routes exists for almost all participants, although to varying degrees. But to do so, they need the mentioned basic requirements like the European booking platform and lower ticket prices to be able to drive by train trough Europe. With the above-mentioned additional requirements, they imagine rail travel as an attractive means of transport of the future, which they would always like to use. As the study gives a purely German view of a very small sample size of five participants, results could be different with other German users and vary from country to country. Therefore, more data should be examined in further qualitative and also quantitative studies in more European countries. Furthermore, the requirements mentioned by the participants only refer to objective factors like travel time and comfort. However, the psychological factors such as habits, social influence, and attitudes might not be changed by measures that address the mentioned requirements of the participants. Therefore, further studies should aim at integrating a wider variety of factors which can then be positively influenced regarding trans-European rail travel.

Finally, the measures discussed in this study, such as the European mobility platform, European passenger rights, and the European timetable of the European Commission provide a first impression of possible steps towards promoting sustainable travel.

Acknowledgements. We would like to thank all the participants in the focus group for their time and openness in the discussion, without which the study would not have been possible.

References

1. European Union: Sustainable & Smart Mobility Strategy. Putting European transport on track for the future. European Union (2020)
2. Umweltbundesamt: Vergleich der durchschnittlichen Treibhausgas-Emissionen einzelner Verkehrsmittel im Personenverkehr in Deutschland. TREMOD, 6.21 (2021)
3. Eurostat: Air transport of passengers by country (yearly data). (2022). https://ec.europa.eu/eurostat/databrowser/view/ttr00012/default/line?lang=en. Accessed 15 July 2022
4. Boon, I.: A transfer in international train travel:. Enhancing passenger comfort while changing trains during cross-border travel. Delft University of Technology (2017)
5. Gamon, W., Naranjo Gómez, J.M.: Main problems of railway cross-border transport between Poland Germany and Czech Republic. Sustainability **11**, 4900 (2019). https://doi.org/10.3390/su11184900

6. Donners, B.: Erasing Borders Delft University of Technology European Rail Passenger Potential (2016)
7. European Union: Sustainable & Smart Mobility Strategy. The Transport and Mobility Sector. European Union (2020)
8. European Commission: European Green Deal. Transport and Green Deal (2022). https://ec. europa.eu/info/strategy/priorities-2019-2024/european-green-deal/transport-and-green-dea l_de. Accessed 24 Jan 2022
9. Pagliara, F., Vassallo, J.M., Román, C.: High-speed rail versus air transportation: case study of Madrid-Barcelona Spain. Transp. Res. Record **2289**, 10–17 (2022)
10. Park, Y., Ha, H.K.: Analysis of the impact of high-speed railroad service on air transport demand. Transp. Res. Part E Logistics Transp. Rev. **42**, 95–104 (2006). https://doi.org/10. 1016/j.tre.2005.09.003
11. Witlox, F., Zwanikken, T., Jehee, L., Donners, B., Veeneman, W.: Changing tracks: identifying and tackling bottlenecks in European rail passenger transport. Eur. Transp. Res. Rev. **14**(1), 1–12 (2022). https://doi.org/10.1186/s12544-022-00530-9
12. Linnartz, M., Dufner, Y., Fricke, N.: Information presentation in autonomous shuttle busses: –what and how? In: Wölfel, M., Bernhardt, J., Thiel, S. (Eds.) ArtsIT, Interactivity and Game Creation. ArtsIT 2021. Lecture Notes of the Institute for Computer Sciences, Social Informatics and Telecommunications Engineering, pp. 413–423, vol. 422. Springer, Cham (2022). https://doi.org/10.1007/978-3-030-95531-1_28
13. Román, C., Espino, R., Martín, J.C.: Analyzing competition between the high speed train and alternative modes. The case of the Madrid-Zaragoza-Barcelona corridor. J. Choice Model. **3**, 84–108(2010). https://doi.org/10.1016/S1755-5345(13)70030-7
14. Risser, R., et al.: Verkehr ist Verhalten. Psychologische Theorien zu Verkehr und Mobilität (2019)
15. Bühlmann, M., Vogel, T.: Verkehrsmittelwahl bei Urlaubsreisen. Eine empirische Analyse der Kriterien und Gründe der Verkehrsmittelwahl für Urlaubsreisen im europäischen Raum. Fachhochschule Nordwestschweiz (2020)
16. Jonas, K., Stroebe, W., Hewstone, M.: Sozialpsychologie. Springer, Berlin (2014)
17. Myers, D.G.: Psychologie. Springer, Berlin (2014)
18. van Doorn, K.: The influence of user-generated content on intention to use holiday train travel. Exploring a way to stimulate more sustainable holiday transportation choices. Wageningen University & Research (2020)
19. Dziekan, K., Schlag, B., Jünger, I.: Barrieren der Bahnnutzung – Mobilitätshemmnisse und Mobilitätsbedürfnisse. In: Schlag, B. (ed.) Verkehrspsychologie, Lengerich (2004)
20. van Overhagen, L.: A design vision towards seamless European train journeys. Making the train the default option to travel within Europe. Delft University of Technology (2021)
21. Tomeš, Z., Jandová, M.: Open access passenger rail services in Central Europe. Res. Transp. Econ. **72**, 74–81 (2018)
22. Schulz, M.: Quick and easy!? Fokusgruppen in der angewandten Sozialwissenschaft. In: Schulz, M., Mack, B., Renn, O. (eds.) Fokusgruppen in der empirischen Sozialwissenschaft, pp. 9–23. VS Verlag für Sozialwissenschaften, Wiesbaden (2012)
23. Zwick, M., Schröter, R.: Konzeption und Durchführung von Fokusgruppen am Beispiel des BMBF-Projekts „Übergewicht und Adipositas bei Kindern, Jugendlichen und jungen Erwachsenen als systemisches Risiko". In: Schulz, M., Mack, B., Renn, O. (eds.) Fokusgruppen in der empirischen Sozialwissenschaft, pp. 24–48. VS Verlag für Sozialwissenschaften, Wiesbaden (2012)

24. Lee, K., Hwang, E.-J., Yeom, S.-H., Kim, M.-H., Jo, H.-J.: The effect of high-speed rail-way station facilities and train related services on customer satisfaction: based on KTX user experience. J. Korean Society Railway (2016). https://doi.org/10.7782/JKSR.2016.19.3.351
25. Bundesregierung: Mehr Nachtzüge für Europa (2021). https://www.bundesregierung.de/breg-de/aktuelles/mehr-nachtzuege-fuer-europa-1992404. Accessed 15 July 2022

Adaptive Dimming of Highway Lights Using Recurrent Neural Networks

Angelos Kolaitis[1], Georgios Alexandridis[1(✉)] (iD), Panagiota Adam[2],
Petros Alexandridis[2], Grigoris Chasanis[3], and Fabrice Breton[3]

[1] Artificial Intelligence and Learning Systems Laboratory, School of Electrical
and Computer Engineering, National Technical University of Athens,
157 80 Zografou, Greece
`akolaitis@mail.ntua.gr`, `gealexandri@islab.ntua.gr`
[2] Extrabit L.P., 97 Nikolaou Plastira str, 122 42 Egaleo, Greece
{`nota.adam,petros.alexandridis`}`@extrabit.gr`
[3] Olympia Odos S.A., 4 Rizareiou str, 152 33 Chalandri, Greece
{`gchasanis,fbreton`}`@olympiaodos.gr`
`https://www.ails.ece.ntua.gr/`, `https://www.extrabit.gr/`,
`https://www.olympiaodos.gr/`

Abstract. Highway operators are in a constant search of techniques and
methodologies that can reduce their energy footprint. In this respect,
the installation of dimmable light-emitting diode lights on the open
road section of highways appears to be a promising solution, due to the
reduced energy consumption (compared to high pressure sodium lamps)
and the ability to adjust their brightness at various levels, based on the
road's traffic load. However, setting the desired level of light intensity
cannot be performed instantly, due to safety and contractual reasons
that a highway operator must follow. For this reason, an adaptive and
intelligent system is proposed in this work, that models traffic load and is
able to predict its future trend, based on current load and light intensity
measurements. In this way, the unnecessary use of the lighting equipment
is avoided, as brightness is dropped to a minimum level when traffic load
is predicted to be low. The proposed model is based on recurrent neural
networks and more specifically on long short-term memory cells that are
able to model complex dependencies in data with temporal correlations,
like traffic load measurements. The overall approach is evaluated on relevant data provided by Olympia Odos S.A. that operates the Elefsina-
Korinthos-Patra highway in Greece, with promising results.

Keywords: Traffic load prediction · Highway Lighting · LED
Lighting · Intelligent Traffic Control Systems · Recurrent Neural
Networks · Long Short-Term Memory

© ICST Institute for Computer Sciences, Social Informatics and Telecommunications Engineering 2023
Published by Springer Nature Switzerland AG 2023. All Rights Reserved
A. L. Martins et al. (Eds.): INTSYS 2022, LNICST 486, pp. 114–128, 2023.
https://doi.org/10.1007/978-3-031-30855-0_8

1   Introduction

The transportation sector, along with the organization and operation of road networks and traffic management, is of pivotal importance for the economic development of countries and the improvement of the quality of life of their citizens. Nowadays, in a period of rapid development and application of innovative solutions in transportation technologies, the ability to integrate smart systems that can tackle complex problems and enhance the level of the provided services is challenging.

Especially in the area of highway lighting, new possibilities emerge, as light-emitting diode (LED) lights allow the adjustment of their brightness, a process also known as dimming [6]. In contrast, traditional lighting methods, such as high pressure sodium (HPS) lamps incur high operating costs, due to their increased energy consumption and corresponding equipment maintenance and replacement needs [5]. Additionally, their environmental footprint must be also taken into account, since the inability to adjust their brightness results in light pollution that affects negatively both the residents of the neighboring areas adjacent to highways, as well as the local flora and fauna.

Even though LED lights can be dimmed, this process cannot be performed instantly, based on the current traffic load, as it requires a certain amount of time during which the traffic load and consequently the light intensity requirements may change. For this reason, the development of a machine learning (ML) algorithm that will be able to model and predict the traffic load for near-future time windows (e.g. within the next hour), based on current traffic data and lighting conditions, is necessary. In this manner, the available equipment is used in an energy efficient way, as brightness is limited to a minimum level when the road traffic is predicted to be low.

This work predominately focuses on the development of an ML algorithm that predicts future traffic load. The said algorithm is going to be part of a broader intelligent architecture that ingests predictions along with weather data and road incidents and selects the desired dimming level, based on a decision making process and a rule set defined by the concessionaire of the highway (Fig. 1). The developed system has been tested on data from the Elefsina-Korinthos-Patra highway in Greece, which are provided by the concessionaire, Olympia Odos S.A. The expected benefits of the overall intelligent lighting system, apart from being an end-to-end solution for brightness management in open highways, are energy savings, reduction of the CO_2 footprint as well as light pollution, while at the same time assessing the desired levels of safety and traffic quality, especially during low visibility time periods (night, cloudy weather, etc).

The rest of the paper is organized as follows; Sect. 2 overviews related work, Sect. 3 outlines the benefits of LEDs over other legacy technologies and Sect. 4 presents Intelligent Traffic Control Systems. Section 5 discusses the traffic load prediction module, starting from the data acquisition process (Sect. 5.1), continuing with the machine learning algorithm (Sect. 5.2), the description of the optimal model (Sect. 5.3) and the evaluation the obtained results (Sect. 5.4). Finally the paper concludes in Sect. 6.

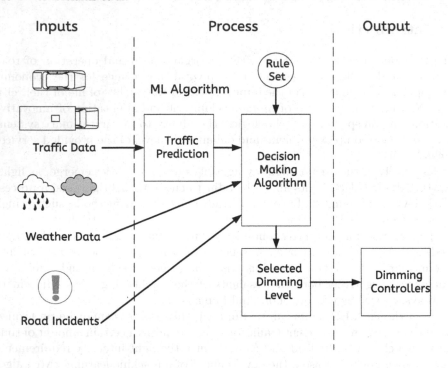

Fig. 1. The overall intelligent lighting system architecture

2   Related Work

Traffic prediction has been extensively studied, especially in the framework of smart cities [18]. The main objective in this case is to employ machine learning methodologies in order to predict traffic jams and other road incidents that might hinder the flow of traffic. This type of information is particularly useful to urban planners, transportation authorities and to individuals and parties involved in the planning and development of the transportation infrastructure and services within cities.

Recently, highway traffic prediction has also emerged as an active research field, especially with the availability of both private and public relevant datasets. For example, private data provided by South Korean highways have been used in [31], where the authors employed long short-term memory cells for highway vehicle speed prediction, along with bayesian optimization and meta-learning for hyper-parameter tuning. Or in [2], where real-time traffic flow is modelled by a Bayesian classifier and support vector regression. In [16], structural state space models are utilized for short-term highway traffic state prediction and are evaluated on data from the northern Taiwan highway network.

Many works are based on public data provided by the California Department of Transportation Caltrans Performance Measurement System (PeMS)[1]. In [30], the authors propose an intelligent system based on empirical mode decomposition and least-squares support vector machines. The spatial and temporal correlations existent in PeMS traffic data are also examined in the context of diffusion convolutional recurrent neural networks [15], graph convolutional networks [27] or attention-based periodic-temporal neural networks [25].

Finally, in [17], the authors have a similar objective to our own; they propose a smart highway lighting system based on road occupancy. Nevertheless, their actual approach is rather simplistic as they develop a probabilistic model which is evaluated on simulated data. To the best of our knowledge, our proposed methodology is among the first to study the problem of highway traffic prediction using machine learning techniques and for the purpose of adjusting the intensity of the lighting systems.

3 Light Emitting Diodes

Reducing the operating costs of highways while at the same time complying with safety levels defined by national and international regulations, is one of the biggest challenges faced by all parties involved in the infrastructure of transportation networks (states, construction companies, operating and management companies). In particular, highway management companies put a constant effort in modernizing their equipment by adopting smart methods to reduce their energy footprint, such as replacing traditional lighting devices with dimmable LEDs.

Even though initially LEDs exhibited greater life cycle costs compared to HPS luminaire [29], recent developments, such as the price drop of LED lamps thanks to higher production and more players in the market (particularly from China), as well as their better efficacy, compared to other technologies, have resulted in an increased market penetration [8]. In particular, from $120 \frac{lm}{W}$, which was comparable to the $90{-}100 \frac{lm}{W}$ of the legacy technologies, LEDs achieve efficacies of more than $160 \frac{lm}{W}$ on professional lighting applications like in highways, parking lots, etc [5].

The use of dimmable LED lighting on highways ensures a significant reduction in energy consumption - and hence operating costs - without reducing the light quality or affecting road safety [13]. A reduction in energy consumption is still possible even when no new lighting studies have been performed and the old equipment is just replaced with the new one [33]. This is attributed to two factors; (i) the better efficacy of the LED lamps and therefore the need to use considerably smaller installed power, compared to other lamp types (e.g. HPS), in order to achieve the same light coverage, (ii) their ability to be used in a selective and controlled manner, according to the actual requirements of each occasion. Moreover, the correct use of the dimming feature can contribute to

---

[1] https://pems.dot.ca.gov/.

further increasing the efficiency of LED lights, while this ability can also contribute to the reduction of light pollution, which disturbs the ecological balance, as it has a great effect on the animal life and well-being [28].

4   Intelligent Traffic Management Systems

Intelligent traffic management systems (ITMS) are systems that monitor road networks and whose use can aid operators draw dynamic conclusions. ITMS collect data from a multitude of sources, such as cameras, sensors, mobile phones etc, that are subsequently processed in order to draw insight out of them. ITMS constitute an active, multidisciplinary research field, as they make use of technologies like big data analytics, machine learning, Internet of Things (IoT) and others. A number of studies in the relevant literature summarize useful conclusions from pilot applications of such systems [12,22].

The benefits of ITMS can be visible in various aspects, including the effective use of real-time data [11], the capability of managing big data loads from various sources [19,24], the automatic adaptation to traffic loads [7,14], the constant adaptation to changes in their environment and the possibility of preemptive predictions [21,26]. Their application in adjusting the brightness of the lights of the open road section of highways can be seen as achieving the optimum tradeoff between road safety and energy consumption [7,20]. On the one hand, the highway operators seek to reduce operational costs as much as possible. On the other hand, street lighting is necessary for the safety of the road users, while regulations mandate that it should be set above certain thresholds, depending on current traffic conditions. At the same time, dimming the LED lights can not be performed instantly, but requires a time frame of 10 minutes in order for the brightness to reach the desired level. Obviously, continuously alternating brightness levels is not productive at all.

In this respect, an intelligent and adaptive lighting system that reads current traffic conditions and predicts their trend for the near-future (e.g. the next couple of hours) can be very useful. Based on the said predictions, the operator can lower the brightness level when necessary, reducing operational costs and achieving energy savings, without affecting road safety. In the current work, the adaptive lighting system is studied with respect to the traffic prediction module. More specifically, ML algorithms are going to be implemented, based on recurrent neural networks with long-short term memory units. The respective models are going to be trained on traffic data from the Elefsina-Korinthos-Patra highway in Greece, provided by Olympia Odos S.A.

5   Traffic Load Prediction

This Section presents the key components of the traffic prediction module, that is an integral part of the overall intelligent lighting system architecture (Fig. 1). Initially, data acquisition is discussed (Sect. 5.1), proceeding with the description of the implemented ML algorithms (Sect. 5.2), following with the description

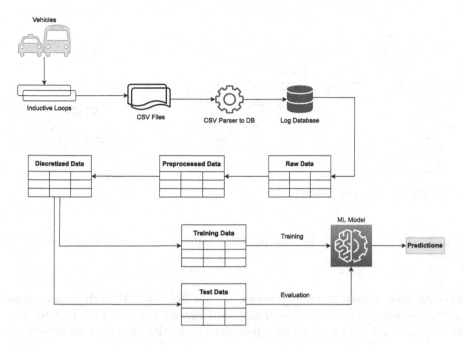

Fig. 2. The Traffic Load Prediction module

of the optimal model (Sect. 5.3) and finally ending with the evaluation of its performance (Sect. 5.4). The overall procedure is depicted on Fig. 2.

The traffic data for the consecutive analysis originate from the Elefsina-Korinthos-Patra (Olympia Odos) highway in Greece, have been collected in 2018 and are provided by Olympia Odos S.A. The full length of the highway is depicted in Fig. 3, along with the toll stations.

5.1   Data Acquisition

Traffic load data acquisition can be performed in a number of ways, either *intrusive* or *non-intrusive*, including magnetic field detectors (magnetometers), pressure detectors, cameras, microwave radars, bluetooth and GPS trackers. In the case of the Olympia Odos highway, the chosen solution are inductive loop detectors, placed on the road surface (Fig. 2, top left). Those devices are comprised of a coil, through which an electric current passes. The presence of metallic objects or other sources of electromagnetic interference around the coil alter its self-inductance and therefore permit it to function as a vehicle detector. An inductive loop detector is comprised of a controller, along with the accompanying cable which is mounted on the road surface (at the highway intersections in the examined case - Fig. 3).

The raw data from the controllers of the inductive loops are read in comma-separated value (CSV) format and are subsequently stored on a log database (Fig. 2, top row). Every entry in the database corresponds to one of the 40

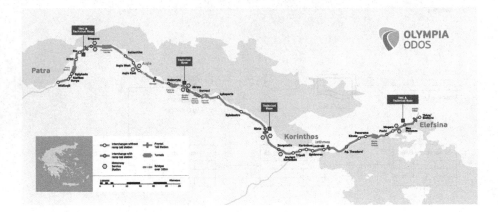

Fig. 3. The full length of the Olympia Odos highway in Greece, along with the toll stations

measurement points in each direction of the highway. At each measurement point, sensors are placed on each lane and are equipped with a counter that stores the number of vehicles that pass over it. In the analysis that follows, we have selected only the main highway sensors, as their information is more relevant to those on the exit ramps, when predicting the traffic load of the highway. The selected group of sensors can detect the vehicle type (e.g. motorbike, car, lorry), their average speed and the occupancy degree (percentage) of the road. Every six minutes, each sensor stores the contents of its counter into the database (Table 1).

Table 1. Sensor data stored in the database (every 6 min)

Feature	Example
Timestamp	2018-01-04 10:12:00
Sensor location	VDS ZEV M T96,6
Highway direction	EPT-T
Highway lane	1
Lane occupancy (%)	1.3%
Average speed of vehicles	126 $\frac{km}{h}$
Total number of vehicles	24

Prior to providing the data as input to the machine learning algorithms, a number of preprocessing steps are necessary (Fig. 2, second row). Initially, the data are inspected for missing or corrupted values, which are subsequently removed from the dataset. Then, the measurements for each lane are aggregated per sensor location and direction, in order to obtain the total traffic load. Figure 4 displays the average daily traffic load at the EPI-E location (Epidavros, direction to Elefsina) for the examined time period (February 2018 to November 2018), after it has been preprocessed.

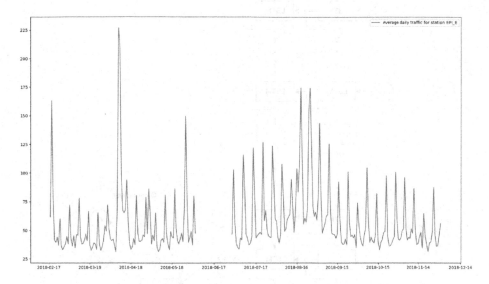

Fig. 4. Average daily traffic for the examined time period (February 2018 to November 2018) at the EPI-E location (Epidavros, direction to Elefsina)

A closer inspection of the displayed data reveals the expected temporal correlations in traffic load. For example, there are evident two main seasonalities in the data; namely, weekdays and weekends. Weekends exhibit larger traffic volumes and this is especially characteristic of Sundays, when many travelers return to Athens via Elefsina. Other sources of seasonal data (increased traffic loads) are holiday seasons (Easter, summer), public and national holidays, as well as random events (e.g. accidents) that may occur on the highway. It is also worth mentioning that the "gap" appearing around June 2018 is due to a malfunctioning of the given induction loop for the said period, which has been detected (and the corresponding values removed) during the preprocessing phase.

5.2   Machine Learning Algorithms

As it is evident both from the analysis in Sect. 5.1 and Fig. 4, the nature of the examined problem is that of *time series forecasting* [3]. In simpler words, the objective is to predict the evolution of the time series (here, the traffic load) over time, implying that, as there is a temporal correlation between the current traffic load and its past values, there should also be a correlation between present values and future ones. If we are able to predict future traffic loads with a certain confidence for the next hour, then we are able to proactively increase the brightness levels and reactively decrease them, based on those predictions.

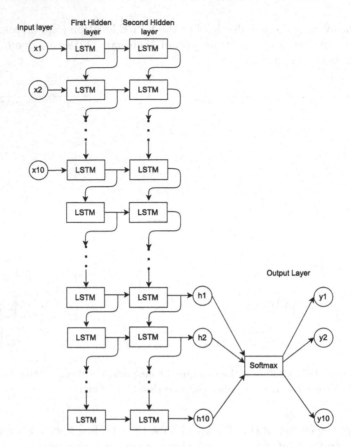

Fig. 5. The implemented machine learning model (recurrent neural network with LSTM cells)

Time series forecasting has been extensively studied in the framework of machine learning algorithms, employing a variety of techniques, including regression, neural networks, support vector machines and random forests [1]. Among the most prominent methodologies are recurrent neural networks (RNNs) [9], which are an extension to feed-forward, artificial neural networks (ANNs), where a feedback loop has been added between the output of each neuron and its input. The presence of the said feedback loop is considered to address the temporal dependencies in sequences of data [23].

The building blocks of RNNs are the recurrent neurons, which are also called units and are stacked in layers from the network input to output (Fig. 5), in a similar fashion to the ordinary neurons of ANNs. The most popular RNN units are the long short-term memory (LSTM) cells [10] and the gated recurrent units (GRUs) [4]. In this work, we have experimented with networks featuring both types of recurrent neurons.

The input to the RNN network is the past traffic load data, in temporal order and its output are the predicted traffic load values, again in temporal order. According to the analysis of Sect. 5.1, the measurement period is 6 min, therefore, if the objective is to predict traffic for the following hour, then the subsequent 10 values need to be predicted. Consequently, the network output is of size 10. The network input size is related to how far it is necessary to "look back" in time in order to be able to produce accurate predictions for the future. If the time window (in the past) is very short, we might miss useful correlations for our analysis; on the other hand if it is too long, we might introduce noise into the model, in the form of unnecessary information. After an initial experimentation, it has been found out that the optimal time window in the past is also one hour; that is, the model reads the past hour's measurements (10 values) in order ot predict the following hour's load (10 predictions). In essence, the overall RNN architecture falls in the category of a *many-to-many* prediction, where the input size is equal to the output size (Fig. 5).

Finally, the type of the predicted values need to be determined. An obvious choice would be to treat the problem of traffic prediction in the form of regression; that is to output the exact value of the future traffic load. However, such a modelling is not fit for the case we are examining, as we are interested in determining the traffic level (and subsequently, adjust the brightness of the LED lights) rather than a precise value. For this reason, apart from studying it in the context of regression, we have also decided to discretize the output to categories of N cars; that is, to treat it in the form of multiclass classification (i.e. in the first category fall predictions of up to N cars, in the second between N and $2N$ and so forth - Fig. 2 second row, left).

5.3 Optimal Model

Having determined the main aspects of the proposed architecture in Sect. 5.2, we proceed with tuning its parameters and hyper-parameters in order to obtain as accurate predictions as possible. These include the activation functions used in the recurrent (hidden) layers and in the output layer. In the former case, the hyperbolic tangent has been chosen, as its smoothness has been found to be helpful during network training. In the latter case, the softmax function has been chosen, as the problem is multiclass and because it can convert the output of the neurons into probabilities (that sum up to 1). Finally, categorical cross-entropy has been used as the loss function, as it is common for classification problems.

Other hyper-parameters include the number of hidden layers, the number of neurons per hidden layer, the type of the recurrent units in the hidden layers, the Dropout rate and the number of training epochs. Their optimal values have been determined from an initial search space through exhaustive grid search and cross-validation. Table 2 summarizes both the search space for the said hyper-parameters, along with their optimal values.

Figure 5 displays the architecture of the optimal model. It is comprised of two hidden layers of 70 LSTM neurons each (2nd and 3rd columns). The outputs

Table 2. Hyper-parameter search space and optimal values

Hyper-parameter	Search space	Optimal value
Number of hidden layers	[1, 2, 3]	2
Number of neurons per hidden layer	[30, 40, 50, 60, 70]	70
Recurrent unit types	[LSTM, GRU]	LSTM
Dropout rate	[0, 0.01, 0.1]	0
Number of training epochs	[10, 20, 30]	30

of the 10 last LSTM cells of the second hidden layer are aggregated in the output layer (last column).

5.4 Evaluation

The optimal model of Sect. 5.3 has been trained on inductive loop data, according to the process described in Sect. 5.1. In order to avoid overfitting, the model has been trained on data from one location (KOR_E - Corinth, direction to Elefsina) and has been evaluated on two other locations, on both directions of the highway (AKO_E - Ancient Corinth, direction to Elefsina and AKO_T - Ancient Corinth, direction to Patras). Table 3 summarizes model performance on the training and the test data. The examined metrics are the *mean absolute error* (MAE), the *root mean square error* ((RMSE) and the *mean absolute precentage error* (MAPE) [32]. Those metrics are defined in Eqs. 1–3 below

$$MAE \ = \frac{1}{M} \sum_{i=1}^{M} |\hat{y}_i - y_i| \tag{1}$$

$$RMSE = \sqrt{\frac{1}{M} \sum_{i=1}^{M} (\hat{y}_i - y_i)^2} \tag{2}$$

$$MAPE = \frac{1}{M} \sum_{i=1}^{M} \left| \frac{\hat{y}_i - y_i}{y_i} \right| (\%) \tag{3}$$

where M are the total measurements in the training/test datasets, $\hat{y}_i$ is the prediction and y_i is the actual measurement. MAE and RMSE are regression metrics (by their definition correlated), quantifying the deviation between predicted and actual values (RMSE penalizes larger deviations more) and their optimal value is zero (therefore the smaller MAE and RMSE values, the better). MAPE, on the other hand, is the normalized version of MAE. Accuracy measures how many times $\hat{y}_i$ is equal to y_i in the training/test dataset and we also provide results for the discretized accuracy (multiclass classification problem described in Sect. 5.2); that is when we model system output in categories of N cars each.

A closer examination of the results presented on Table 3 validates the performance of the proposed approach. When traffic prediction is examined as a regression problem (first 4 result rows of Table 3), the optimal model of Sect. 5.3

Table 3. Model evaluation on the training (2nd column) and test data (3rd-4th columns)

Metric	Performance		
	KOR_E	AKO_E	AKO_T
MAE	10.15	8.68	9.30
RMSE	17.05	14.94	15.98
MAPE	20.33%	28.21%	28.40%
Accuracy	57.96%	61.82%	59.85%
Accuracy ($N = 20$)	93.01%	95.50%	94.99%
Accuracy ($N = 40$)	98.70%	99.50%	99.19%
Accuracy ($N = 60$)	99.69%	99.87%	99.72%

is able to make predictions that are only a few vehicles apart from the actual load. On the other hand, when the same problem is treated as (multiclass) classification (last 3 result rows of Table 3), the performance, in terms of the accuracy metric, is excellent, exceeding 99% in both the training and the test data. As discussed earlier (Sect. 5.2), the discretization of the network output into categories (classification problem) facilitates its integration into the overall intelligent lighting system (Fig. 1), without sacrificing the quality of the obtained predictions.

6 Conclusions

In this work, a machine learning model for traffic prediction, based on recurrent neural networks, has been presented. The said model is a component of a greater architecture, an intelligent lighting system, that adjusts the brightness of dimmable LED lights on the open road section of highways, reducing energy costs, as well as the overall environmental footprint of the road operators. The obtained results, both qualitative and quantitative, are very encouraging and the overall architecture is currently implemented on a larger scale, on the Elefsina-Korinthos-Patra highway in Greece.

Naturally, the current implementation can be further extended. For example, more data may be integrated into the model, in the form of domain knowledge (e.g. certain days that are expected to witness high traffic loads, like public holidays). Additionally, outlier detection can be useful as a further preprocessing step, as it has been observed that certain values recorded by the inductive loops are out of the ordinary and may be attributed to errors/interference during data acquisition. Finally, it is worth building more complex models, that consider data input from more than one locations.

Acknowledgements. This research was co-financed by the European Union and Greek national funds through the Operational Program Competitiveness, Entrepreneurship, and Innovation, under the call RESEARCH CREATE INNOVATE (project name: IntelliLight, project code: MIS-5055986).

References

1. Ahmed, N.K., Atiya, A.F., Gayar, N.E., El-Shishiny, H.: An empirical comparison of machine learning models for time series forecasting. Econometric Rev. **29**(5–6), 594–621 (2010). https://doi.org/10.1080/07474938.2010.481556
2. Ahn, J., Ko, E., Kim, E.Y.: Highway traffic flow prediction using support vector regression and bayesian classifier. In: 2016 International Conference on Big Data and Smart Computing (BigComp), pp. 239–244 (2016). https://doi.org/10.1109/BIGCOMP.2016.7425919
3. Chatfield, C.: Time-Series Forecasting. Chapman and Hall/CRC, Boca Raton (2000)
4. Cho, K., van Merrienboer, B., Bahdanau, D., Bengio, Y.: On the properties of neural machine translation: encoder-decoder approaches. CoRR abs/1409.1259 (2014). https://arxiv.org/abs/1409.1259
5. Davidovic, M., Kostic, M.: Comparison of energy efficiency and costs related to conventional and led road lighting installations. Energy **254**, 124299 (2022). https://doi.org/10.1016/j.energy.2022.124299, https://www.sciencedirect.com/science/article/pii/S0360544222012026
6. Djuretic, A., Skerovic, V., Arsic, N., Kostic, M.: Luminous flux to input power ratio, power factor and harmonics when dimming high-pressure sodium and led luminaires used in road lighting. Lighting Res. Technol. **51**(2), 304–323 (2019). https://doi.org/10.1177/1477153518777272
7. Fanoon, A., Shafana, A.: Smart lighting system for efficient street lighting. J. Technol. Value Addition **1**(2), 36–47 (2020)
8. Zissis, G., Bertoldi, P., Serrenho, T.: Update on the status of led-lighting world market since 2018 (KJ-NA-30500-EN-N (online)) (2021). https://doi.org/10.2760/759859
9. Hewamalage, H., Bergmeir, C., Bandara, K.: Recurrent neural networks for time series forecasting: current status and future directions. Int. J. Forecast. **37**(1), 388–427 (2021). https://doi.org/10.1016/j.ijforecast.2020.06.008, https://www.sciencedirect.com/science/article/pii/S0169207020300996
10. Hochreiter, S., Schmidhuber, J.: Long short-term memory. Neural Comput. **9**(8), 1735–1780 (1997). https://doi.org/10.1162/neco.1997.9.8.1735
11. Jacob, S., Rekh, A., Manoj, G., Paul, J.: Smart traffic management system with real time analysis. Int. J. Eng. Technol. (UAE) **7**, 348–351 (2018)
12. Janušová, L., Čičmancová, S.: Improving safety of transportation by using intelligent transport systems. Procedia Eng. **134**, 14–22 (2016). https://doi.org/10.1016/j.proeng.2016.01.031, https://www.sciencedirect.com/science/article/pii/S1877705816000345. tRANSBALTICA 2015: PROCEEDINGS OF THE 9th INTERNATIONAL SCIENTIFIC CONFERENCE. May 7-8, 2015. Vilnius Gediminas Technical University, Vilnius, Lithuania
13. Jägerbrand, A.K.: Led (light-emitting diode) road lighting in practice: an evaluation of compliance with regulations and improvements for further energy savings. Energies, **9**(5), 357 (2016). https://doi.org/10.3390/en9050357, https://www.mdpi.com/1996-1073/9/5/357
14. Kumar, R., Gupta, K.: ITMS (intelligent traffic management system). In: Pant, M., Deep, K., Bansal, J., Nagar, A., Das, K. (eds.) Proceedings of Fifth International Conference on Soft Computing for Problem Solving. Advances in Intelligent Systems and Computing, vol. 436, pp. 487–495. Springer, Singapore (2015). https://doi.org/10.1007/978-981-10-0448-3_40

15. Li, Y., Yu, R., Shahabi, C., Liu, Y.: Diffusion convolutional recurrent neural network: data-driven traffic forecasting (2017). https://doi.org/10.48550/ARXIV. 1707.01926, https://arxiv.org/abs/1707.01926
16. Lu, C.C., Zhou, X.: Short-term highway traffic state prediction using structural state space models. J. Intell. Transp. Syst. **18**(3), 309–322 (2014). https://doi.org/ 10.1080/15472450.2013.836929
17. Mustafa, A.M., Abubakr, O.M., Derbala, A.H., Ahmed, E., Mokhtar, B.: Towards a smart highway lighting system based on road occupancy: model design and simulation. In: Sucar, E., Mayora, O., Muñoz de Cote, E. (eds.) Applications for Future Internet. LNICST, vol. 179, pp. 22–31. Springer, Cham (2017). https://doi.org/10. 1007/978-3-319-49622-1_4
18. Nagy, A.M., Simon, V.: Survey on traffic prediction in smart cities. Pervasive Mob. Comput. **50**, 148–163 (2018). https://doi.org/10.1016/j.pmcj.2018.07.004, https:// www.sciencedirect.com/science/article/pii/S1574119217306521
19. Nallaperuma, D., et al.: Online incremental machine learning platform for big data-driven smart traffic management. IEEE Trans. Intell. Transp. Syst. **20**(12), 4679–4690 (2019). https://doi.org/10.1109/TITS.2019.2924883
20. Palša, J., Vokorokos, L., Chovancová, E., Chovanec, M.: Smart cities and the importance of smart traffic lights. In: 2019 17th International Conference on Emerging eLearning Technologies and Applications (ICETA), pp. 587–592 (2019). https://doi.org/10.1109/ICETA48886.2019.9040086
21. Pečar, M., Papa, G.: Transportation problems and their potential solutions in smart cities. In: 2017 International Conference on Smart Systems and Technologies (SST), pp. 195–199 (2017). https://doi.org/10.1109/SST.2017.8188694
22. Saedi, R., Khademi, N.: Travel time cognition: exploring the impacts of travel information provision strategies. Travel Behav. Soc. **14**, 92–106 (2019). https://doi.org/10.1016/j.tbs.2018.09.007, https://www.sciencedirect. com/science/article/pii/S2214367X17300509
23. Schäfer, A.M., Zimmermann, H.G.: Recurrent neural networks are universal approximators. In: Kollias, S.D., Stafylopatis, A., Duch, W., Oja, E. (eds.) ICANN 2006. LNCS, vol. 4131, pp. 632–640. Springer, Heidelberg (2006). https://doi.org/ 10.1007/11840817_66
24. Sharif, A., Li, J., Khalil, M., Kumar, R., Sharif, M.I., Sharif, A.: Internet of things - smart traffic management system for smart cities using big data analytics. In: 2017 14th International Computer Conference on Wavelet Active Media Technology and Information Processing (ICCWAMTIP), pp. 281–284 (2017). https://doi.org/10. 1109/ICCWAMTIP.2017.8301496
25. Shi, X., Qi, H., Shen, Y., Wu, G., Yin, B.: A spatial-temporal attention approach for traffic prediction. IEEE Trans. Intell. Transp. Syst. **22**(8), 4909–4918 (2021). https://doi.org/10.1109/TITS.2020.2983651
26. Singh, V., Unadkat, V., Kanani, P.: Intelligent traffic management system. Int. J. Recent Technol. Eng. **8**(3), 7592–7597 (2019)
27. Song, C., Lin, Y., Guo, S., Wan, H.: Spatial-temporal synchronous graph convolutional networks: a new framework for spatial-temporal network data forecasting. In: Proceedings of the AAAI Conference on Artificial Intelligence, vol. 34, no. 1, pp. 914–921 (2020). https://doi.org/10.1609/aaai.v34i01.5438, https://ojs.aaai. org/index.php/AAAI/article/view/5438
28. Stone, E.L., Harris, S., Jones, G.: Impacts of artificial lighting on bats: a review of challenges and solutions. Mamm. Biol. **80**(3), 213–219 (2015). https://doi.org/10. 1016/j.mambio.2015.02.004, https://www.sciencedirect.com/science/article/pii/ S1616504715000233. special Issue: Bats as Bioindicators

29. Tähkämö, L., Räsänen, R.S., Halonen, L.: Life cycle cost comparison of high-pressure sodium and light-emitting diode luminaires in street lighting. Int. J. Life Cycle Assess. **21**(2), 137–145 (2016). https://doi.org/10.1007/s11367-015-1000-x

30. Wang, Z., Chu, R., Zhang, M., Wang, X., Luan, S.: An improved hybrid highway traffic flow prediction model based on machine learning. Sustainability **12**(20), 8298 (2020). https://www.mdpi.com/2071-1050/12/20/8298

31. Yi, H., Bui, K.H.N.: An automated hyperparameter search-based deep learning model for highway traffic prediction. IEEE Trans. Intell. Transp. Syst. **22**(9), 5486–5495 (2021). https://doi.org/10.1109/TITS.2020.2987614

32. Yin, X., Wu, G., Wei, J., Shen, Y., Qi, H., Yin, B.: Deep learning on traffic prediction: methods, analysis, and future directions. IEEE Trans. Intell. Transp. Syst. **23**(6), 4927–4943 (2022). https://doi.org/10.1109/tits.2021.3054840

33. Ylinen, A.M., Tähkämö, L., Puolakka, M., Halonen, L.: Road lighting quality, energy efficiency, and mesopic design - led street lighting case study. LEUKOS **8**(1), 9–24 (2011). https://doi.org/10.1582/LEUKOS.2011.08.01.001

Berth Allocation Problem in Export Tidal Bulk Ports with Inventory Control

Cassio Linhares[1]($\boxtimes$), Jorge Silva[1], Marcos Azevedo[2], Glaubos Climaco[2], and Alexandre César Muniz de Oliveira[2]

[1] [PPGCC]Laboratory of Artificial Cognition Methods for Optimisation and Robotics - LACMOR, São Luís, MA, Brazil
`cassio.diniz@discente.ufma.br, jorge.silva@lacmor.ufma.br`
[2] Departament of Informatics – DEINF,
[UFMA]Federal University of Maranhão – UFMA, São Luís, MA, Brazil
`{marcos.azevedo,alexandre.cesar}@ufma.br`

Abstract. This paper presents the problem of allocating berth positions for vessels in tidal bulk port terminals (BAPTBI), considering the specific export scenario and robust control over goods' stock levels. An integer linear mathematical model is proposed for the discrete case (time and quay). The model controls the minimal and maximum inventory levels. A dataset of 59 instances was generated based on data obtained from a relevant bulk terminal in São Luís, Brazil. Through the experiment using the Gurobi solver, it is noticed that some medium-sized instances take more than 1 h to be solved.

Keywords: Berth allocation problem · Tidal ports · Inventory level constraints · Integer Programming · Mixed Integer Programming

1 Introduction

Bulk cargo is transported unpacked in large quantities of liquid (e.g., petroleum, gasoline, caustic soda, and chemicals) or dry (e.g., coal, grain, iron ore, and bauxite ore). In 2020, about 70% of the seaborne trade volume in tonnes loaded was dry bulk cargo, including iron ore and grains, of which Brazil is a great exporter, reaching in both 23% of world markets [1]. In bulk ports, vessels are loaded using excavators, conveyor belts, or pipelines. Silos or inventory piles for the bulk cargo are often alongside the berth or disposed of in large areas around the port [2].

In Brazil, the total port handling in 2021 was solid bulk 706,635,947 ton, liquid bulk 314,750,969 ton, containerised cargo 132,991,636 ton and general Load 60,004,915 ton, totalling 1,214,383,467 ton that represents 5.09% of increasing when compared to 1,155,608,201 ton in 2020. Ponta da Madeira terminal handled 182.36 million tons, Santos terminal 113.28 million tons, and Tubarão terminal 64.14, from which iron ore (370.57 million tons), oil and results (195.73million tons), and container (132.99million tons) [3].

© ICST Institute for Computer Sciences, Social Informatics and Telecommunications Engineering 2023
Published by Springer Nature Switzerland AG 2023. All Rights Reserved
A. L. Martins et al. (Eds.): INTSYS 2022, LNICST 486, pp. 129–138, 2023.
https://doi.org/10.1007/978-3-031-30855-0_9

In Maranhão state, the operational scenario at the maritime industrial port complex of São Luís is shaped by the public terminal of Itaqui port and the private terminals of Ponta da Madeira (Vale Mining Company), Aluminum Consortium of Maranhão (Alumar Alumina refinery), all currently in operation, as well as two new port terminals: the São Luís port terminal, headed by the company WPR, a subsidiary of the WTorre Company; and the Alcântara terminal port headed by GPM (Grão-Pará Multimodal) company [4].

A berth is a quay location equipped with one or more ship loaders. Generally, the more ship loaders, the greater throughput the berth has. The physical space dedicated to the berth can be continuous or discretised. In tidal ports, such as the ones in São Luís, vessels may need to wait for tidal conditions for mooring even when a berth position is available. Thus, the transit from waiting areas to the berth position is done in time windows at regular time intervals, previously known, in general, during high tides [5].

The decision to be taken must consider when (tidal time window) and where to berth a vessel, following the enterprise's berthing politics that considers berth capabilities and throughput, ship features and cargo, etc., and performance measures as overall quay utilisation, turnaround time, and incurred demurrage.

This work is devoted to the heterogeneous berth case of the Berth Allocation Problem in Tidal Bulk ports with Inventory level conditions (briefly named as BAPTBI or BAPTBS [5]), for which is assumed a dynamic BAP on a given discretised planning horizon. The quay is also discretised in berth positions with different load or unload throughput.

The vessels are allocated to time windows with favourable tidal conditions and berth availability regarding the inventory level of bulk cargo transported from/to the mining/refining company yard [5]. It is assumed that each vessel can load or unload multiple bulk cargo types without changing the berth, keeping the same throughput. For loading operations, inventory must be enough to be loaded onto the vessel. Unloading operations prioritise those vessels carrying raw materials at a critical inventory level.

Despite satisfactorily representing a standard bulk port terminal in tidal ports, the proposal in [6,7] differs from the present one mainly because they do not consider operational scenarios related to large mining companies, which work with large volumes of bulk and make decisions based on the levels of inventory in their storage yards. A recent literature review found no studies addressing stock-constrained ports, especially moving bulk in tidal windows [8].

This paper is organized as follows: in Sect. 2, a flat bibliographic review is presented; the mathematical model is proposed in Sect. 3; the instance generator, the instance dataset, and the main computational results are depicted in Sect. 4; the main finding are highlighted in Sect. 5.

2   Related Works

The problem of planning and scheduling integrated guaranteeing that products are stored and shipped within the established schedule has been approached in [9]. A mathematical model was formulated as a Product Flow Planning and Scheduling Problem, solved by a column generation procedure and a branch-and-price algorithm.

The results have shown that the proposed method can reach optimal solutions in small and medium instances, producing upper and lower bounds for medium and large sizes instances related to operational scenarios where optimisation packages are not effective [9].

A mathematical model that deals with tidal constraints was proposed by [7], specifying aspects such as allocation of sections of quays and arrival-departure of vessels. The quay boundary is discretised into sections with the same length, each equipped with only one fixed quay crane. Depending on the vessel's length, one or two quay cranes can load or unload the vessel. CPLEX and a Genetic Algorithm were able to solve the model. The latter was proposed to deal with the above 20 vessels [7].

[10] proposes a model dealing with berth locations on an opposite or adjacent side in a continuous quay. Hence the model manages spatial constraints limiting the mooring and departure of vessels. Such real-world restrictions are not taken into account in the literature. The authors have proposed a mixed-integer linear programming formulation and a heuristic-based solver algorithm to obtain optimal or near-optimal solutions using instances inspired by an actual tank terminal in Belgium.

A stochastic version of a previous deterministic model [11] has been proposed based on a network berth-flow, dealing with delays on the planning horizon. The model considers different arrival times for each vessel, and a network is constructed for each type of berth. The results have shown that the stochastic model surpasses the manual allocation.

In [12], a mathematical model is presented, assuming a dynamic arrival of vessels, discrete berths, and operations without interruption before service completion. The work presented the results of a mathematical model validated through numerical experiments over six instances inspired by data of the bulk port of *Sfax*, Tunisia. The model considers specific features like length and draft of vessel, length and draft of berth, and security control time between vessels. The authors compared the results obtained by CPLEX solver with those obtained by the Sidi Youssef Port's planning process (SYPP), reaching a total service time saved from 6% to 17% [12].

Based on the port of Jorf Lasfar [13], the largest in Africa, a model was proposed to deal with the restrictions of routes made between the storage hangars and the berths with different water depths and heterogeneous berth speeds. The model's objective is to maximise the difference between dispatch and demurrage for all berthed vessels. Even being inspired by a specific port, the model is flexible to be easily adapted to any bulk port.

Despite satisfactorily representing a standard bulk port terminal in tidal ports, the proposal in [6, 7] differs from the present one mainly because they do not consider operational scenarios related to large mining companies, which work with large volumes of bulk and make decisions based on the levels of inventory in their storage yards. A recent literature review found no studies addressing stock-constrained ports, especially moving bulk in tidal windows [8].

3   Mathematical Modelling

The Berth Allocation Problem in Tidal Bulk ports with Inventory levels constraints (BAPTBI) is a lineup decision problem on a set of vessels with an Estimated Time of Arrival (ETA) within a given planning horizon. The lineup is a set of decisions that leads to the vessels' Estimated Time of Berthing (ETB). Once the berth and the docking TTW are assigned, it is possible to define the Estimated Time of Sailing (ETS).

The Berth Allocation Problem in Tidal Bulk ports with Inventory levels constraints (BAPTBI) has been modelled with time, and berth discretised [5]. A Tidal Time Window (TTW) happens in a regular and known time frequency, contemplating high tides or even low tides but under particular current conditions in which it is possible to tow a large ship through the narrow sea channel safely. The planning horizon is divided by M TTW and all the time scale (vessel's arrival times, days on hand, etc.) is discretised and expressed as a multiple of TTW.

For convenience, TTWs happen in a regular and known time-frequency TF ($TF \cong 12$ h, if contemplating only high tides). The planning horizon is divided by M TTWs and the time scale (vessel's arrival times, days on hand, etc.) is discretised and expressed as a multiple of TTW. Such assumption is sufficiently flexible to represent fine or coarse-grained discrete times. Even eventual not regular TTWs, like those with low tidal currents, can be represented by reducing the time-frequency (fine-grained discrete-time) and including constraints that disable specific low tide windows.

The data for BAPTBI is given by [5]:

- N: set of ships, $n = |N|$;
- M: set of TTWs, $m = |M|$;
- L: set of berth positions, $l = |L|$
- a_i: expected arrival time (ETA) of the ship i (TTW);
- h_{il}: handling time of the ship i if berthed at l (TTW);
- d_i: demurrage for ship i;
- e_k: the initial stock level for the raw material k;
- w_k: the amount of consumption or production for raw material k;
- q_{ik}: the cargo capacity of the ship i with respect to raw material k.

The bulk k may be imported or exported (input or output cargo). Hence, the operation type (unload or load) is defined by the signal of w_k and q_{ik}.

- importation: $w_k, q_{ik} > 0$;
- exportation: $w_k, q_{ik} < 0$;

Handling time, h_{il} is given by:

$$h_{il} = \frac{\sum_{k \in K} q_{ik}}{v_l} \tag{1}$$

The BAPTBI mathematical model is decided by the variable y_{ijl} that represents the relationship between vessels, TTWs and berths (Eq. 2).

$$y_{ijl} = \begin{cases} 1 \text{ if ship } i \text{ is allocated to TTW } j \text{ and allocated to berth } l \\ 0 \text{ otherwise} \end{cases} \tag{2}$$

Equations 3 and 4 ensure that each vessel may be moored in a berth, at a TTW, after the ETA. Equation 5 avoids a vessel to be moored before the previous vessel is out of the berth. The last service TTW can be obtained by $j + h_{il} - 1$.

$$\sum_{j=1}^{a_i-1} \sum_{l=1}^{|L|} y_{ijl} = 0, \qquad \forall i \in N \tag{3}$$

$$\sum_{j=a_i}^{|M|} \sum_{l=1}^{|L|} y_{ijl} = 1, \qquad \forall i \in N \tag{4}$$

$$\sum_{\substack{n=1 \\ n \neq i}}^{|N|} \sum_{\substack{m=j \\ m \leq |M|}}^{j+h_{il}-1} y_{nml} \leq (1 - y_{ijl})|N||M|, \qquad \forall i \in N, j \in M, l \in L \tag{5}$$

$$\sum_{i=1}^{|N|} \sum_{l=1}^{|L|} \sum_{z=a_i}^{j} \frac{\min(j - a_i + 1, h_{il})}{h_{il}} \times q_{ik} \times y_{izl} \leq j \times c_k + e_k, \qquad \forall j \in M, k \in K \tag{6}$$

$$\sum_{i=1}^{|N|} \sum_{l=1}^{|L|} \sum_{z=a_i}^{j} \frac{\min(j - a_i + 1, h_{il})}{h_{il}} \times q_{ik} \times y_{izl} \geq j \times c_k \mid c_k \quad Q_k, \qquad \forall j \subset M, k \subset K \tag{7}$$

Equation 6 refers to inventory control in an importation port, i.e., incoming vessels arrive loaded with the raw material necessary for the manufacturing activities that take place in the industry that manages the port (usually large transnational enterprises). On the other hand, Equation represents an exportation port inventory constraint in which the incoming vessels only may berth if there is a sufficient amount of bulk cargo to be loaded in.

The minimisation of the service time (Eq. 8) is defined as the sum of the waiting time, $j - a_i$, added to the handling time, h_{il}, for each ship. Note that TTW j meets the expected berth time (ETB).

$$\min \sum_{i=1}^{|N|} \sum_{j=1}^{|M|} \sum_{l=1}^{|L|} (j - a_i + h_{il}) \times y_{ijl} \tag{8}$$

4   Computational Experiments

In this section, the results of computational experiments are presented to enable the assessment of the proposed mathematical model. It is important to mention that the new proposition maintains the same realistic elements modelled previously, however featuring a better running time for resolution.

In order to define a more challenging dataset for a commercial solver and eventually for approximate algorithms, an instance generator is proposed for the BAPTBI.

4.1   Instance Generator

We have run an instance generator for building problem instances based on the operational scenarios in the private bulk port terminals in São Luís: Ponta da Madeira port (Vale Mining Company), Alumar port (Alumina refinery). The former mainly exports large volumes of *sinter-feed* iron ore through six ship-loaders that feature four berths. The latter imports raw materials, such as caustic soda and bauxite, through all two-berth positions. Nevertheless, occasionally Alumar port employs a single berth that is the only one equipped for load operations, and exports refined alumina destined to big manufacturers worldwide.

4.2   Instance Dataset

We have provided a total of 59 export instances[1], ranging combinations from $N \in [10, 50]$, $L \in [4, 6]$, and $K \in [4, 6]$. Such ranges of values cover parameters that well represent port terminals that are slightly smaller or larger than those found in São Luís' port terminal. All vessels handle only one bulk cargo at a time.

Allocating berths to ships affects handling times and consequently can expose the inventory to critical levels (close to zero or above Q_{max}), especially in scenarios where each ship only transports one raw material per trip. In these cases, it is more likely situations where it is required to prioritise ships with cargo whose inventory level is reaching a critical level. However, sometimes there is no possible decision that saves the instance from unfeasibility.

The problem instances are named in the form nnN.bB.kK to specify nn vessels, b berths and k different cargo.

4.3   Commercial Solver

Exact methods play an essential role in validating heuristic algorithms, as they serve as a baseline for comparing results. In this work, we use Gurobi's solver, version 9.5.1 with academic license[2].

---

[1] dataset available at http LACMOR.
[2] https://www.gurobi.com/academia/academic-program-and-licenses/.

The solver uses simplex or barrier methods for continuous models and branch-and-cut for MILP[3]. The user can modify a significant number of parameters allowing different configurations.

This particular solver was chosen by the resources available, the detailed documentation, and the library provided in many programming languages besides performance.

4.4 Computational Experiment

In the second computational experiment, we run the solver GUROBI on the dataset considering the turnaround time objective function (Eq. 8) in the time limit of $4,800s$.

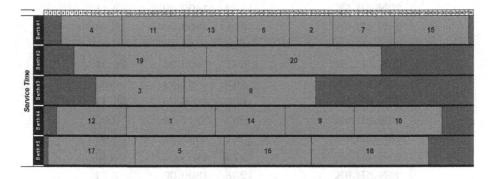

Fig. 1. Solution Service Time for instance 20N.5B.5P.20D

Table 1. Computational Experiment Results Using GUROBI

Instance	Solution (TTW)	Time (s)	GAP (%)
10N.4B.5K	236	3.66	0.00
10N.4B.6K	285	7.90	0.00
10N.5B.4K	167	2.63	0.00
10N.5B.5K	190	2.12	0.00
10N.5B.6K	210	2.73	0.00
10N.6B.4K	107	0.94	0.00
10N.6B.5K	136	1.45	0.00
10N.6B.6K	151	1.91	0.00

(*continued*)

---

[3] https://www.gurobi.com/documentation/9.5.1/refman/cpp_grbmodel_optimize. html.

Table 1. (*continued*)

Instance	Solution (TTW)	Time (s)	GAP (%)
15N.4B.4K	501	82.31	0.00
15N.4B.5K	644	77.90	0.00
15N.4B.6K	845	125.49	0.00
15N.5B.5K	620	117.80	0.00
15N.5B.6K	765	90.77	0.00
15N.6B.4K	217	12.47	0.00
15N.6B.5K	317	20.94	0.00
15N.6B.6K	396	37.90	0.00
20N.4B.4K	1016	236.32	0.00
20N.4B.5K	1122	4800.00	2.41
20N.4B.6K	1311	4800.00	0.23
20N.5B.4K	523	54.30	0.00
20N.5B.5K	671	4800.00	36.07
20N.6B.4K	465	41.89	0.00
20N.6B.5K	605	4800.00	39.34
20N.6B.6K	807	147.59	0.00
25N.4B.4K	1251	395.35	0.00
25N.4B.5K	1273	4800.00	3.30
25N.5B.6K	1258	4800.00	1.74
25N.6B.5K	991	4800.00	29.87
30N.5B.4K	922	4800.00	51.19
30N.5B.6K	1119	4800.00	0.45
30N.6B.5K	1413	930.68	0.00
30N.6B.6K	1192	4800.00	0.76
35N.4B.4K	922	284.07	0.00
35N.4B.5K	1172	622.62	0.00
35N.4B.6K	1435	4800.00	0.84
35N.5B.4K	1242	4800.00	30.19
35N.5B.5K	1452	659.00	0.00
35N.5B.6K	1637	4800.00	0.49
35N.6B.6K	2061	4800.00	0.44
40N.4B.4K	1742	4800.00	28.76
40N.4B.5K	2294	4800.00	0.22
40N.4B.6K	2114	4800.00	0.99
40N.5B.4K	1995	4800.00	0.40
40N.5B.5K	2290	4800.00	3.49

(*continued*)

Table 1. (*continued*)

Instance	Solution (TTW)	Time (s)	GAP (%)
40N.5B.6K	2470	4800.00	1.70
40N.6B.5K	2062	4800.00	0.63
45N.4B.4K	1854	4800.00	54.64
45N.4B.5K	1640	4800.00	40.24
45N.4B.6K	2180	4800.00	1.01
45N.5B.4K	1957	994.93	0.00
45N.5B.5K	2128	4800.00	0.61
45N.5B.6K	2460	4800.00	0.53
50N.4B.4K	1871	4800.00	0.11
50N.4B.5K	2403	4800.00	58.43
50N.4B.6K	2804	4800.00	69.72
50N.5B.5K	2929	4800.00	58.01
50N.5B.6K	3474	4800.00	37.25

5 Conclusion

This work shows a slightly better response of GUROBI for the new maximum inventory level constraint tested for 81 instances. It happens due to the reduction of the search space with the inclusion of this new constraint, so the solver can spend its total time for new areas, reducing the final gap. From 81 instances tested 21 were considered infeasible by the solver, or 4800 was not enough time to find a solution.

Table 1 above shows the results obtained for the instances, the total time used by GUROBI to reach the best solution and the final gap of the search space.

Already in Fig. 1 we have a graphic example of solution obtained by the solver where we can see the proper distribution of vessels along berths and tidal windows. To reach the minimum service time, the proposed solution agglutinate the vessels without free TTW between them to find the lower value for the objective function. For the 20N.5B.5P instance, the solution prioritise the faster berths (#1, #4 and #5) to attend the vessels, reducing the time usage for the slower berths (#2 and #3)

Future researches can improve the instance generator quality, working with higher number of vessels and comparing larger datasets with controlled differences between them. Other point is to apply heuristics and metaheuristics that can compete against the commercial solvers or work with them inside hybridization strategies to reach better results.

References

1. United Nations Conference on Trade and Development. Review of Maritime Transport 2021. Review of maritime transport. United Nations, Geneva (2021). ISBN 978-92-1-113026-3
2. Ribeiro, G.M., Mauri, G.R., de Castro Beluco, S., Lorena, L.A.N., Laporte, G.: Berth allocation in an ore terminal with demurrage, dispatch and maintenance. Comput. Ind. Eng. **96**(C), 8–15 (2016). ISSN 0360–8352. https://doi.org/10.1016/j.cie.2016.03.005
3. National waterway transportation agency (ANTAQ). https://anuario.antaq.gov.br/ea/index.html. Accessed February 2022
4. Sant'Ana, H.A.D., Alves, E.D.J.P.: Mining-railroad-port: at the end of the line a City in Question. Virtual Brazilian Antropology. V14N2, Part 2 (2017). ISSN 1809–4341
5. Barros, V.H., Costa, T.S., Oliveira, A.C., Lorena, L.A.: Model and heuristic for berth allocation in tidal bulk ports with stock level constraints. Comput. Ind. Eng. **60**(4), 606–613 (2011). https://doi.org/10.1016/j.cie.2010.12.018
6. Cheimanoff, N., Fontane, F., Kitri, M.N., Tchernev, N.: A reduced vns based approach for the dynamic continuous berth allocation problem in bulk terminals with tidal constraints. Expert Syst. Appl. **168**, 114215 (2021). https://doi.org/10.1016/j.eswa.2020.114215
7. Liu, M., Liu, R., Chu, F., Chu, C.: Mathematical model and solution approach for berth allocation problem in tidal bulk ports with different vessel draft requirements. In: 2018 15th International Conference on Service Systems and Service Management (ICSSSM), pp. 1–6. IEEE (2018). https://doi.org/10.1109/ICSSSM.2018.8465036
8. Mnasri, S., Alrashidi, M.: A comprehensive modeling of the discrete and dynamic problem of berth allocation in maritime terminals. Electronics **10**(21), 2684 (2021). ISSN 2079–9292. https://doi.org/10.3390/electronics10212684
9. Menezes, G.C., Mateus, G.R., Ravetti, M.G.: A branch and price algorithm to solve the integrated production planning and scheduling in bulk ports. Eur. J. Oper. Res. **258**, 926–937. Elsevier (2017). https://doi.org/10.1016/j.ejor.2016.08.073
10. Correcher, J.F., Van den Bossche, T., Alvarez-Valdes, R., Berghe, G.V.: The berth allocation problem in terminals with irregular layouts. Eur. J. Oper. Res. 1096–1108 (2019). https://doi.org/10.1016/j.ejor.2018.07.019
11. Yan, S., Lu, C.-C., Hsieh, J.-H., Lin, H.-C.: A dynamic and flexible berth allocation model with stochastic vessel arrival times. Netw. Spat. Econ. **19**(3), 903–927 (2019). https://doi.org/10.1007/s11067-018-9434-x
12. Lassoued, R., Elloumi, A.: The discrete and dynamic berth allocation problem in bulk port. In: 6th International Conference on Control, Decision and Information Technologies (CoDIT), pp. 1976–1980 (2019). https://doi.org/10.1109/CoDIT.2019.8820590
13. Bouzekri, H., Alpan, G., Giard, V.: A dynamic hybrid berth allocation problem with routing constraints in bulk ports. In: IFIP International Conference on Advances in Production Management Systems, pp. 250–258 (2020). https://doi.org/10.1007/978-3-030-57993-7_29

Intelligent Transportation and Electric Vehicle

Bus Journey Time Prediction: A Comparison of Whole Route and Segment Journey Time Predictions Using Machine Learning

Laura Dunne(✉) ⓘ and Gavin McArdle ⓘ

School of Computer Science, University College Dublin, Belfield Dublin 4, Ireland
laura.dunne2@ucdconnect.ie, gavin.mcardle@ucd.ie

Abstract. Accurately predicted bus journey times are essential for bus network reliability and making bus transport attractive. The most common approach when predicting bus journey times with machine learning (ML) is to predict journey times for each stop pair segment. Segment data can be very noisy, leading to inaccuracies. To investigate this, this paper compares the classic stop pair segment approach to three other methods. Firstly, a naive method of calculated historical averages is introduced as a baseline. We then explore two methods based on predicting the whole bus route journey time from origin to terminus. To estimate a passenger's journey, where the whole route is not travelled, we estimate the proportion of the whole journey time the passenger's journey will take. The first of these methods calculates this proportion from similar historical journeys, and the second proposed method trains an ML model to predict this proportion for each segment of the passenger's journey. The results show that this novel proposed approach results in less error across most metrics, when compared to the segment prediction method. An interesting insight from the analysis shows the proposed approach has enhanced benefits during peak travel time and during the working week. Gains in prediction accuracy at these times would benefit the most commuters. This research can be applied to make robust scheduling decisions that will increase bus network reliability, improve bus network satisfaction and uptake, and lead to more sustainable cities.

Keywords: bus journey time prediction · machine learning · random forest

1 Introduction

Scheduled bus services are an important component of the transportation network in an increasingly urban world. Many urban centres are rapidly expanding and have exceeded the road and parking infrastructure for every inhabitant to have a private car [11] even if air quality issues could be overcome by increased

© ICST Institute for Computer Sciences, Social Informatics and Telecommunications Engineering 2023
Published by Springer Nature Switzerland AG 2023. All Rights Reserved
A. L. Martins et al. (Eds.): INTSYS 2022, LNICST 486, pp. 141–156, 2023.
https://doi.org/10.1007/978-3-031-30855-0_10

or complete electrification of personal vehicles. As stated by UN Sustainable Goal 11.2 [26], more sustainable forms of transport are necessary for continued development. Walking and cycling are ideal for shorter journeys in mild weather, as they require minimal infrastructure and have health benefits associated with active transportation [17]. For many reasons, much of the population will continue to depend on public bus and rail services. Buses have several advantages over rail transport; buses are cheaper for the same quality of service [2], require far less infrastructure, and are more flexible as buses can easily be rerouted as urban centres evolve. However, buses are not without limitations and often lack reliability compared to rail services. They operate in more complex and less controlled environments than trains, stopping more regularly and interacting with other traffic and cyclists. Many governments have policies encouraging switches to more sustainable transport since the Paris Agreement in 2015 [4]. Many of these policies focus on improving the bus network to promote its use. Since resources are not infinite, the bus services must also be optimised within the existing infrastructure. The most significant factor for passengers is a low waiting time [19] which is directly related to the reliability of the bus network [23], and accurately predicting journey times for bus scheduling and real-time passenger information (RTPI) is key to a reliable bus network [3].

The prediction of bus journey times is the subject of much research. The main techniques used are simple historical averages [15], statistical methods including regression models, Kalman filters and Machine Learning (ML) [21]. The literature in this area has several weaknesses; there is a lack of standard syntax, and the studies tend to be small due to the complexity of bus data [18,21,27]. There is also no standard benchmark dataset to allow comparisons between studies. Comparing one study with another is usually impossible as bus routes have different characteristics, affecting the error metrics. The longer the bus route, the higher the absolute error will be [10]. Bus routes on networks with low reliability will have a higher level of irreducible error regardless of the prediction methods employed [8,21].

A common approach in many studies that predict bus journey times with ML is training multiple models for each consecutive stop pair segment. Generally, a model is built to predict the journey time for the segment between every two consecutive stops on the bus network [7,10,16,20,21,27]. This approach will result in a number of models that is one less than the number of stops on the route. There are many reasons for this segment prediction approach: stops are where bus arrival times are often monitored with Automatic Vehicle Location (AVL) systems and are typically the only place passengers can embark and disembark. Stop arrival time is most relevant to the service user, and it is a natural and intuitive way to conceptualise bus routes. However, real-world data is messy, and the measurement of bus location can be inexact. The GPS readings themselves are not exact and have reported errors up to 30m depending on the age of the GPS unit, local conditions and the speed of the bus. [28]. Many GPS units deployed on buses are old, and buses often operate in densely urban areas. The presence of tall buildings, or the so-called 'urban canyons', is known to impact the accuracy of GPS readings [14]. A recent study [25] showed a 13-second discrepancy between the GPS recorded time of arrival of a bus at bus stops and the actual time of arrival. There is also the compounding factor of the frequency of recording of position. Often this is around 30 s but can be longer, so the timing of arrival at stops is often interpolated [22]. These factors will likely create significant noise in the data regarding journey times between individual stops, increasing errors in the predictions from models trained on segment data. We observed that studies that predicted both longer and shorter sections of the same route tended to have lower error metrics for longer sections [5,6,12,20,21]. We conducted a provisional experiment to test the theory that whole route prediction methods were more accurate than segment prediction methods. Two methods predicted the whole route journey time. The first method had a single Random Forest (RF) model trained on the whole journey times between the origin and terminus stop. The second method trained an RF model for each consecutive stop pair segment on the route and returned the sum of these models' predictions to estimate the whole journey time. The evaluation revealed the first method was superior across multiple error metrics. Predicting by segment resulted in a mean absolute error (MAE) of 286 s versus 266 s for whole journey prediction. Segment prediction had a mean absolute percentage error (MAPE) of 0.099 and a coefficient of determination (R^2) of 0.877, and the corresponding values for whole journey prediction were 0.094 and 0.895, respectively.

These results motivated further exploration, as regardless of the accuracy of whole journey time predictions, they are only useful for predicting journey times for bus schedules. They are not useful for predicting individual passenger trip times (i.e. partial journeys). Partial journey predictions are needed for journey planning and RTPI. We sought to harness the accuracy of whole journey time predictions to improve partial journey time predictions. An experiment was designed to compare four methods of journey time prediction for several bus routes in Dublin, Ireland. The methods were a naive historical averages (HA) method, the most common method: segment prediction (SP) and two methods based on whole journey prediction. Both of these methods predict the whole route journey time and estimate the proportion of the whole route journey time the partial journey is likely to take. As described in [8], the first of these methods calculates the historical average proportion similarly to how HA calculates journey time and is called Whole Journey Prediction with Calculated Proportion (WJP-C). The novel second method uses an RF model to predict the proportion and this method is called Whole Journey Prediction with Predicted Proportion (WJP-P).

This paper makes the following contributions:

- Challenges the status quo regarding how bus routes are treated conceptually for ML modelling by assessing the SP method, an approach often used without much discussion of the rationale.
- Presents an approach for predicting partial journey times that significantly improves upon the SP method on most metrics with the consumption of similar computing resources.

– Performs deep analysis of the results of the four methods and examines the results by segment length, bus route, time of day and day of the week.

The remainder of this paper is organised as follows: Sect. 2 describes the data processing, Sect. 3 outlines the methodology used, Sect. 4 demonstrates the results and discusses the analysis, and Sect. 5 presents the conclusions of this study and discusses the planned further work.

2   Data

The National Transport Authority (NTA) in Ireland provided the historical bus data used in this study. As is typical with AVL data, there were some data quality issues, such as the bus stop arrival events not being recorded or duplicate arrival events at the same stop. As a result, not every unique trip had the same stop sequence; some trips were invalid and could not be included in the analysis. When selecting a subset of these routes for analysis, the routes with the highest quality data were desired. The inclusion criteria for this study were that the bus routes had at least 80% valid unique trips and at least 3000 unique trips in total. Based on these criteria, 16 bus routes were selected from the Dublin Bus network. These were eight head sign pairs for route numbers: 4, 27A, 32, 42, 56A, 79A, 120, and 184. The final dataset was all valid data for these routes for a year from January 1st to December 31st 2018. The Dublin Bus network in 2018 contained 253 routes and served over 1.3 million people in the Dublin area.

The most common stop sequence present on each route in the data was found, and this stop sequence was confirmed to be correct by comparison to the GTFS (General Transit Feed Specification) data published by Dublin Bus. The raw data was structured as bus arrival events at bus stops. Trips that contained extreme outliers, such as whole journey times or segments with journey time outliers greater than twelve standard deviations (SD) from the mean were removed, as were trips with impossible values such as negative journey times. Less than one and a half per cent of data was lost at this step. Additional features for the time, day of the week, and month were extracted from the timestamps. The time group feature had variable granularity. Peak travel periods are 30 min, and off-peak travel periods are 60 min long and are encoded from 0 to 29 starting at midnight. This was to avoid too coarse a granularity during rapidly changing peak travel periods yet allow for enough data in each time group during off-peak periods when there are fewer buses on the network. This approach was benchmarked against homogenous 30-minute and 60-minute granularities and was found to improve error metrics. Further details on the data cleansing procedure can be found in [8].

The cleaned and preprocessed data format is shown in Table 1. Following processing, the data was split into a training set and a testing set in the ratio of 85:15. This could not be done using a standard test/train split as many rows in the dataset refer to the same unique trip. To maintain data integrity, 15% of the trip IDs were randomly selected, and all rows with those trip IDs became the test set. The training set was then further processed in three ways. Firstly,

Table 1. Sample of the data after preprocessing. The stop arrival times are defined in seconds after midnight and journey time is in seconds. Day 0 is Monday and Month 1 is January. Time groups 9 and 10 are 30-minute periods during the morning peak travel period from 08:00 to 08:30 and 08:30 to 09:00

TripID	First Stop	Second Stop	First Stop Arrival Time	Second Stop Arrival Time	Month	Day	Time Group	Journey Time
20858	324	327	30579	30669	1	0	9	90
20858	327	7113	30669	30745	1	0	10	76
20858	7113	127	30745	30812	1	0	10	67
20858	127	112	30812	30877	1	0	10	65
20858	112	113	30877	30958	1	0	10	81
20858	113	114	30958	30964	1	0	10	6

the training set is used to create a Reference Dataset. This contains the average journey time and the average proportion of the full journey for each unique segment on each route for each combination of time/day in our dataset. An example of the resulting Reference Dataset is shown in Table 2.

Table 2. Sample of the Reference Dataset. All of these samples are from Route 4 in direction 1, and take place on a Monday (Day = 0) between 13:00 and 17:30 in the afternoon (time groups 15 through 20) on the segment between stops 273 and 405. The Reference Dataset contains the mean journey time and mean proportion of the whole journey time for each day/time combination.

Day of Week	Time Group	First Stop	Second Stop	Mean Journey Time	Mean Proportion
0	15	273	405	249.79	0.058591
0	16	273	405	253.63	0.059462
0	17	273	405	251.87	0.059878
0	18	273	405	262.81	0.058941
0	19	273	405	257.38	0.059040
0	20	273	405	263.17	0.060619

Secondly, the training set undergoes further processing to train RF models to predict whole journey times. It is restructured to represent unique journeys instead of arrival events. All arrival events except for the first and last were dropped for predicting whole journeys. The target feature, the historical journey time, is calculated for each journey in the dataset. The resulting data structure is shown in Table 3 and contains three temporal features: month, day and time group.

Traffic volume and passenger load have the most significant impacts on bus journey times [24]. These features are difficult to measure directly, but as they offer a cyclical pattern, they are encoded in temporal features [1]. The training data is also used to structure the data for segment prediction, similar to for whole journey predictions, but the details of the intermediate bus stops are not removed.

Table 3. Sample of the data prior to modelling

Month	Day	Time Group	Total Journey Time
3	3	10	5442
1	2	7	5097
1	2	15	4799
1	2	26	2807
4	4	19	5402

3   Methodology

Once the dataset was processed, four methods were implemented to predict journey time as shown in Fig. 1. These four methods are described in this section.

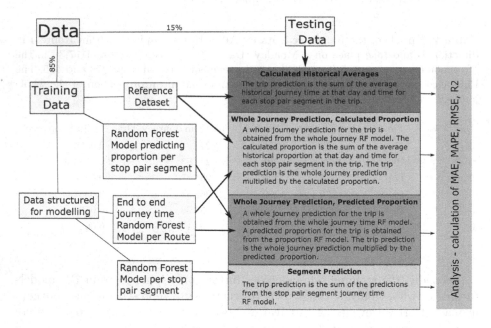

Fig. 1. Methodology Flow Diagram

3.1   Historical Averages (HA)

The Reference Dataset described in Sect. 2 was used in two ways. Firstly, it was used in the naive baseline method, HA. To produce an estimate for a passenger's partial trip time, this method references the Refernce Dataset for each segment at the time and day that the partial trip occurs and sums these historical average times to get a total. HA is shown in Eq. 1 where n is the number of segments in the trip and $\overline{T}$ is the average historical journey time for the day of the week, d and time of day, t that the trip takes place.

$$\sum_{i=1}^{n} \overline{T}_{i,dt} \tag{1}$$

3.2 Whole Journey Prediction with Calculated Proportion (WJP-C)

Secondly, the Reference Dataset is used to calculate the proportion of the whole journey, the passenger's partial journey historically represented. The dataset is referenced for each segment on the partial journey at the time and day the trip takes place and the sum of these historical average proportions for the segments is returned. This value will always be a ratio between 0 and 1 depending on how much of the whole journey the passenger travels. It is multiplied by the prediction returned from the whole journey RF model to get an estimate for the passenger's journey time. That model has been trained on the whole journey dataset restructured for modelling as described in Fig. 3. RF was used throughout as it needs minimal hyperparameter tuning, is scalable and has previously been shown to be the best of the traditional ML algorithms for this dataset [8]. WJP-C is shown in Eq. 2 where $\hat{W}$ is the whole journey time prediction from the random forest model, n is the number of segments in the trip and $\overline{P}$ is the average historical proportion for the day of the week, d and time of day, t that the trip takes place.

$$\hat{W} \cdot \left(\sum_{i=1}^{n} \overline{P}_{i,dt}\right) \tag{2}$$

3.3 Whole Journey Prediction with Predicted Proportion (WJP-P)

An RF model is trained for each segment on the route that will predict the proportion of the whole journey that the segment will take. The training data is sequentially filtered to just the data corresponding to the relevant stop pair, and an RF model is trained for each pair. The number of models trained depends on the length of the route and is always one less than the number of stops. WJP-P is shown in Eq. 3 where $\hat{W}$ is the whole journey time prediction from the RF model, n is the number of segments in the trip and $\hat{P}$ is the predicted proportion.

$$\hat{W} \cdot \left(\sum_{i=1}^{n} \hat{P}_i\right) \tag{3}$$

3.4 Segment Prediction (SP)

In a similar way to how WJP-P builds a model to predict the proportion of each segment, the SP method sequentially filters the data to each consecutive stop pair segment and builds an RF to predict journey time, and like before, the number of models trained will be one less than the number of stops on the route. SP is shown in Eq. 4 where $\hat{S}$ is the segment prediction from the RF model and n is the number of segments in the trip.

$$\sum_{i=1}^{n} \hat{S}_i \qquad (4)$$

3.5 Testing

It was not possible to access real passenger journeys for this experiment, so a simulated passenger journey was extracted from each of the 21706 test journeys. A random sequence of stops was generated from each unique journey in our test set. This was achieved by choosing two random indices from a sequential list of stops for the route the unique journey is from. We check that the same index has not been chosen twice, and the lower index becomes the boarding stop and the higher index becomes the disembarking stop of the pseudo passenger. This is similar to the approach used in [8,13]. Quotas were used to ensure the distribution of the length of the partial sample journeys was uniform from each route, with a similar number of journeys for each possible number of segments.

For each test journey, four predictions were made - one for each of the four methods. Analysis was then performed, including the calculation of MAE, MAPE, root mean squared error (RMSE), mean percentage error (MPE) and R^2. The resulting predictions were also assessed for skew and were found to be right skewed with skew values of between 0.97 and 0.999. Since the dataset was not normally distributed, one-way ANOVA and Kruskal-Wallis tests were performed on the predicted values of the methods to evaluate statistical significance. The results were analysed to show the results of the method by segment length, route, day of the week and time of day. The results are presented and discussed in the next Section.

4 Results and Discussion

As can be seen in the results presented in Table 4, the proposed method WJP-P outperforms the other methods using MAE, MAPE, RMSE and R^2, the results of the commonly used SP are comparable to WJP-P, and both outperform the other two methods on all metrics. The MAE for WJP-P is a 5% improvement over the commonly used SP method. The MAPE is 2.5% better for WJP-P compared to SP. WJP-P surpasses SP by 6.4% on RMSE. R^2 is high for all methods due to the size and quality of the data, and WJP-P surpasses the other methods with an R^2 of 0.954.

The magnitude of the error is of primary importance, but the bias or direction of the error is also important and is rarely reported in the literature. MPE is not a good metric for assessing the accuracy of the results, as even large positive and negative error values could negate each other. Still, it was included in our analysis as it is a good indicator of the bias in the results. We can see from the MPE results in Table 4 that all methods return a small positive MPE. HA and WJP-C return smaller MPE values than SP and WJP-P. A negative MPE means the method tends to overpredict journey time instead of underpredicting it. If a bus journey is underpredicted, the bus will arrive later than expected, and if a bus journey is overpredicted, the bus will arrive earlier than expected. When bus scheduling is taking place, methods of prediction that overestimate should be used as this reduces the likelihood of late departure on the return journey, which is one of the causes of unreliability on bus networks [9]. For journey planning without arrival-time bound transfers (e.g. arriving in the office by 9 am), methods that overpredict are superior.

The results were statistically significant with ANOVA and Kruskal-Wallis tests with p-values of 0.013 and 0.019, respectively. These results were stable over multiple runs with different test/train splits and various test/train sizes. The remainder of this Section will discuss a deeper analysis of the performance of the methods by the number of segments travelled, by the route and by temporal features.

Table 4. Full Results

Metric	HA	SP	WJP-C	WJP-P
MAE/s	164.88	154.15	159.92	**146.36**
MAPE	0.1309	0.1276	0.1298	**0.1245**
RMSE/s	289.46	245.81	275.52	**229.98**
MPE	-0.01099	-0.02309	**-0.01069**	-0.02298
R^2	0.927	0.948	0.934	**0.954**

4.1   Impact of Number of Segments

As shown in Figs. 2 and 3, WJP-P outperforms the other methods on all lengths of journey that exceed 9 segments in length. Up to 9 segments in length, WJP-C and HA methods are superior. This threshold is likely due to the cumulative noise in the data. It can be considered that methods involving calculated averages, especially HA, perform well on short trips and especially WJP-P but also SP, perform well on medium and long trips.

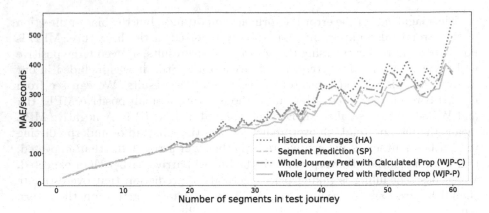

Fig. 2. The number of stop pair segments in the partial journey vs MAE. WJP-P outperforms all other methods for trips with a length of greater than 9 segments. The number of segments in the test journey in this chart has no relationship to where in the whole bus journey the test journey is. There could be a test journey of 1 segment at the beginning or the end of the whole bus journey.

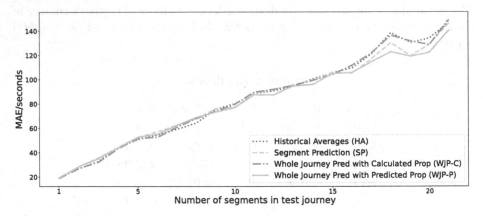

Fig. 3. The number of stop pair segments in the partial journey vs MAE: trips with a segment length of 1 to 22. This enlarged part of Fig. 2 more clearly shows HA and WJP-C outperforming the other methods until the number of segments in the trip exceeds 9 and WJP-P outperforming other methods for trips longer than 9 segments.

4.2 Impact of Route

Generalising from the findings in Fig. 2 and 3, it was theorised that the methods using calculated averages, HA and WJP-C, would perform best on short routes and WJP-P would perform best on medium and longer routes. This was largely found to be the case, as can be seen in Table 5 and Fig. 4. Even though HA was included as a naive baseline method, and performed poorest overall, it was the best performing method on four routes. These routes were all short routes, with an average length of 30.5 segments, and were four of the six shortest routes.

WJP-P was the top scoring method on nine routes which have an average length of 50.89 segments. Despite being the dominant method in the literature, SP was the superior method on only two routes, the 184 in both directions. WJP-C was the top-performing method on one route, the longest one. It was also observed that some of the routes had very minimal differences in the MAE between the methods, and others had wide variation. The column *Max minus Min MAE* in Table 5 shows the remainder when the MAE of the best performing method is subtracted from the MAE of the worst performing method. Several factors were examined to try to elucidate the cause of this instability between methods including the percentage of data retained after outlier removal, SD, variance, skew, kurtosis and the number of outliers at various thresholds. None of the factors studied showed a strong correlation or had a linear relationship with the *Max minus Min MAE*. However, it can be seen in Table 5, which is arranged in order of increasing SD, that the routes with a large difference in the performance of methods all have an SD larger than 60 s. The results across these sixteen routes echo what is seen across the literature, with different methods performing better on different datasets. It is clear that bus routes shouldn't be treated as a homogenous group when assessing methods for the prediction of journey times.

4.3   Impact of Temporal Variables

An analysis of MAE by time of day and the day of the week was conducted for the two best-performing methods overall, WJP-P and SP, as shown in Figs. 5 and 6. A pattern emerged that seemed to correspond to peak and off-peak travel times/days on the bus network, so this was quantified with a reliability index, defined as one divided by the SD of the whole journey times on the network, as described by Sterman and Schofer [24]. Figure 5 shows WJP-P outperforming SP, especially during the morning and evening peak travel periods when the network reliability is low. The left section of the graph shows WJP-P outperforming SP

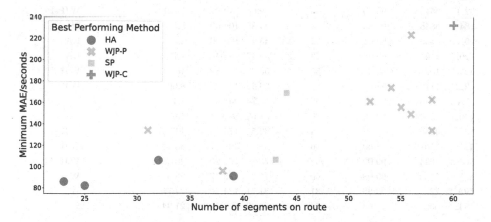

Fig. 4. The best method by the number of segments on the bus route and the MAE of the best performing method.

from time group 5 to 12 (5 am to 11 am) and again from time group 20 to 25 (5 pm to 9 pm). There is minimal difference between the two methods during off-peak times. Similarly, Fig. 6 shows WJP-P outperforming SP from Monday to Friday. During the conventional working week and especially during peak travel times is the time with the greatest number of passengers are on the network, and improving journey times at these times will benefit the most people. This is an important finding and is a strong argument for WJP-P over SP.

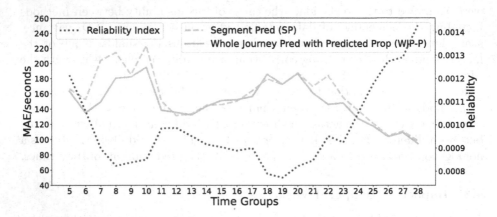

Fig. 5. The time groups in the study vs MAE and reliability

Table 5. Results by Route

Route	Num Trips	Percent Data	Num Segs	SD	Min MAE	Max minus Min MAE	Best Method
27A_1	8775	99.51	39	31.73	91.15	7.93	HA
32_2	6423	98.75	58	32.89	134.30	6.46	WJP-P
32_1	6512	98.20	56	39.66	149.37	17.21	WJP-P
184_1	6848	98.85	43	44.88	106.60	8.83	SP
79A_1	7566	99.01	32	45.43	106.00	2.42	HA
120_2	13618	99.52	23	52.47	86.04	2.79	HA
42_1	10200	98.25	55	53.38	155.89	16.77	WJP-P
42_2	11164	98.67	58	56.32	163.08	8.06	WJP-P
27A_2	8436	99.45	38	56.74	96.15	7.19	WJP-P
120_1	13944	99.18	25	58.62	82.15	1.90	HA
56A_1	4238	97.85	54	62.51	174.12	147.37	WJP-P
4_1	15016	98.69	56	69.59	223.77	30.49	WJP-P
56A_2	4294	99.02	52	73.85	161.25	201.51	WJP-P
4_2	15629	99.08	60	75.94	232.77	23.54	WJP-C
79A_2	7240	99.38	31	81.71	134.20	22.77	WJP-P
184_2	6361	98.63	44	88.43	169.19	21.34	SP

4.4   Computational and Storage Resources

The computational and storage resources consumed in this experiment are presented in Table 6. All methods were tested on the same partial journeys on a 2017 MacBook Pro with a 3.3 GHz Intel Core i5 processor and 16 GB of memory. Data processing time has been provided separately from training time because after the initial year of data is processed, the time taken for processing additional daily data would be minimal. HA does not do any ML model training, so its average training time is zero. WJP-C trains a single RF model per route, and a short training time of 0.51 s reflects this. WJP-P and SP show similar prediction times with 42.91 s and 45.40 s, respectively. Both of these methods train a model per segment, but the training time for WJP-P is shorter than SP. The average prediction time is likely the most significant of these measurements for journey planning applications and RTPI, as this will determine the speed at which information is returned to passengers. HA and WJP-C are very similar and over 40 times faster than WJP-P and SP, which are also very similar to each other. The same pattern is seen for storage with the models and data required for HA and WJP-C 18 times smaller than the other two methods. These results are specific to RF models, which have a larger storage size and a shorter training time than neural network models.

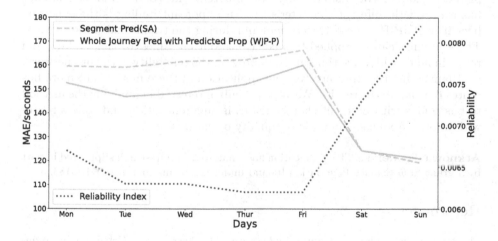

Fig. 6. The days of the week in the study vs MAE and reliability

Table 6. Computational and storage resources consumed by the different methods

Measurement	HA	SP	WJP-C	WJP-P
Data Processing/Route (in seconds)	54.83	20.32	102.7	132.29
Training Time/Route (in seconds)	0.00	45.40	0.51	42.91
Prediction Time/Test case (in seconds)	0.0157	0.6719	0.0156	0.6735
Storage /Route (in megabytes)	846.30	16017.62	852.80	16739.08

5   Conclusion

From the results of our experiments and analysis, we conclude that the commonly used SP method is not the best approach. It is not the best approach overall, nor on the majority of the bus routes, across multiple metrics. We also conclude bus routes are not a homogenous population and that attempting to define a single best algorithm for predicting bus journey times will result in sub-optimisation. The optimum method for journey time predictions should be determined based on many factors, including those identified in this study: the application, the trip's length, the temporal features of the trip, and also possible factors related to the bus route characteristics and data profile.

The novel method we present in this paper represents a significant contribution as WJP-P outperforms SP on most metrics, and on the majority of bus routes at a similar computational cost. The other method based on whole journey time prediction, WJP-C, has an overall reduction of 3.7% MAE compared to SP but at a significantly reduced computational cost. We suggest this as a good value option, balancing the accuracy of predictions with computational and storage costs.

Analysis of the results has provided important insights into the nature of bus journey time prediction regarding the bias in and variability between methods predicting for trips of different lengths, at different times of day and week and for bus routes with different characteristics. An important finding is the enhanced benefit of WJP-P at peak travel times and during the traditional working week. These findings can be applied to predict bus journey times for timetabling, and result in more achievable timetables, improving the reliability of the bus network.

Planned further work involves the application of these methods to more bus routes to validate the results. We are especially interested in applying the method to bus routes with different characteristics in different cities, and to bus routes with a lower frequency and a lower quality of data.

Acknowledgements. This publication has emanated from research supported in part by a grant from Science Foundation Ireland under Grant number 18/CRT/6183.

References

1. Almeida, F., Lobo, A., Couto, A., Ferreira, J.P., Ferreira, S.: Urban factors influencing the vehicle speed of public transport. Transp. Res. Procedia **62**, 318–324 (2022). 24th Euro Working Group on Transportation Meeting
2. Avenali, A., Catalano, G., Gregori, M., Matteucci, G.: Rail versus bus local public transport services: a social cost comparison methodology. Transp. Res. Interdiscip. Perspect. **7**, 100200 (2020)
3. Cats, O., Loutos, G.: Evaluating the added-value of online bus arrival prediction schemes. Transp. Res. Part A Policy Pract. **86**, 35–55 (2016)
4. Chakhtoura, C., Pojani, D.: Indicator-based evaluation of sustainable transport plans: a framework for Paris and other large cities. Transp. Policy **50** (2016)
5. Chen, G., Yang, X., An, J., Zhang, D.: Bus-arrival-time prediction models: link-based and section-based. J. Transp. Eng. **138**(1), 60–66 (2012)

6. Chien, S.I.J., Ding, Y., Wei, C.: Dynamic bus arrival time prediction with artificial neural networks. J. Transp. Eng. **128**(5), 429–438 (2002)
7. Cristóbal, T., Padrón, G., Quesada-Arencibia, A., Alayón, F., de Blasio, G., García, C.R.: Bus travel time prediction model based on profile similarity. Sensors **19**(13), 2869 (2019)
8. Dunne, L., McArdle, G.: A novel post prediction segmentation technique for urban bus travel time estimation. In: Proceedings of the Tenth International Workshop on Urban Computing (2021)
9. El-Geneidy, A.M., Horning, J., Krizek, K.J.: Analyzing transit service reliability using detailed data from automatic vehicular locator systems. J. Adv. Transp. **45**(1), 66–79 (2011)
10. Gal, A., Mandelbaum, A., Schnitzler, F., Senderovich, A., Weidlich, M.: Traveling time prediction in scheduled transportation with journey segments. Inf. Syst. **64**, 266–280 (2017)
11. Gössling, S.: Why cities need to take road space from cars - and how this could be done. J. Urban Des. **25**(4), 443–448 (2020)
12. He, P., Jiang, G., Lam, S.K., Sun, Y.: Learning heterogeneous traffic patterns for travel time prediction of bus journeys. Inf. Sci. **512**, 1394–1406 (2020)
13. He, P., Jiang, G., Lam, S.K., Tang, D.: Travel-time prediction of bus journey with multiple bus trips. IEEE Trans. Intell. Transp. Syst. **20**(11), 4192–4205 (2019)
14. Ma, L., et al.: Estimating urban road GPS environment friendliness with bus trajectories: a city-scale approach. Sensors **20**(6), 1580 (2020)
15. Maiti, S., Pal, A., Pal, A., Chattopadhyay, T., Mukherjee, A.: Historical data based real time prediction of vehicle arrival time. In: Proceedings of the 17th International IEEE Conference on Intelligent Transportation Systems, pp. 1837–1842 (2014)
16. Mazloumi, E., Rose, G., Currie, G., Sarvi, M.: An integrated framework to predict bus travel time and its variability using traffic flow data. J. Intell. Transp. Syst. **15**(2), 75–90 (2011)
17. Morabia, A., et al.: Potential health impact of switching from car to public transportation when commuting to work. Am. J. Public Health **100**(12), 2388–2391 (2010)
18. Nimpanomprasert, T., Xie, L., Kliewer, N.: Comparing two hybrid neural network models to predict real-world bus travel time. Transp. Res. Procedia **62**, 393–400 (2022). 24th Euro Working Group on Transportation Meeting
19. dell' Olio, L., Ibeas, A., Cecin, P.: The quality of service desired by public transport users. Transp. Policy **18**(1), 217–227 (2011)
20. Pandurangi, A., Byrne, C., Anderson, C., Cui, E., McArdle, G.: Design and development of an application for predicting bus travel times using a segmentation approach. In: Proceedings of the 6th International Conference on Geographical Information Systems Theory, Applications and Management 2020, pp. 72–80 (2020)
21. Pałys, L., Ganzha, M., Paprzycki, M.: Machine learning for bus travel prediction. In: Computational Science - ICCS 2022, pp. 703–710 (2022)
22. Singh, N., Kumar, K.: A review of bus arrival time prediction using artificial intelligence. WIREs Data Min. Knowl. Discov. e1457 (2022)
23. Soza-Parra, J., Muñoz, J.C., Raveau, S.: Factors that affect the evolution of headway variability along an urban bus service. Transportmetrica B Transp. Dyn. **9**(1), 479–490 (2021)
24. Sterman, B.P., Schofer, J.L.: Factors affecting reliability of urban bus services. Transp. Eng. J. ASCE **102**(1), 147–159 (1976)

25. Sutandi, A.C., Dermawan, A.: Accuracy of bus timetable using information communication and technology GPS to inform trans metro bandung bus passenger. In: Proceedings of the 6th International Conference on Civil, Offshore and Environmental Engineering, pp. 725–734 (2021)
26. U.N.: Goal 11 — Department of Economic and Social Affairs. https://sdgs.un.org/goals/goal11. Accessed 15 July 2022
27. Yu, B., Wang, H., Shan, W., Yao, B.: Prediction of bus travel time using random forests based on near neighbors. Comput. Aided Civ. Infrastruct. Eng. **33**(4), 333–350 (2018)
28. Zhao, X., Carling, K., Håkansson, J.: An evaluation of the reliability of GPS-based transportation data. In: Proceedings of the Computer Science Conference, Vienna (2017)

Detection of Distracted Driving: A Smartphone-Based Approach

Giuseppe Cancello Tortora, Mirko Casini, Andrea Lagna, Martina Marino, and Alessio Vecchio(✉) ⓘ

University of Pisa, Pisa 56122, Italy
alessio.vecchio@unipi.it

Abstract. Road accidents cause 1.35 million deaths a year and have now become the leading cause of death between the ages of 5 and 29. CAReful is an application that can be used while driving to detect dangerous behaviors, such as drowsiness, turning the head, using the smartphone, or the presence of excessive noise. CAReful uses different sensors to monitor the driver, such as the microphone, GPS, camera, accelerometer, gyroscope, and magnetometer, and to obtain information about the vehicle's speed and the road. Since driving behavior is privacy-related, all processing and storage of sensitive information occur on the user's device.

Keywords: Road accidents · Distraction detection · Smartphone

1 Introduction

According to the "Global status report on road safety", the number of road traffic deaths is approximately 1.35 million every year, and road accidents are the main cause of death for people aged 5–29 years [18]. A significant fraction of road accidents is known to be caused by distracted driving. The U.S. Department of Transportation's National Highway Traffic Safety Administration (NHTSA) estimates that the number of deaths caused by distraction was ⏐3300 in 2011, whereas the number of injuries was 387000 [15]. The problem is known to be relevant also in other parts of the world [8], and in more recent years the situation did not get better [16].

Distraction can be defined as a specific type of inattention where the driver focuses on non-driving activities. Distractions can be categorized in *visual distractions*, such as looking at the infotainment system of the vehicle, *manual distractions*, such as eating or drinking, and *cognitive distractions*, such as speaking with other passengers [17]. In many cases, a distracting task can span more categories: for instance, reading a text message on a smartphone requires both looking away from the road and using at least one of the hands to control the smartphone. Distractions can also be more or less demanding in terms of cognitive load.

The increasing capabilities of vehicles, in terms of automated driving, can be helpful in the long term, as the driving tasks will be shifted from humans

A. L. Martins et al. (Eds.): INTSYS 2022, LNICST 486, pp. 157–165, 2023.
https://doi.org/10.1007/978-3-031-30855-0_11

to the vehicle's intelligence. However, the level of automation that is currently available, or that will be available in the near future, can be paradoxically an incentive to distraction [12]. In fact, some levels of automated driving require the driver to be attentive and promptly take control of the vehicle in anomalous situations, but being the human relieved most of the time from driving tasks, distracting activities like using a smartphone can occur even more frequently. In addition, the time needed to replace all existing vehicles with fully automated ones is going to take several years.

As a consequence, methods for automatically detecting distracted driving received significant attention during the last years. In this paper, we propose a system for detecting distracted driving that advances the state of the art along the following directions: i) the method identifies a wide range of distracting activities relying on the multiple sensors available on a smartphone (the camera, the microphone, the GPS, the IMU); ii) detected distractions are used to compute a distraction index that can be used by the driver for self-assessing their driving style; iii) the system relies only on a smartphone and all computation and storage of information occur locally. This is important because information about the driving style is of personal nature and it could be used for malevolous purposes (e.g. by insurance companies not authorized by the user). Finally, in some countries, monitoring of workers is not allowed; therefore, a solution like the one we propose can be useful for those professional drivers who are interested in self-assessing their driving style but, at the same time, want to preserve their privacy.

2   Related Work

Because of the social significance of the problem, the detection of distracted drivers received significant attention during the last few years. Several approaches are based on computer vision only. Through computer vision, in fact, it is possible to detect a wide range of distracting behaviors, such as using a smartphone while driving, reaching out objects in the backseat, or looking in the wrong direction. In [6], an approach based on two stages is presented: the first stage relies on a ResNet-101 network to identify and locate the relevant elements in an image, such as hands, face, and a smartphone; the second stage uses features like the distance between the previously identified elements to classify the current behavior as safe or not. The approach was evaluated on a set of images when executed on a standard PC. Another vision-based approach is described in [14], where a camera is used to recognize a set of distracting activities such as texting using the phone, operating the radio, doing makeup, reaching behind, or talking with other passengers. The focus of the study was on the best performance that can be obtained using a number of well-known deep learning methods in terms of accuracy and execution speed on embedded computers. The problem of optimizing a Convolutional Neural Network (CNN) is faced in [3], where the number of parameters is reduced compared to other CNN-based approaches. Also in this case, the approach is based only on images of the driver to recognize the unsafe behaviors included in the dataset provided in [7].

Detection of unsafe behaviors that is specifically designed for being executed on smartphones is described in [19]. Unsafe behaviors are not restricted to inattentive driving, but also include careless change of lane, tailgating another vehicle, and lane weaving. One of the main goals of the system is to select the most appropriate camera depending on the current context. The reason is due to the inability of the adopted smartphones to activate the front-facing camera when, at the same time, the rear one is in use. The front-facing camera is used to recognize the possible drowsiness of the driver or the direction of the head, whereas the other camera is needed to observe the trajectory of the car across lanes and the distance from the preceding vehicle. The approach focuses on a wide range of danger sources, but does not specifically target the possibly different distracted driving behaviors.

SafeDrive is a wearable system able to detect a number of distracting actions [11]. SafeDrive relies on the IMU available on smartwatches to monitor the right-hand movements of the driver, to understand if she is interacting for too much time with the car controls, she is searching items located at the passenger's seat or at the backseat, or she is eating. The approach uses, as the main source of information, the rotation angle of the driver's hand on the horizontal plane, integrated with information collected by the smartphone. The latter, in particular, is useful to monitor the vehicle's dynamics. Another approach based on wearable devices is the one described in [13], where the position of the smartwatch is derived using the RSSI of Bluetooth Low Energy (BLE) communication. The basic idea is that the smartwatch communicates with the passengers' smartphones so that its position can be estimated without relying on IMUs (the rationale is that IMUs are also influenced by vehicle dynamics). The set of distracting actions again includes using a smartphone, eating or drinking, searching onboard items, and operating the vehicle systems. IMUs were used in [9], where the considered distracting activities were all related to the use of a smartphone (being involved in a call, two-way texting, and reading a message).

The reader is forwarded to [12], where existing literature about the detection of driver's distraction is reviewed and taxonomized.

3   CAReful: An App for Detecting Distracting Behaviors

CAReful is an Android application for smartphones able to measure the level of inattention of the user while driving. The app makes use of the different sensors typically available on a smartphone to collect information about the behaviour of the driver and about the environment around her (e.g., tortuosity of the road). The distracting behaviors that CAReful is able to detect are: drowsiness, turned head, usage of smartphone, smartphone fall, and excessive noise. The device is supposed to be positioned in front of the user as it is commonly done when using a smartphone as a navigation aid. The main sensors used by CAReful are: the GPS, the microphone, the camera and all the motion-related sensors, such as the accelerometer, the gyroscope and the magnetometer. Beside the distracting behaviors, CAReful combines the presence of such activities with the vehicle speed and the tortuosity of the travelled road. The idea is that distracting behaviors are much more dangerous as the speed increases or when the road is non-rectilinear. The output is a single index that can be used to evaluate the general risk associated to distractions. The index is computed during a trip and saved to keep note of the user's behavior. In the following, we describe how the considered distracting activities are detected.

3.1   Drowsiness

The front camera is used for the detection of the driver drowsiness. In particular, drowsiness is recognized by computing the fraction of time the eyes of the driver are closed. The camera sampling rate is set 10 Hz, as a trade-off between detection accuracy and resource consumption. To recognize the features of the driver's face, we rely on the Google ML Kit [10]. In particular, we make use of the Face Detection APIs to detect the points of interest within a face and then to estimate the fraction of time the eyes are kept open or closed. Whenever the driver's eyes are kept closed for 20 consecutive frames ($\sim$2 s), then a drowsiness counter is incremented. Such a counter is then combined with similar ones concerning the other possibly distracting activities to obtain the final index.

3.2   Turned Head

The same camera is used also to understand if the driver has turned her head to the left or to the right, looking away from the road. Also in this case, we relied on the Face Detection APIs as it is highly optimized for being executed on mobile devices. The driver's head is considered to be turned when the module of the Euler Y angle of the head is greater than a threshold (40°). The threshold has been set considering that when the Euler Y angle is greater that 36°, only the right eye is visible from the camera. The same applies when the angle is less than $-36°$. Once the driver has turned her head in one of the two directions for at least 4 s, the counter related to this distracting behavior is increased.

3.3   Usage of Smarthphone

The IMU of the smartphone provides information useful to detect if the device is used by the driver. In particular, we adopted a simple approach based on detecting a rotation of the device, corresponding to when the smartphones is removed from the holder where it is supposed to be placed. The listener of the gyroscope is activated with a period of $\sim$200 ms. If the module of the angular velocity becomes greater than the threshold, the distracting activity is detected.

3.4   Smartphone Fall

We decided to include the fall of the smartphone in the set of distracting activities because picking up the device from the vehicle floor can be extremely dangerous. To detect a fall, the magnitude of the acceleration vector is computed and stored in a buffer. We decided to use the magnitude of the acceleration vector, and not all the three components, to keep the method simple and independent from the possible rotations of the device when falling [1,2,5]. The magnitude values in the buffer are then compared with two thresholds – *lowTh* and *highTh* – to detect the free fall of the smartphone and then its impact onto the floor. Every time a new value is added to the circular buffer, the algorithm searches in the array for a value lower than *lowTh*, corresponding to the free fall phase. Then, if the free fall phase is detected, the algorithm searches for a value higher than *highTh* in the remaining part, caused by the impact of the device onto the floor.

3.5   Excessive Noise

The microphone of the smartphone is used to capture the level of noise in the vehicle. The *android.media AudioRecord* class is used to sample the sound level every 500 ms, encoded as 16 bit PCM. The mean value of the samples is computed to make the system tolerant to possible short spikes in the signal. The mean value is then compared to a reference value to obtain the level of noise on a dB scale. The reference value used is the minimum value that the device is able to measure. Unfortunately, the result cannot be easily translated into a dB Sound Pressure Level[1] (SPL) because the latter assumes a reference level of $20\mu Pa$ and the samples are collected through an uncalibrated smartphone. For this reason, we finally compared the result to an empirically derived threshold. A study demonstrated that reasonably accurate measurements can be carried out when using iOS devices as the different models share many similarities from the point of view of the audio subsystem [4].

3.6   Trip Logging and Road Tortuosity

Every trip has departure and arrival coordinates, collected via GPS. The GPS is also used to retrieve the speed of the vehicle which is used as a multiplying factor when computing the distraction index, as discussed in Sect. 4. The rotation vector, derived from the accelerometer and magnetometer readings, is used to compute the curvature index of the road covered during the trip. The azimuth is sampled every 200 ms and the difference between adjacent samples is used as an indication of the direction change in the considered period. Finally, the average module of the differences is used as an indication of the overall road tortuosity. The result is then compared to a set of empirically-defined thresholds to obtain the curvature index.

---

[1] dB SPL is typically used to express the threshold of discomfort or pain for humans.

Table 1. Contribution of every distraction counter and multiplier in the score formula

	Role	Range	Description
Tortuosity	multiplier	1–3	Difficulty of the road
Speed	multiplier	1–4	Speed of the vehicle
Drowsiness	counter	0–30	How many times eyes are closed
Head turned	counter	0–15	How many times head is turned
Usage	counter	0–1	Phone is used
Fall	counter	0–1	Phone falls
Noise	counter	0–12	How many times noise is detected

4   Distraction Score

As mentioned, the distraction score quantifies the level of distraction of the driver at a given time during the trip. The distraction score d is computed according to the following formula:

$$d = (\frac{Speed}{4} + \frac{Tortuos.}{3}) \cdot (\frac{Head}{15} + \frac{Drowsiness}{30} + \frac{Noise}{12} + Fall + Usage) \quad (1)$$

Speed and tortuosity act as a multiplying factor. The other term, instead, expresses the amount of the driver's distracting behaviors. The speed index is supposed to be in the 1–4 range as we identified 4 different speed limits to be typically adopted (urban road, extra-urban road, main extra-urban road, and motorway). Road tortuosity is expressed by a value in the 1–3 range, as we wanted to classify roads into easy, medium, and difficult ones. The counters related to drowsiness, turned head, and smartphone usage are normalized in the range 0–1 by dividing their actual values by the theoretically maximum values obtainable in a minute. The range of possible values for the different counters is shown in Table 1. This is done to compute the fraction of time a specific behavior has been detected. Fall and usage of smartphones are considered binary values, as they are associated with particularly distracting behaviors. During the whole trip, the attention level is re-computed every minute (and the counters are reinitialized). This enables identifying specific parts of the trip that have been characterized by distractions.

Equation 1 is used to compute the "istantaneous" disattention level. However, to provide a more readable feedback to the driver, variations are smoothed through an exponential moving average:

$$d_i = (\alpha \cdot d) + (1 - \alpha) \cdot d_{i-1}$$

The value of d_i is then shown to the user using a range of colors as depicted in Fig. 1b. To be more specific, what is actually presented to the user is the attention level, as we feel that providing positive feedback to the driver is better than highlighting bad behaviors.

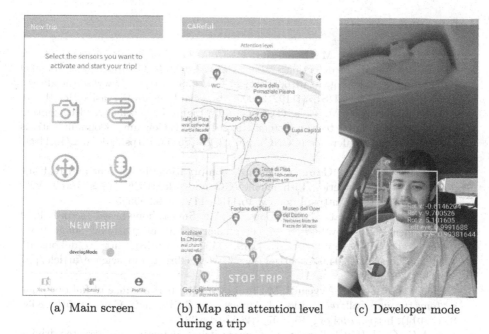

(a) Main screen   (b) Map and attention level   (c) Developer mode
                              during a trip

Fig. 1. Screenshots of the app.

5   Conclusion

CAReful is an application that does not store any sensitive data, all the information collected about the driver and the surrounding environment is processed in real-time and not stored. Processing occurs locally using just the smartphone resources, and without transmitting any information to external services. The only information stored is a summary of the trip: departure and arrival location, departure and arrival time, and aggregate score. We believe that self-assessing the users' driving style while preserving their privacy is key to the widespread adoption of tools like the one we propose and, in the end, to improve safety on the roads.

Some screenshots of the app are shown in Fig. 1. In particular, Figs. 1a and 1b show the main screen and the map that is visualized when driving. Figure 1c instead shows the development mode of the app, where information about collected data and intermediate results is reported.

Future work will concern the evaluation of the app. As also pointed out by the literature summarized in Sect. 2, the evaluation of systems aimed at detecting distractions when driving is particularly troublesome because real tests are too risky. A possible solution is represented by realistic driving simulators, possibly integrated with a trace-driven execution as far as the motion sensors are concerned.

References

1. Abbate, S., Avvenuti, M., Bonatesta, F., Cola, G., Corsini, P., Vecchio, A.: A smartphone-based fall detection system. Pervasive Mob. Comput. **8**(6), 883–899 (2012). https://doi.org/10.1016/j.pmcj.2012.08.003, https://www.sciencedirect.com/science/article/pii/S1574119212000983. special Issue on Pervasive Healthcare

2. Abbate, S., Avvenuti, M., Cola, G., Corsini, P., Light, J., Vecchio, A.: Recognition of false alarms in fall detection systems. In: 2011 IEEE Consumer Communications and Networking Conference (CCNC), pp. 23–28 (2011). https://doi.org/10.1109/CCNC.2011.5766464

3. Baheti, B., Talbar, S., Gajre, S.: Towards computationally efficient and realtime distracted driver detection with mobileVGG network. IEEE Trans. Intell. Veh. **5**(4), 565–574 (2020). https://doi.org/10.1109/TIV.2020.2995555

4. Celestina, M., Hrovat, J., Kardous, C.A.: Smartphone-based sound level measurement apps: evaluation of compliance with international sound level meter standards. Appl. Acoust., **139**, 119–128 (2018). https://doi.org/10.1016/j.apacoust.2018.04.011, https://www.sciencedirect.com/science/article/pii/S0003682X17309945

5. Cola, G., Vecchio, A., Avvenuti, M.: Improving the performance of fall detection systems through walk recognition. J. Ambient Intell. Humaniz. Comput. **5**(6), 843–855 (2014). https://doi.org/10.1007/s12652-014-0235-x

6. Dey, A.K., Goel, B., Chellappan, S.: Context-driven detection of distracted driving using images from in-car cameras. Internet Things, **14**, 100380 (2021). https://doi.org/10.1016/j.iot.2021.100380, https://www.sciencedirect.com/science/article/pii/S254266052100024X

7. Eraqi, H.M., Abouelnaga, Y., Saad, M.H., Moustafa, M.N.: Driver distraction identification with an ensemble of convolutional neural networks. J. Adv. Transp. **2019**, 4125865 (2019). https://doi.org/10.1155/2019/4125865

8. European Respiratory Society Observatory. European Commission. Road safety thematic report - driver distraction, D.G.f.T. (2022)

9. Goel, B., Dey, A.K., Bharti, P., Ahmed, K.B., Chellappan, S.: Detecting distracted driving using a wrist-worn wearable. In: 2018 IEEE International Conference on Pervasive Computing and Communications Workshops (PerCom Workshops), pp. 233–238 (2018). https://doi.org/10.1109/PERCOMW.2018.8480282

10. Google: Ml kit. https://developers.google.com/ml-kit. Accessed 15 Sept 2022

11. Jiang, L., Lin, X., Liu, X., Bi, C., Xing, G.: SafeDrive: detecting distracted driving behaviors using wrist-worn devices. Proc. ACM Interact. Mob. Wearable Ubiquit. Technol. **1**(4), 1–22 (2018). https://doi.org/10.1145/3161179

12. Kashevnik, A., Shchedrin, R., Kaiser, C., Stocker, A.: Driver distraction detection methods: a literature review and framework. IEEE Access **9**, 60063–60076 (2021). https://doi.org/10.1109/ACCESS.2021.3073599

13. Mewborne, T., Zhang, L., Tan, S.: A wearable-based distracted driving detection leveraging BLE. In: Proceedings of the 19th ACM Conference on Embedded Networked Sensor Systems, pp. 365–366. SenSys 2021, Association for Computing Machinery, New York (2021). https://doi.org/10.1145/3485730.3492872

14. Tran, D., Manh Do, H., Sheng, W., Bai, H., Chowdhary, G.: Real-time detection of distracted driving based on deep learning. IET Intell. Transp. Syst. **12**(10), 1210–1219 (2018). https://doi.org/10.1049/iet-its.2018.5172, https://ietresearch.onlinelibrary.wiley.com/doi/abs/10.1049/iet-its.2018.5172

15. Department of Transportation, N.H.T.S.A.: Traffic safety facts - research note - distracted driving 2011 (2011)
16. Department of Transportation, N.H.T.S.A.: Distracted driving (2020). https://www.nhtsa.gov/risky-driving/distracted-driving. Accessed 14 July 2022
17. Vegega, M., Jones, B., Monk, C., et al.: Understanding the effects of distracted driving and developing strategies to reduce resulting deaths and injuries: a report to congress. Technical report, United States. Office of Impaired Driving and Occupant Protection (2013)
18. (WHO), W.H.O.: Global status report on road safety (2018)
19. You, C.W.,et al.: CarSafe app: alerting drowsy and distracted drivers using dual cameras on smartphones. In: Proceeding of the 11th Annual International Conference on Mobile Systems, Applications, and Services, pp. 13–26. MobiSys 2013, Association for Computing Machinery, New York (2013). https://doi.org/10.1145/2462456.2465428

Detection of Invisible/Occluded Vehicles Using Passive RFIDs

Ricky Yuen-Tan Hou[✉]

Guangdong Provincial Key Laboratory of Interdisciplinary Research and Application for Data Science, Faculty of Science and Technology, BNU-HKBU United International College, Zhuhai 519000, China
rickyhou.hk@gmail.com

Abstract. Vehicle detection in autonomous driving could be very challenging under adverse road conditions. The problem has been studied intensively. However, recent studies have shown that the problem remains unsolved, especially when the vehicles are occluded or under low-light conditions. This paper adopts a different approach to vehicle detection by taking advantage of RFID technology. Specifically, RFID tags are attached to the vehicle's surfaces, and then a system is designed to detect, locate, and track those tags dynamically. In addition, RFIDs are allowed to store user data on chips. To fully utilize this feature, this paper develops an algorithm to select and store the most critical information in tags for recovering the boundaries of occluded vehicles and finding the vehicle's location and orientation. The proposed method achieves the following objectives: (1) Vehicles could be detected at a relatively long distance in any conditions (including low-light or adverse weather). (2) The boundary of the occluded vehicle could be recovered. (3) Vehicles are still detectable even if they are turned off. (4) The implementation is relatively simple. The evaluation results have shown that the proposed method is able to detect a vehicle's orientation and rotation and recover the boundary for an occluded vehicle.

Keywords: Autonomous driving · RFID tags · shape approximation · orientation estimation · vehicle detection · vehicle safety

1 Introduction

In recent years, due to the popularity of autonomous driving, the related accidents also increased [1, 2]. According to a report [2], the accidents were caused by detection defections, such as the driving systems failing to detect other vehicles or recognize surrounding objects.

1.1 Challenges of Vehicle Detection

Autonomous vehicles are required to identify and track other vehicles around them and properly handle each detected vehicle. However, there are many challenges to recognizing those vehicles on roads correctly. The most significant challenges of vehicles detection are summarized as follows:

A. L. Martins et al. (Eds.): INTSYS 2022, LNICST 486, pp. 166–181, 2023.
https://doi.org/10.1007/978-3-031-30855-0_12

Vehicle detection is especially challenging in heterogeneous traffic or adverse road conditions, in which the size and type of vehicles vary significantly. When vehicular traffic density is high, it leads to frequent occlusion. Occlusions increase the difficulty of learning the visual representations of vehicles. The tracker may fail to follow the target under occlusions since the occlusions prevent the tracker from learning the complete appearance representation of the target [3]. Furthermore, complex backgrounds, weather conditions, and cast shadows make identifying and tracking a vehicle difficult [4].

1.2 Related Works

Although on-road vehicle detection is challenging, significant progress has been made for general problems in recent years [5, 6]. Autonomous vehicles integrate multiple sensors onboard for information acquisition about road conditions. Those sensors can be classified into two main categories: active and passive [5].

The most common approaches to detecting vehicles by active sensors include radar-based and laser-based. Millimeter-wave radar is widely used for vehicle detection, in which a frequency-modulated continuous waveform signal is emitted. Its reflections are received and demodulated, and frequency content is analyzed [6]. Radar sensing generally features a narrow angular field of view, and measurements are quite noisy, requiring extensive filtering and cleaning [6].

Lidar-based systems emit and receive lasers at wavelengths generally between 600 and 1000 nm. The distance to the detected object could be derived based on how far the photons have traveled round trip [5]. Laser-based systems are accurate; however, they do not perform well in rain and snow [7]. When a large number of vehicles are moving simultaneously in the same direction, interference among sensors of the same type poses a big problem [7].

A passive vision-based system such as a camera is utilized to track approaching and preceding vehicles more effectively than active sensors as visual information can provide a brief description of the surrounding vehicles [5]. Optical sensors can also be used for lane detection, traffic sign recognition, or object identification [5].

Multiple sensor approaches are more likely to progress and achieve more reliable and secure systems than a single sensor. In the fusion process, either two types of sensors perform detection simultaneously and then validate each other's results, or one sensor detects while the other validates [5].

Imaging technology is the mainstream of vehicle detection methods [6], which could be divided into two broad categories: appearance-based and motion-based methods. Appearance-based methods recognize vehicles directly from images. However, motion-based approaches require a sequence of images to recognize vehicles [6]. Therefore, monocular vehicle detection often relies on appearance features and machine learning, while stereo vehicle detection often relies on motion features, tracking, and filtering [6].

Several recent studies investigated the detection problem under special scenarios, such as nighttime and low-light [8, 9]. The studies have shown that complex road and ambient lighting conditions and camera configurations can significantly impact the effectiveness. If vehicles are occluded by nearby objects or under very bad weather, the detection problem could be even more challenging. Current benchmarks indicate that recent detection algorithms can detect approximately 90% of partially occluded and 80% of heavily occluded vehicles [3]. One popular occlusion handling method is the analysis of motion cues, such as frame comparison reasoning, which analyzes continuous image data and identifies objects by comparing data between frames [3]. However, this method is restricted in cases of static occlusion where the variation of occlusion between frames is small [3, 10]. Some other popular methods of occlusion handling combine a number of the following occlusion cues or image characteristics to assess if an object boundary is recognized or recovered [3]. The weaknesses of the existing methods are obvious: (1) the success rates heavily rely on the visual quality or road conditions; (2) the occluded parts are very difficult to be recovered in cases of static occlusion because the related information is limited.

1.3 Proposed Solution for Detection of Invisible/Occluded Vehicles

This paper proposes a method to detect invisible/occluded vehicles by taking advantage of the new developments in radio frequency identification (RFID) technologies. The main idea is to attach passive RFID tags to a vehicle's surfaces to add new electromagnetic visibility to the vehicle. Furthermore, each tag is allowed to store a vehicle's 3D model on the chip. So that the RFID reader can remotely retrieve the 3D model from a tag when a vehicle is invisible or occluded; in addition, based on the tags' returned signals, the vehicle's boundary, location, and orientation could be derived. Compared to optical systems, RFID is independent of weather conditions and the time of the day [16].

The remaining sections of this paper is organized as follows. Section II analyzes the characteristics of RFIDs and explains the use of RFID technologies to make vehicles detectable in adverse road conditions. The storage space in a tag is very limited and varies in different brands. Section III shows how to dynamically minimize the storage space required for the 3D model of a vehicle. Section IV designs a data structure to support effective detection and computation in consideration of limited storage space in RFID tags. Section V proposes methods to estimate an occluded vehicle's direction, distance, and orientation. Section VI is the performance evaluation for the proposed method.

2   Make Vehicles Detectable by Using RFIDs

RFID is designed to be attached to equipment or objects for easier detection, location, and tracking. RFIDs are highly reliable yet have low implementation complexity [13, 24]. For instance, multiple RFID tags are attached to an object to enhance availability and detection accuracy in inventory applications [25]. An RFID system usually contains one or more RFID tags and a reader. A tag consists of a silicon microchip attached to a small antenna, mounted on a substrate, and encapsulated in a plastic or glass veil. A reader consists of a scanner with antennas to transmit and receive signals, is responsible for communication with the tag, and receives the information from the tag. A reader can scan multiple tags at a time. Figure 1 is the illustration of interactions between a reader and multiple tags. However, it can also detect each tag individually. RFID tags are not necessary to communicate within line of sight. This characteristic is useful when the vehicle is partially occluded.

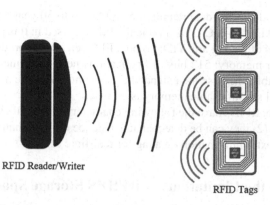

RFID Reader/Writer

RFID Tags

Fig. 1. An RFID reader can turn on multiple tags simultaneously over a long distance.

2.1 Durability and Detection Range of Passive RFIDs

There are two types of RFID systems in operation: active and passive. In an active system, the tag has its power source. The battery life could be up to a few years. However, the tag has no internal power supply in a passive system; therefore, it can be much smaller [15]. Passive tags contain circuitry that gains power from radio waves emitted by readers in their vicinity. They use this power to give a reply to the reader. Passive tags have no moving parts or internal power sources. The chance of breakdown within the tag itself is extremely low. Therefore, passive tags can last for the entire lifespan of the vehicles to which they are mounted [13].

The communication distance of RFID depends on the active or passive RFID, RF output power of reader/writer, the antenna gain of tag and reader/writer, and the user environment. In general, the communication distance for active tags could be up to 100 m [11]. For the passive type, although the reachable distance of radio waves depends on the conditions related to the antenna size and the signal strength, generally speaking, the higher frequency bands (UHF) have larger communication distances. For instance, in the mainstream market, some UHF RFID tags' ranges can reach 20 m [12] or 30 m [13]. Recent studies have shown that the new passive RFID could be reached at an unprecedented range of up to 64 m [14, 15].

2.2 User Memory on RFID Tags

An RFID tag is composed of four types of memories in a tag. They are (1) reserved memory, (2) TID (tag ID is written by manufacturers), (3) EPC (electronic product code) can be written by users, and (4) user memory. Type (3) and (4) can be rewritten by users. Storing extra information (other than ID number) in an RFID tag allows users to access records in real-time without connecting to a reference database. When a reader scans an RFID tag, it can retrieve the ID and the stored data.

Different RFID tags have varying amounts of storage available. The capacity of RFID tags ranges from 60 bytes to 64K bytes [19]. Typically, a tag carries about 2 KB of data (e.g., Fujitsu chip MB89R118). However, some industrial passive UHF tags can store

4 KB or 8 KB of data. The data retention could be up to 30 years. Invengo RFID Tag (Model No. XC-TF8102-B-C43) is a typical RFID tag used in this paper's experiment. The specifications of the tag are: TID: 96 bits, EPC (electronic product code) memory: 256 bits, and user memory: 512 bits. If applications need more memory than the EPC section has available, they use the extended user memory to store more information. In this case, the total size of usable memory is 96 bytes.

To summarize, RFIDs have the following characteristics: (1) their lifespan can be as long as 30 years; (2) they can be detected at a distance of more than 60 m; (3) users are allowed to store extra information on a tag for real-time access.

3   Overcome the Limitations of RFID'S Storage Space

One of the solutions to detect invisible/occluded vehicles is to increase every vehicle's visibility to other vehicles. There are several advantages to attaching passive RFID tags to a vehicle's surfaces. Those tags can be detected reliably under different road conditions [16]. Secondly, the vehicle's identifier, 3D model, etc., are stored in each tag for real-time access. So that vehicles can easily detect and locate the invisible/occluded vehicles, they can also recover the boundaries of the occluded vehicles. The storage requirement of a vehicle's 3D model should be minimized to overcome the limitation of RFID's storage space and achieve better computational efficiency. The following sub-sections are to develop an algorithm to simplify the 3D expression.

3.1   Vehicle Segmentation

In 3D modeling, a vehicle is scanned into a point cloud which usually consumes a lot of storage space. A vehicle's point cloud is divided into multiple parts to simplify the vehicle bounding's expression. A tight bounding box is generated for each part. As a result, the tags' positions will tightly align with the virtual boundary. Then the resulting bounding boxes are joined together to create a 3D vehicle model.

Edge-Based Segmentation
Several existing algorithms can be used to divide a point cloud into logical parts [20, 21]. For instance, there are edge-based segmentation, region growing segmentation, segmentation by model fitting, etc. Different algorithms have their advantages. Vehicles usually have simple shapes; they are easier to be divided into parts. In this paper, edge-based segmentation is chosen as it is a fast algorithm to speed up the computation [21]. The edge-based segmentation algorithms have two main stages: (1) edge detection to outline the borders of different regions and (2) grouping of points inside the boundaries to deliver the final segments [21]. Edges in a given point cloud are defined by the points where changes in the local surface properties exceed a given threshold. Figure 2 shows two examples of dividing a car and a truck into segments.

Fig. 2. Two examples: (a) a car is divided into two segments; (b) a truck is divided into three segments.

3.2 Shape Selection

After segmentation, each part of the vehicle will be converted into a bounding box to simplify the 3D expression.

Building the Shape Database

First, a database of simple 3D geometric shapes is built to store a set of representative shape exemplars. The selection of those shape exemplars is straightforward. The common shapes that appear in the vehicles are selected. It is important to ensure that those shapes have multiple flat surfaces, which will be easier for the algorithm to estimate the vehicle's pose at a later stage. The database can be updated if the shapes of vehicles have changed. The following is an example (Fig. 3):

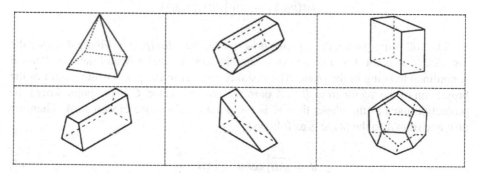

Fig. 3. Database of 3D geometric shapes with flat surfaces.

Initial Shape Selection

Instead of directly reconstructing shape representations, the proposed method operates indirectly by selecting shape exemplars. More precisely, after segmentation, for each segment, the algorithm is to select one shape exemplar among a set of K shape exemplars from a given shape database. The goal is to approximate the realistic shape for each segment yet consume minimum storage space. After each selection of shape exemplars, the exemplar's parameters can be manipulated to fit the bounding box as perfectly as possible. A loss function is developed to evaluate the fitness of the approximation. This polygonal model could be used in different types of vehicles. By careful selection, all shapes consist of limited flat surfaces, and each surface is a plane that is a flat (not curved) two-dimensional space.

3.3 Distance Calculation and Parameters Fine-Tuning

A function is used to evaluate the effectiveness of the resulting 3D geometric shape. The distance is measured between each point of the point cloud and the surface (plane) of the 3D shape. The following model is proposed: let $P = \{p_1, \cdots, p_i, \cdots, p_m\}$ is the point cloud, and $S = \{s_1, \cdots, s_j, \cdots, s_n\}$ denote flat surfaces (planes) of the resulting 3D model. Define $dist(p_i, S)$ to be the distance function point p_i to S. The objective is to minimize the total distance from P to S.

$$d(P, S) = \text{minimize} \sum_{i=1}^{m} dist(p_i, S) \qquad (1)$$

Then the problem can be decomposed into the following set of sub-problems:

- Develop a function $dist(p_i, s_j)$ that calculates the distance between a point p_i and an arbitrary plane s_j.
- Calculate the distances between point p_i and each flat surface (each side is a plane) and take the shortest of the distances:

$$dist(p_i, S) = \min_{s_j \in S} \{dist(p_i, s_j)\} \qquad (2)$$

The following paragraph explains how to calculate $dist(p_i, s_j)$. Figure 4 shows the distance from point A to a plane determined by normal vector N and point B. Point B is confined to being in the plane. The distance from A to the plane is the length of the projection of the vector from B to A onto the normal vector. C is the point where the projection touches the plane, then C is the point on the plane closest to A. Then the distance from A to the plane is as follows:

$$d = \left|\vec{AB}\right| \cos \theta = \left|\vec{AB} \cdot \frac{\vec{N}}{|N|}\right| \qquad (3)$$

Iterative Closest Point Fine-Tuning for Each Segment
For each segment, the parameters of a 3D geometric shape (such as lengths of dimensions and orientation) are fine-tuned to match the corresponding point cloud by using the Iterative Closest Point method (ICP), which is used to align two free-form shapes [22]. Then the problem is formulated as follows: given two corresponding free-form shapes (shape S and point cloud P). The goal is to fine-tune the shape parameters to minimize the sum of distance $d(P, S)$. After that, all segments are put together to form the final shape for the vehicle. Some methods are proposed to identify key points for more efficient computation [23]. The trade-off between accuracy and computational time is dependent on the number of key points selected.

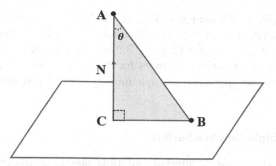

Fig. 4. Illustrate the distance from point P to a plane.

4 Design of Data Structure for RFID Tags

4.1 Data Structure in a Tag

Application developers can use the software development kits provided by reader man-ufacturers to write data into memory. The following information is stored in a tag to facilitate vehicle detection. They are the vehicle's 3D segment shapes, tags' positions on the surfaces, the total number of tags on a specific surface (this number will be used to calculate the weighting of the surface for the pose estimation later), the coordinates of polygons that form the vehicle's 3D model. The above information could allow us to achieve the following objectives: (1) recover the vehicle's 3D model; (2) calculate the portion of detected tags on each surface; (3) estimate the vehicle's orientation.

The following example gives a conceptual idea of the storage requirement for a typical passenger car. The car in Fig. 5 is divided into two segments: two square frustums. A 3D square frustum bounding box takes four parameters. Assume that a floating-point number is used for each parameter. It takes 8 bytes to represent a box. Then two segments take a total of 16 bytes for the 3D representation. Each 3D object also takes 6 bytes to specify the coordinates in the 3D space. As a result, two 3D objects consume another 12 bytes.

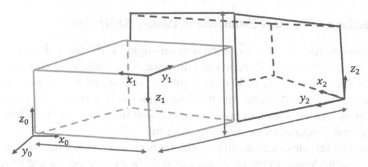

Fig. 5. All 3D objects share the same coordinate system.

There are many ways to represent a rotation for the orientation representation: 3 × 3 matrices, Euler angles, rotation vectors (axis/angle), quaternions, etc. Take the Euler angle as an example; it uses a sequence like (x, y, z) to specify the rotation of the x-axis, y-axis, and z-axis, respectively (see Fig. 5). Each object takes 6 bytes for orientation representation. That takes another 12 bytes. Based on the above rough calculations, the data storage requirement is about 50 bytes for the above example. This example also shows that the proposed algorithm can dynamically adjust the storage requirement for each vehicle.

4.2 Attach Multiple Tags to a Surface

Based on the previous studies, attaching multiple tags to an object can significantly improve the reliability and accuracy of detection [25]. In the ideal case, the tags should be attached to a vehicle's surfaces uniformly. However, this requirement is impractical in the design of vehicles. The strategy is to divide the usable area on each surface into grids to maximize the vehicle's visibility from different angles. A tag is attached to each grid. Depending on the design of a vehicle, the density of tags may be different on each surface. The surface's exposure is measured by counting the percentage of tags that have been detected to overcome the problem of heterogeneous density.

A vehicle's 3D model is divided into different separated surfaces. A total number of tags on each surface is stored in the tag. This number will be used to compare with the number of detectable tags in the scanning process. If the surface is 100% directly facing the detector in the detection range, the detector should be able to receive signals from all tags on this particular surface. Otherwise, the surface is not 100% facing the detector, or a part of the surface is blocked.

5 Detection of Invisible/Occluded Vehicles

The following information is available to detect an invisible or occluded vehicle: (1) the vehicle's 3D model; (2) the distance and direction to the detector; (3) its orientation to the detector. For point (1), the model can be retrieved from an RFID tag. For points (2) and (3), the following sub-sections elaborate on details of the proposed methods.

5.1 Direction and Distance Estimation of Passive RFID Tags

This section describes the details of the time-of-flight (TOF) method for estimating a group of passive RFID tags' direction and distance. Two readers are arranged horizontally at a vehicle's two front ends to perform the TOF-based localization. The above arrangement is to avoid collision with the front vehicles. However, the readers could be mounted at the vehicle's back to avoid collision with the rear vehicles. When multiple tags are present, readers can process a tag at a time.

For on-road vehicle detection, all the vehicles are on the roads which are on the same or similar ground levels. In the proposed method, only the direction and distance of a specific tag are required (not the position in 3D space). Therefore, 2D TOF estimation is adopted in this paper (see Fig. 6). The RFID tag emits a signal, which propagates through the air toward the two readers. The distance between two readers is k. Since the distance from the tag to the reader can be measured separately, therefore, the tag's direction to the vehicle can be estimated. The synchronization between two sensors in TOF measurements is a challenging issue; Medina et al. [18] proposed a TDMA-based method with compensation of the clock drifts and the random variation of the start time.

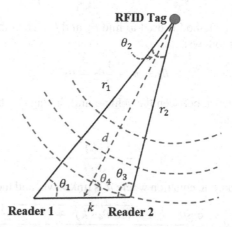

Fig. 6. Measurement of the distance and direction.

In the above figure, two readers and one tag are the three points of a triangle. θ_1, θ_2, and θ_3 are the inner angles of the triangle, respectively. r_1 and r_2 are the distances from the tag to readers 1 and 2, respectively. The goal is to find the distance (d) and direction (θ_4) between the vehicle and the tag. There are different ways [26] to measure the distance between two points, such as time-of-arrival (TOA), time-difference-of-arrival (TDOA), and received-signal-strength (RRS), etc. Although more complicated positioning systems (such as GPS) can be used in the vehicle, they still cannot fulfill all the requirements in this application. For instance, GPS signals are not available in a tunnel. A new method, time-of-flight (TOF), is proposed to address the ranging issue in RFID systems [27, 28]. It measures the time-of-flight of the signal traveling from the transmitter to the measuring unit and back. It performs ranging with a single antenna and could work with standard EPC Generation-2 tags. According to [27], at a distance of 40 m, their study achieved 1-m ranging accuracy outdoors. In another paper [28], their study achieved a ranging precision below 10 cm for a MIMO system at a bandwidth of 100 MHz indoors. In TOF, the distance between the reader and the tag can be estimated by dividing the total traveling time by 2.

$$\tau = \frac{t_1 - t_0}{2} \tag{4}$$

where t_0 and t_1 are the starting time and end time of the signal traveling. There is only one hop in this application, and the tag only gives a simple reply to the reader; the delay spent on routing and processing can be ignored. So, the distance between the reader and the tag can be given by $D = c\tau$, where c is the speed of light.

r_1, r_2 are measured by using TOF, and k is given. Then θ_1 can be expressed in the following equation by using the law of cosine:

$$\theta_1 = \cos^{-1}\left(\frac{r_1^2 + k^2 - r_2^2}{2kr_1}\right) \tag{5}$$

Similarly, the same method is used to find θ_2 and θ_3. Then the direction of arrival, θ_4, can be obtained as follows:

$$\theta_4 = \pi - \frac{1}{2}\theta_2 - \theta_3 \tag{6}$$

Moreover, the distance between the vehicle and the tag can be calculated by using the law of cosine again:

$$\cos\theta_4 = \frac{d^2 + \left(\frac{1}{2}k\right)^2 - r_2^2}{d \cdot k} \tag{7}$$

The above is a quadratic equation where d is unknown, and the answer is as follows:

$$d = \frac{\cos\theta_4 \cdot k \pm \sqrt{(\cos\theta_4 \cdot k)^2 - k^2 - 4r_2^2}}{2} \tag{8}$$

There are two solutions in (8), but one of them will be discarded based on the constraints. A reader can read multiple tags (say, n) at a time. θ_4 and d can be calculated for each tag. Thus, the direction of arrival and the distance between the vehicle and the tag could be estimated as the average values of detected tags:

$$[\theta, d]_{avg} = \left[\frac{1}{n}\sum_{i=1}^{n}\theta_4{}^i, \frac{1}{n}\sum_{i=1}^{n}d^i\right] \tag{9}$$

5.2 Estimation of Vehicle's Orientation

The relative positions of the detected ID tags can be used to estimate the vehicle's orientation. Those IDs are organized in hierarchies. An ID in each tag is formulated in the following format {Vehicle ID, Polygon ID, Surface ID, Tag serial no}. Based on the ID format, a tree structure is organized for fast searching.

Localization registration is to determine the orientation of a set of tags for the pre-built global 3D map. In the matching process, it is computationally expensive. Different approaches are proposed to accelerate the search [29]. The ordered tree comparison is suitable for localization registration [17]. The pre-built global 3D map could be organized as a tree (T_1) that consists of several polygons, and each polygon consists of several surfaces. Each surface has an attribute of the total number of tags attached. The detected tags could also be organized as an ordered tree (T_2) which consists of the detected polygons, and each polygon consists of the detected surface, and each surface consists of the detected tags. Therefore, the problem can be transformed into an ordered-tree comparison. A recent study proposed a linear-time algorithm comparing two similar ordered rooted trees with node labels. They have shown that an optimal mapping that uses at most k insertions or deletions could then be constructed in $O(nk^3)$ where n is the size of the trees [17].

6 Performance Evaluation

6.1 Experiment Configurations

The experiment aims to study the effectiveness of the proposed detection method when the vehicle is invisible or occluded. Due to the budget constraint, a small-scale experiment is implemented in this paper. The setup of the experiment consists of two major components: a reader and a box for simulating a car. These two components can be separated at a maximum distance of 5 m. The box was made based on a car's three dimensions, i.e., 0.46-m length, 0.18-m width, and 0.17-m height. The box has a total of 6 flat surfaces. Multiple tags are attached to each surface. The inner surfaces of the box are covered by aluminum foil, which is to simulate the metal body frame of a car. There is a distance of 4 cm between the two tags. The number of tags for Surface {1, 3, 4, 5} are {5, 12, 12, 12}, respectively (see Fig. 7).

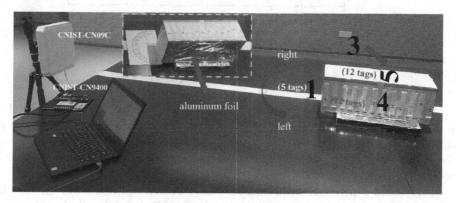

Fig. 7. Experiment Setup.

Before the experiment, a product code was written to each tag for identification. The format of the product code is specified in the previous sections. The antenna is fixed at a position; the box changes the position and orientation. The following is the hardware used:

- Reader: CNIST-CN9400 (model no.). The query interval is 25 ms for each antenna. There is a total of 8 antennas in each unit. A software development kit is installed on a notebook.
- Antenna: CNIST-CN09C (model no.)
- RFID Tag: Invengo RFID Tag (XC-TF8102-B-C43, model no.): working frequency: 860–960 MHz, EPC memory: 256 bits, and user memory: 512 bits.

6.2 Effectiveness of RFID Detection

This sub-section is to study the detection effectiveness when the vehicle is moving. The first experiment detects the vehicle's front surface at different distances. The goal is to count how many tags have been detected for each surface. Figure 8 shows the detectability at a specific angle (see Fig. 7) at different distances. The percentage of detected tags is counted at each distance.

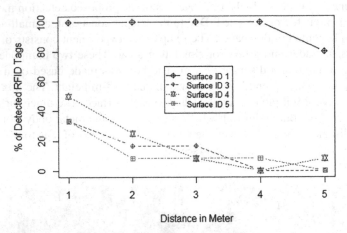

Fig. 8. Distance sensitivity experiment.

The results show that the front surface (Surface ID 1) can be detected successfully at different distances. When the distance increases to 5 m, the percentage of detected tags decreases to 80%, but the success rate is still at a high level. The experiment also shows that, at a short distance, the reader can detect tags from other surfaces which are not directly facing the detector.

The second experiment studies the sensitivity of detected tags when the vehicle changes its orientation. The box is fixed at a distance of 2 m, and then the box is slowly rotated from left to right for 90° (see Fig. 7).

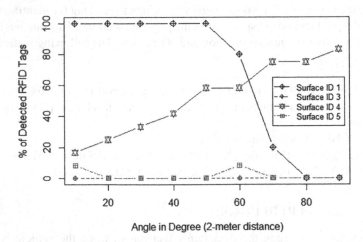

Fig. 9. Sensitivity on rotation.

In Fig. 9, the box is rotated 10° from left to the right at a time (that means Surface 1 will gradually flash out, and Surface 4 will gradually flash in) (see Fig. 7). The percentage of Surface 1 starts declining at 50°, and the reading drops to zero at 80°. However, for Surface 4, the percentage increases steadily when the vehicle rotates. When the degree reaches 90°, the level reaches the top. The changes in the percentages of those two surfaces show that the vehicle is rotating.

6.3 Effectiveness of Occluded Object Detection

This experiment is to study the effectiveness of vehicle detection when nearby objects occlude the vehicle. An object is arranged to slowly move from left to right in the front of the vehicle. The detected tags' percentage is measured in each movement when the occluded surface increases from 10% to 100% at 2 m. Surface 4 is used as a test case in the experiment; because it has the largest surface so that the most significant result could be observed. Figure 10 shows the detection sensitivity of the simulating box.

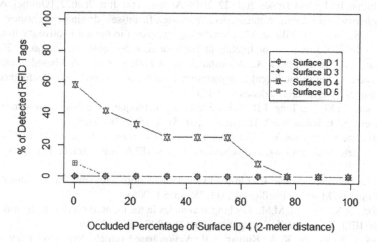

Fig. 10. Sensitivity on occlusion.

Figure 10 shows that the percentage of detected tags decreases proportionally to the percentage of the occluded surface. This experiment demonstrates the importance of using multiple tags.

7 Conclusion

We identify the challenges for vehicle detection under adverse driving conditions. This paper takes advantage of RFID technology to improve the vehicles' visibility and proposes a solution to overcome the weakness of vision-based detection methods. An algorithm is developed to convert a point cloud into a simple 3D model, which then is stored in tags for recovery of the vehicle's boundary. The proposed method has the following advantages: vehicle detection is not sensitive to light, weather, or occluded conditions;

vehicles can be detected at a relatively long distance; the implementation is relatively simple. Finally, a small-scale experiment is set up to evaluate the performance of the proposed method. The results have shown that, by using multiple passive RFID tags, the proposed method is able to detect a vehicle's orientation at various distances; distinguish whether a vehicle is rotating; recover the boundary for an occluded vehicle.

Acknowledgement. This work was supported in part by the Guangdong Higher Education Upgrading Plan (2021–2025) UICR400001–22 and UICR0400025–21.

References

1. Krisher, T.: Feds probe New York Tesla crash that killed man changing flat tire. The Associated Press, Sept. 3, 2021. Accessed on: Jun. 7, 2022, [Online]. Available: https://www.cnbc.com/2021/09/03/feds-probe-new-york-tesla-crash-that-killed-man-changing-flat-tire-.html
2. Chang, L., Dormehl, L.: 6 self-driving car crashes that tapped the brakes on the autonomous revolution. In: Digital Trends, June 22, 2018. Accessed on: Jun. 7, 2022, [Online]. Available: https://www.digitaltrends.com/cool-tech/most-significant-self-driving-car-crashes/
3. Gilroy, S., Jones, E., Glavin, M.: Overcoming occlusion in the automotive environment - a review. IEEE Transactions on Intelligent Transportation Systems, vol. 22, no. 1 (2021)
4. Tourani, A., Shahbahrami, A., Akoushideh, A.: Challenges of video-based vehicle detection and tracking in intelligent transportation systems. In: International Conference on Soft Computing, Yogyakarta, Indonesia (2017)
5. Mukhtar, A., Xia, L., Tang, T.B.: Vehicle detection techniques for collision avoidance systems: a review. IEEE Trans. Intell. Transp. Syst. **16**(5), 2318–2338 (2015)
6. Sivaraman, S., Trivedi, M. M.: Looking at vehicles on the road: a survey of vision-based vehicle detection, tracking, and behavior analysis. IEEE Trans. Intell. Transp. Syst. **14**(4), 1773–1795 (2013)
7. Sun, Z., Bebis, G., Miller, R.: On-road vehicle detection: a review. Transactions on Pattern Analysis and Machine Intelligence, vol. 28, no. 5 (2006)
8. Satzoda, R.K., Trivedi, M.M.: Looking at vehicles in the night: detection & dynamics of rear lights. IEEE Trans. Intell. Transp. Syst. **20**(12), 4297–4307 (2019)
9. David, S. A., Kumar, K. A., Kumar, S. R.: Vision-based vehicle detection survey. iJES, vol. 4, issue 1 (2016)
10. Du, S., Zhang, P., Zhang, B., Xu, H.: Weak and occluded vehicle detection in complex infrared environment based on improved YOLOv4. IEEE Access, vol. 9 (2021)
11. Daily RFID, "100 meters reading range powerful RFID reader," Daily RFID Co. Limited, July 5, 2017. Accessed on: Jun. 7, 2022, [Online]. Available: https://www.rfid-in-china.com/news-detail-1511.html
12. Dima, C.: Passive RFID using UHF delivers long-range benefits in the IoT. Avnet Silica, June 20, 2018. Accessed on: Jun. 7, 2022, [Online]. Available: https://www.avnet.com/wps/portal/silica/resources/article/ passive-rfid-using-uhf-delivers-long-range-benefits-in-the-iot/
13. Kitayoshi, H., Sawaya, K.: Long range passive RFID-tag for sensor networks. In: 2005 IEEE 62nd Vehicular Technology Conference, Dallas (2005)
14. Hester, J., Tentzeris, E. M., Eid, A.: Fully passive, long-range radio-frequency identification (RFID) via 5G. Georgia Institute of Technology. Accessed on: Jun. 7, 2022, [Online]. Available: https://licensing.research.gatech.edu/pdf/1932
15. Wang, J., Zhang, J., Saha, R.: Pushing the range limits of commercial passive RFIDs. In: The 6th USENIX Symposium on Networked Systems Design and Implementation, Boston (2019)

16. Reichardt, L., Adamiuk, G., Jereczek, G., Zwick, T.: Car-to-infrastructure communication using chip-less, passive RFID tags. In: IEEE Antennas and Propagation Society International Symposium, Toronto, Canada (2010)
17. Touzet, H.: Comparing similar ordered trees in linear-time. Journal of Discrete Algorithms 5(4), 696–705 (2007)
18. Medina, C., Segura, J. C., Torre, A. D. L.: Accurate time synchronization of ultrasonic TOF measurements in IEEE 802.15.4 based wireless sensor networks. Ad Hoc Networks, vol. 11, 442–452 (2013)
19. Ahuja, S., Potti, P.: An introduction to RFID technology. Commun. Netw. 2(03), 183–186 (2010)
20. Che, E., Jung, J., Olsen, M. J.: Object recognition, segmentation, and classification of mobile laser scanning point clouds: a state of the art review. Sensors (Basel), vol. 19(4) (2019)
21. Grilli, E., Menna, F., Remondino, F.: A review of point clouds segmentation and classification algorithms. International Archives of the Photogrammetry, Remote Sensing and Spatial Information Sciences, vol. XLII-2/W3, 339–344 (2017)
22. Wu, L.S., Wang, G.L., Hu, Y.: Iterative closest point registration for fast point feature histogram features of a volume density optimization algorithm. Measurement and Control 53(1–2), 29–39 (2020)
23. Zhang, W., Qi, C.: Pose estimation by key points registration in point cloud. In: The 3rd International Symposium on Autonomous Systems, Shanghai, China (2019)
24. Zhang, Y., Amin, M. G., Kaushik, S.: Localization and tracking of passive RFID tags based on direction estimation. International Journal of Antennas and Propagation (2007)
25. Bolotnyy, L., Krize, S., Robins, G.: The practicality of multi-tag RFID systems. In: Proceedings of the 1st International Workshop on RFID Technology - Concepts, Applications, Challenges, Funchal, Portugal (2007)
26. Beham, A. R.: A review on RFID localization techniques for IoT. International Journal for Scientific Research & Development, vol. 4, issue 10 (2016)
27. Lanzisera, S., Zats, D., Pister, K.S.J.: Radio frequency time-of-flight distance measurement for low-cost wireless sensor localization. IEEE Sens. J. 11(3), 837–845 (2011)
28. Hinteregger, S., Kulmer, J., Goller, M., Galler, F., Arthaber, H., Witrisal, K.: UHF-RFID backscatter channel analysis for accurate wideband ranging. In: IEEE RFID 2017, Phoenix, the United States (2017)
29. Geppert, M., Liu, P., Cui, Z., Pollefeys, M., Sattler, T.: Efficient 2D-3D matching for multi-camera visual localization. In: The 2019 International Conference on Robotics and Automation, Montreal (2019)

Predictive Energy Management for Battery Electric Vehicles with Hybrid Models

Yu-Wen Huang[1,2], Christian Prehofer[1], William Lindskog[1(✉)], Ron Puts[1], Pietro Mosca[1], and Göran Kauermann[2]

[1] DENSO Automotive, Eching, Germany
yu.huang@campus.lmu.de, {c.prehofer,w.lindskog,
r.puts}@eu.denso.com, p.mosca@electravehicles.com
[2] LMU München, Munich, Germany
goeran.kauermann@stat.uni-muenchen.de

Abstract. This paper addresses the problem of predicting the energy consumption for the drivers of Battery electric vehicles (BEVs). Several external factors (e.g., weather) are shown to have huge impacts on the energy consumption of a vehicle besides the vehicle or powertrain dynamics. Thus, it is challenging to take all of those influencing variables into consideration. The proposed approach is based on a hybrid model which improves the prediction accuracy of energy consumption of BEVs. The novelty of this approach is to combine a physics-based simulation model, which captures the basic vehicle and powertrain dynamics, with a data-driven model. The latter accounts for other external influencing factors neglected by the physical simulation model, using machine learning techniques, such as generalized additive mixed models, random forests and boosting. The hybrid modeling method is evaluated with a real data set from TUM and the hybrid models were shown that decrease the average prediction error from 40% of the pure physics model to 10%.

Keywords: Hybrid modeling · Energy consumption · Battery electric vehicles · Statistical Modelling

1 Introduction

Battery Electric Vehicles (BEVs) are fully electric vehicles with rechargeable batteries with the aim to reduce energy consumption and CO_2 emissions [12]. Compared to vehicles with combustion engines, the heating needed to be provided by electrical energy, which can account for more than 30% of the overall energy consumed [23]. In addition, the battery capacity and efficiency are heavily affected by ambient temperature and external environmental conditions. All of the reasons mentioned above lead to the problem of "range anxiety", which is the concern from the drivers that the car will not have enough energy to reach its final destination or the next recharging station. This is a significant barrier to market acceptance of battery electric vehicles (BEVs) [19].

© ICST Institute for Computer Sciences, Social Informatics and Telecommunications Engineering 2023
Published by Springer Nature Switzerland AG 2023. All Rights Reserved
A. L. Martins et al. (Eds.): INTSYS 2022, LNICST 486, pp. 182–196, 2023.
https://doi.org/10.1007/978-3-031-30855-0_13

The purpose of this paper is to utilize a hybrid modeling approach to improve the accuracy of energy consumption prediction. The novelty of this approach consists is the combination of a physics-based model, to capture the basic vehicle and powertrain dynamic, with a data-driven model (e.g., generalized additive mixed models), to account for the other potentially influencing factors that are not covered by the physics-based simulation model.

Evaluation of the results is carried out using leave-one-out cross-validation. The data set used is from TU München [23], which provides detailed trips' information of 72 trips driving around Munich in various ambient driving conditions.

The contribution of the paper is twofold. First, the energy consumption prediction accuracy is improved despite the limited available trips in the data set and unknown number of drivers. Second, the proposed approach separates the vehicle specifics from the external influencing factors, which makes it easier to adapt the model to different vehicle, or to drivers with different driving behaviors.

2 Background and Approach

2.1 Prediction of Energy Consumption

As the available battery capacity and energy consumption of the vehicle are the main influencing factors on the driving range of a BEV, a good deal of effort has been devoted to develop energy consumption estimation models for battery electric vehicles (e.g., [5, 9]). Many influencing factors are found that have impact on the energy consumption of BEVs, such as vehicle characteristics, vehicle speed, road elevation, acceleration, etc. These variables fluctuate greatly in real life, making energy consumption prediction an even more complex problem.

In terms of physics-based simulation methodology, either Newton's Laws (analytical model) are applied to the vehicle as a point-mass, or detailed physical processes are incorporated for each module in an electric vehicle [25]. A number of analytical models were proposed in the literature, for instance, [7] developed a simulation model, for energy estimation and route planning for a Nissan Leaf. [9] developed four simulation models for a city electric bus and validated the models using the data collected from a bus prototype. The drawback of these purely physics-based models is that they don't consider heating and air conditioning in the energy computation, which can have huge impact on the overall consumption [23].

In contrast to physics-based simulation models, a number of purely data-driven models (mostly regression models) were proposed for the energy consumption estimation of BEVs. For instance, [5] took into account many aspects (such as the battery's State of Charge (SOC), speed, weather data, road type, and driver profile) and gathered data from a BEV named Pure Mobility Buddy 09. The authors presented a data mining method for predicting a BEV's driving range that employs regression inside. [3] developed a cascade neural network (NN) regression model for energy consumption prediction.

A recent paper [18] analyzed the same BEV tracking data in VED data set [16] to forecast SOC using deep-learning models, such as LSTM, and Deep Neural Networks. Yet this work does not consider the heating and AC energy.

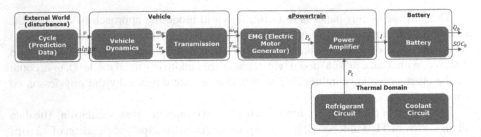

Fig. 1. Schematic view of utilized physic-based simulation model.

Overall, data-driven models also come with shortcomings. For example, large amounts of data are required, and being more sensitive to the settings of hyper-parameters. Even though the prediction accuracy of the models can be high under certain circumstances, the result is not promising if a trip's characteristics are not seen in the training data set. In addition, the results are not physically justifiable due to the lack of interpretability of the black box models.

Therefore, a combination of the two above approaches is proposed. The goal of this work is to show that the proposed method, combining a physical model with a data-driven machine learning model, can be applied successfully and adapted to different driving behaviors and driving conditions.

2.2 Hybrid Modeling for Energy Consumption Prediction

Figure 1 shows a schematic view of the physical model utilized physical model in this paper, following existing work as in [8]. The physics-based simulation model is implemented in MATLAB [15] containing a Battery Electric Vehicle (BEV) model and its components such as motor, high voltage battery, and vehicle dynamics. Regenerative braking or recuperation is the recovery of kinetic energy during braking. It is assumed to be 50% as the data set contains more trips with higher ambient temperature without further tuning.

Figure 2 illustrates the proposed energy consumption prediction method for a specific trip. The physical model takes time, speed, and road inclination from the data as inputs, and calculates parameters containing information related to the battery of the vehicle, such as battery temperature, battery current, and battery voltage based on theories in physics. The whole physics simulation process is done in MATLAB.

For the statistical corrective models to account for the factors not considered by the physical model, longitudinal data models are used. Different methods have been proposed to handle longitudinal data effectively (thus eliminating the problem of dependence between temporal data), for example mixed-effects model [6]. Each mixed model has two parts - fixed effects that are identical for the entire population and random effects which relate to each of the hierarchical levels. Fixed effects in our case describe general input variables e.g. temperature and time (duration of driving).

Random effects, on the other hand, explain the randomness and heterogeneity as a result of known and unknown factors. In this work, this relates to trip specific heterogeneity which is not captured by the fixed effects. These are driver specific effects

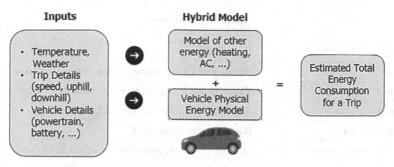

Fig. 2. Energy prediction for a trip utilizing proposed hybrid model.

relating to both driving style and personal comfort temperature in the vehicle cabin. Mixed-effects models use local data to generate one broad flexible model for a certain area, explaining a significant portion of the population model's random variability [1]. In addition, this paper also utilized random forests and boosting, which are widely used in machine learning field for the comparison purpose.

The predictive capabilities of the models are evaluated using leave-one-out cross-validation. That is to say, there are a total of n iterations, where n is the number of the trips in the data set. For every iteration, there is only one testing trip, the remaining are all training data. The training data is used to train the statistical corrective models while the single testing trip is used to do an overall comprehensive evaluation. The evaluation process will repeat n times as there are n trips in the data set, and the calculation results will be averaged.

2.3   Data Set

The TUM data set [23] contains 72 real driving excursions in Munich. The variables in the data are recorded once every 0.1 s using a 2014 BMW i3 (60 Ah) as the testing vehicle. Each trip has time-series data related to environmental signals (temperature, elevation, etc.), vehicle signals (speed, throttle), battery signals (voltage, current, temperature, SoC), heating circuit signals (indoor temperature, heating power) and a timestamp [22]. Table 1 explains the relevant columns available in the TUM data set.

Table 1. Variable descriptions for TUM data set.

Variable	Description
Time	Timestamp for each record in s
Trip.id	Trip identifier
Seasonality	The trip is recorded in summer or winter

(*continued*)

Table 1. (*continued*)

Variable	Description
Weather	Weather when the trip was recording, e.g., cloudy
Velocity	The magnitude of instantaneous velocity in km/h
Elevation	The vehicle's height above sea level in m
Battery temperature	Battery temperature in ∘C
Requested heating power	Heating power requested by the driver in kW
Air conditioner power	Air conditioner power used in kW
Ambient temperature	Outside temperature in ∘C
Battery current	Battery current in A
Battery voltage	Battery voltage in V

3 Evaluation and Results

This section assesses the results of proposed method quantitatively and the overall performance is discussed. The evaluation has been carried out on an ASUS VivoBook, Intel Core i7-8565U, 4 cores, 16 GB RAM. The evaluation process can be summarized below:

1. Calculate physical model energy consumption based on battery's current and voltage simulation results, and add the values as additional column to the trips in the data set.
2. Subtract the real energy consumption by the physical model's predictions (from Step 1), which are named physical model's residuals.
3. Build data-driven models to predict the physical model's residuals calculated.
4. Add the estimated physical model's residuals from the data-driven models to the physical model's predictions from Step 1.

To account for different scales, absolute percentage error is utilized for the cumulative values of the energy consumption at time point T of a trip (i.e., the end time of a trip), and is defined as:

$$\text{APE}_T = \left| \frac{y_T - f_T}{y_T} \right| \tag{1}$$

where y_T is the real value and f_T is the forecast value at time T.

3.1 Generalized Additive Mixed Models (GAMMs)

Generalized additive models are an extension of regression models that allow effects of input variables to be smooth. For generalized additive mixed models, which includes mixed effects allows one to account for unobserved heterogeneity [4], e.g., due to individual driving behavior. Suppose that observations of the ith of n units consist of an outcome variable y_i and p covariates $x_i = (1, x_{i1},..., x_{ip})^T$ associated with fixed effects and a $q \times 1$ vector of covariates z_i associated with random effects. Given a $q \times 1$ vector b of random effects, the observations y_i are assumed to be conditionally independent with means $\mathbb{E}(y_i|b) = \mu_i^b$ and variances $\text{var}(y_i|b) = \phi m_i^{-1} \upsilon(\mu_i^b)$, where $\upsilon(\cdot)$ is a specified variance function, m_i is a prior weight (e.g., a binomial denominator) and ϕ is a scale parameter, and follow a generalized additive mixed model

$$g(\mu_i^b) = \beta_0 + f_1(x_{i1}) + ... + f_p(x_{ip}) + z_i^T b \tag{2}$$

where $g(\cdot)$ is a monotonic differentiable link function, $f_j(\cdot)$ is a centred twice-differentiable smooth function, the random effects b are assumed to be distributed as $\mathcal{N}\{0, D(\theta)\}$ and θ is a $c \times 1$ vector of variance components [14].

The estimates that are based on data that show clear violations of key assumptions for GAMM should be treated with caution, though few papers (e.g., [20]) state that mixed model estimates were usually robust to violations of those assumptions (e.g., normality of random effects).

As the data does contain outliers, the distribution of the response (i.e., physical model's residuals) heavily-tailed. The Student's t family for heavy-tailed data is applied. The density of the Student's t family is given by:

$$f(y_i) = \frac{\Gamma((\nu + 1)/2)}{\Gamma(\nu/2)} \frac{1}{\sqrt{\nu\pi\sigma}} \left(1 + \frac{1}{\nu}\left(\frac{y_i - g(\eta_i)}{\sigma}\right)^2\right)^{-(\nu+1)/2} \tag{3}$$

The model diagnosis for the GAMM with Student's t family fitted on the TUM data set is shown in Fig. 3. The Q-Q plot indicates that the Student's t family is suitable for the TUM data set as the model's residuals from the GAMM match the theoretical quantiles (i.e., the red line). The estimated smooth effects from the GAMM model fit are presented in Fig. 4. The last figure indicates the random effect "Trip Id" of the trips, and they are plotted against Gaussian quantiles. In mixed-effects models, one doesn't directly estimate random effects but assumes they are normally distributed with mean of 0. Therefore, the random effects are checked against Gaussian quantiles for the normally distributed assumption.

The summary of the GAMM model with Student's t family fitted on the TUM data set is shown in Table 2. For the parametric terms of the model, although the p-values indicate that some of the predictors are not significant in terms of assuming threshold of 0.05, those predictors are still kept in the model as the main goal of the paper is to predict the energy consumption of a BEV instead of making explanation out of input variables (it makes little sense to use p-values to determine the variables in a model that is being used for prediction [21]). For the smooth terms of the model, such as time, the coefficient is not printed, as each smooth has several coefficients, one for each basis function. The Effective Degree of Freedom (EDF) represents the complexity of the smooth fit. EDF of 1 is equivalent to a straight line, EDF of 2 is equivalent to a quadratic curve, and so on. With higher EDF describing more wiggly curves.

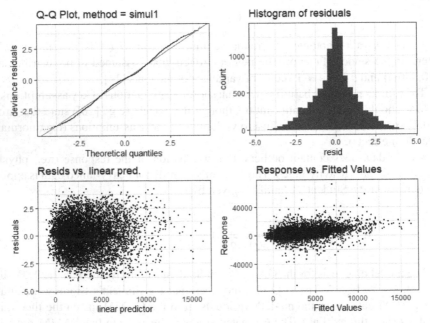

Fig. 3. Model diagnosis for GAMM with Student's t family fitted on TUM data set.

The common way to evaluate a predictive model is by looking at the average error rate from all of the iterations of cross-validation, but it is still interesting to know how the model performs on each iteration. Figure 5 shows the overall error distribution of all the iterations from the leave-one-trip-out cross-validation for the GAMM with Student's t family fitted on the TUM data set.

3.2 Random Forest

For fitting Random Forest on longitudinal data, small modification on the normal random forest algorithm is proposed by [11] utilizing subject-level bootstrapping, which enables the effective use of all data samples and allows for unequal contribution from the subjects.

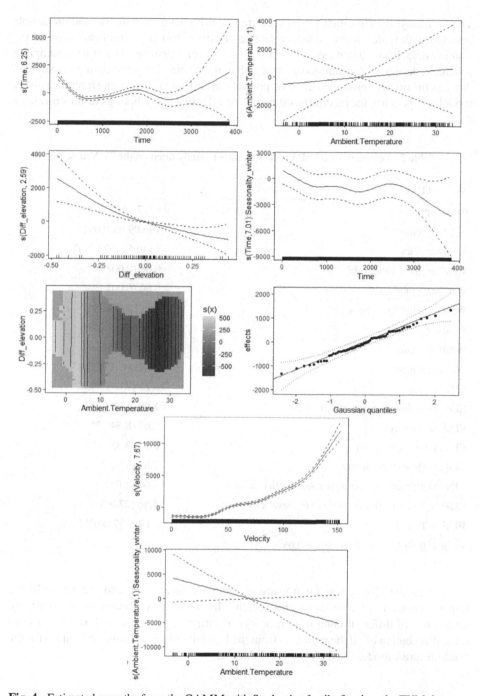

Fig. 4. Estimated smooths from the GAMM with Student's t family fitted on the TUM data set.

That is to say, the algorithm grows each tree on a bootstrap sample (a random sample selected with replacement) at the subject level rather than at the replicate level of the training data. It has advantages for the analysis of longitudinal data because the sampling scheme is designed to accommodate data with multiple measurements for a given subject. Also, as the primary goal of the thesis is prediction, and not in performing inference on the model components, the method has shown to be effective in predicting cluster-correlated data.

Table 2. Summary of GAMM with Student's t family fitted on the TUM data set.

Model TUM	
(Intercept)	1537.44 (938.99)
Weather_cloudy	796.09 (649.09)
Weather_dark	1430.53 (723.35)*
Weather_dark_little_rainy	0.00 (0.00)
Weather_rainy	0.00 (0.00)
Weather_slightly_cloudy	386.27 (582.56)
Weather_sunny	457.96 (573.88)
Weather_sunrise	754.49 (751.99)
Weather_sunset	2322.86 (998.28)*
EDF: s(Time)	6.25 (7.06)***
EDF: s(Ambient.Temperature)	1.00 (1.00)
EDF: s(Velocity)	7.67 (8.54)***
EDF: s(Diff_elevation)	2.59 (3.35)***
EDF: s(Time):Seasonality_winter	7.01 (7.92)***
EDF: s(Ambient.Temperature):Seasonality_winter	1.00 (1.00)
EDF: s(Ambient.Temperature,Diff_elevation)	4.86 (27.00)
EDF: s(Trip.id)	44.40 (57.00)***

$***p < 0.001; **p < 0.01; *p < 0.05$

The random forest was fitted using the package htree in R, and the tuning of the hyper-parameters is done using grid search which attempts to compute the optimum values out of different combination of hyper-parameters. Figure 6 shows the overall error distribution of all the iterations from the leave-one-trip-out cross-validation for the random forest model fitted on the TUM data set.

3.3 Boosting

The boosting model utilized is using traditional gradient boosting method to form a marginal model as Generalized Estimating Equation (GEE). GEE, proposed by [13], is a general statistical approach to fit a marginal model for clustered data analysis. Whereas the mixed-effect model is an individual-level approach by adopting random effects to capture the correlation between the observations of the same subject [2], GEE is a population-level approach based on a quasi-likelihood function and provides the population-averaged estimates of the parameters [24]. In this method, the correlation between measurements is modeled by assuming a working correlation matrix. The estimations from the GEE are broadly valid estimates that approach the correct value with increasing sample size regardless of the choice of correlation model [17].

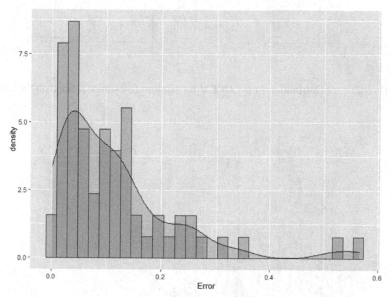

Fig. 5. Overall error distribution from LOOCV for GAMM with Student's t family fitted on the TUM data set.

That is to say, if F_k is the model at the kth boosting iteration, a regression tree is fit to the residuals $r_{ij} = y_{ij} - F_k(x_{ij})$ for $i = 1, ..., n$ and $j = 1, ..., n_i$ (n subjects and ith subject observed at n_i time points). If T_{k+1} denotes this regression tree, then the model is updated by $F_{k+1} = F_k + T_{k+1}$, and the procedure is repeated. Determining the number of boosting iterations is done by using cross-validation with a leave-out-subject approach.

Figure 7 shows the overall error distribution of all the iterations from the leave-one-out cross-validation for the boosting model fitted on the TUM data set.

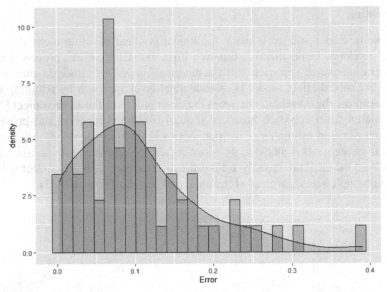

Fig. 6. Overall error distribution from LOOCV for random forest model fitted on the TUM data set.

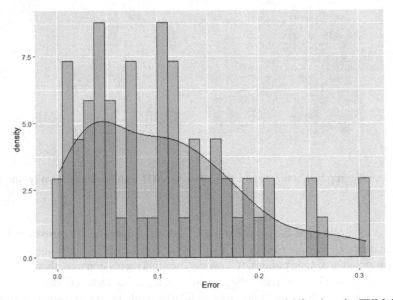

Fig. 7. Overall error distribution from LOOCV for boosting model fitted on the TUM data set.

3.4 Overall Comparison

The box plot for the errors from the models fitted on the TUM data set using Leave-one-out Cross-validation is shown in Fig. 8. Phy_Error is the error from the physics-based simulation without utilizing hybrid modeling approach, Gamm_Error is the error from the GAMM with Student's t family hybrid modeling model, rf_Error is the error from the random forest hybrid modeling model and tb_Error is the error from the boosting hybrid modeling model. The average error rate for the models is shown in Table 3.

From the prediction accuracy perspective, three statistical corrective models don't show a large difference from each other. However, GAMMs have a longer running time compared to the others. In general, the shorter the running time, the better the model would be, as for the practical usage purpose, the drivers are typically not willing to wait for a long time to get a prediction of the cumulative energy consumption at the final destination. Therefore, ensemble learning models would be more preferable in this use case. GAMMs, on the other hand, are useful for observing the effects of each predictor.

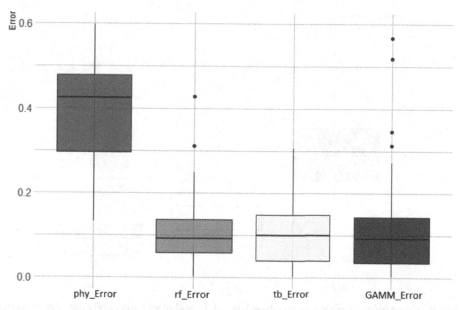

Fig. 8. Comparisons of the models fitted on the TUM data set.

Table 3. Average error rate from LOOCV for the models fitted on the TUM data set.

Model	Average error
Purely Physics-based model	0.379
GAMM with Student's t family	0.115
Random forest	0.106
Boosting	0.103

In addition, as the boosting model has the best overall performance. The purely data-driven approach was constructed as a benchmark against hybrid modeling method utilizing boosting model. The same set of inputs are used to forecast real energy consumption instead of ResidualPhy. The comparison of the error rate between the purely physics-based model's predictions, hybrid model using boosting model's predictions and purely data-driven boosting model's predictions is shown in Fig. 9. Phy_Error is the error from the purely physics based model without any statistical corrective models, tb_without_Error is the error from the purely data-driven approach using boosting model and tb_Error is the error from the hybrid model using boosting, respectively. The purely physics-based model has the highest error, hybrid modeling approach has the lowest error among the three models, and the purely data-driven model has the highest variability compared to the other two, the maximum error rate is almost 0.8 (i.e., 80%), which is really high in the real world.

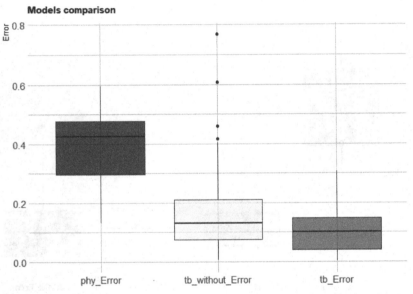

Fig. 9. Comparison of purely physics-based model, hybrid model and purely data-driven model fitted on the TUM data set.

Although the data set comes with restrictions and limitations (e.g., unknown number of drivers, limited sample size issue, only one testing vehicle), the proposed hybrid modeling approach has shown to be very effective to a certain extent with the improvement of over 90% of the total trips' energy consumption prediction accuracy utilizing either one of the corrective models. Despite the fact that the physics-based simulation model shows deviations to reality, it was corrected by the statistical models using less data than required by purely data-driven approaches. The idea of combining simplified physics-based models and data-driven models to achieve better prediction accuracy is therefore worth further investigation based on different scenarios.

4 Conclusions

Given the current deluge of sensor data and advances in statistical models or machine learning methods, the merging of principles from machine learning and physics will play an invaluable role in the future of scientific modeling to address the range anxiety of BEVs and physical modeling problems facing society. In this paper, a physics-based model, representing a rather simple but very efficient model, has been successfully combined with corrective models into a hybrid prediction model to enhance its prediction capability under certain circumstances. While the physics-based model part captures what is actually known about the BEV, the statistical corrective models are responsible for describing the vehicle's excluded features and possible deviations from reality due to the simplified assumptions of the BEV model.

On a realistic, challenging and small data set with a range of temperature and driving styles, the proposed method has shown to be able to achieve roughly 10% average prediction error utilizing either one of the hybrid model. Other works report same accuracy, e.g. [18], however do not consider the effect of AC or heating at all, or another research on energy estimation [10] also reports about 12% error, however does not focus on e-vehicles where cabin (and battery) conditioning has a much stronger effect as it requires extra energy from the battery.

Furthermore, the benefit of the proposed approach is the separation of the effect of powertrain dynamic and the other external factors, which makes it easier to apply trained model from the data obtained from one vehicle to another without sacrificing the prediction accuracy. Also, it can handle cases which are less frequently seen, but where the physical model has a strong effect, e.g. long downhill trips or cold/hot battery temperature.

Acknowledgments. This work was partly supported by the TRANSACT project. TRANSACT (https://transact-ecsel.eu/) has received funding from the Electronic Component Systems for European Leadership Joint Under-taking under grant agreement no. 101007260. This joint undertaking receives support from the European Union's Horizon 2020 research and innovation programme and Austria, Belgium, Denmark, Finland, Germany, Poland, Netherlands, Norway, and Spain.

References

1. Adamec, Z., Adolt, R., Drápela, K., Závodský, J.: Evaluation of different calibration approaches for merchantable volume predictions of Norway spruce using nonlinear mixed effects model. Forests **10**(12), 1104 (2019)
2. Crowder, M.: On the use of a working correlation matrix in using generalised linear models for repeated measures. Biometrika **82**(2), 407–410 (1995)
3. De Cauwer, C., Verbeke, W., Coosemans, T., Faid, S., Van Mierlo, J.: A data-driven method for energy consumption prediction and energy-efficient routing of electric vehicles in real-world conditions. Energies **10**(5), 608 (2017)
4. Everitt, B., Rabe-Hesketh, S.: Generalized additive models. In: Analyzing Medical Data Using S-PLUS. Statistics for Biology and Health, pp. 291–303. Springer, New York (2001). https://doi.org/10.1007/978-1-4757-3285-6_14

5. Ferreira, J.C., Monteiro, V.D.F., Afonso, J.L.: Data mining approach for range prediction of electric vehicle (2012)
6. Fitzmaurice, G.M., Laird, N.M., Ware, J.H.: Applied Longitudinal Analysis, vol. 998. Wiley, New Jersey (2012)
7. Genikomsakis, K.N., Mitrentsis, G.: A computationally efficient simulation model for estimating energy consumption of electric vehicles in the context of route planning applications. Transp. Res. D: Transp. Environ. **50**, 98–118 (2017)
8. Guzzella, L., Sciarretta, A., et al.: Vehicle propulsion systems, vol. 1. Springer, Heidelberg (2007). https://doi.org/10.1007/978-3-642-35913-2
9. Halmeaho, T., et al.: Experimental validation of electric bus powertrain model under city driving cycles. IET Electr. Syst. Transp. **7**(1), 74–83 (2017)
10. Holden, J., Wood, E.W., Zhu, L., Gonder, J.D., Tian, Y.: Development of a trip energy estimation model using real-world global positioning system driving data. Tech. rep., National Renewable Energy Lab. (NREL), Golden, CO (United States) (2017)
11. Karpievitch, Y.V., Hill, E.G., Leclerc, A.P., Dabney, A.R., Almeida, J.S.: An introspective comparison of random forest-based classifiers for the analysis of cluster-correlated data by way of RF++. PLoS ONE **4**(9), e7087 (2009)
12. Kongklaew, C., et al.: Barriers to electric vehicle adoption in Thailand. Sustainability **13**(22), 12839 (2021)
13. Liang, K.Y., Zeger, S.L.: Longitudinal data analysis using generalized linear models. Biometrika **73**(1), 13–22 (1986)
14. Lin, X., Zhang, D.: Inference in generalized additive mixed models by using smoothing splines. J. R. Stat. Soc., B: Stat. Methodol. **61**(2), 381–400 (1999)
15. The Mathworks, Inc., Natick, Massachusetts: MATLAB version 9.3.0.713579 (R2017b) (2017)
16. Oh, G., Leblanc, D.J., Peng, H.: Vehicle energy dataset (VED), a large-scale dataset for vehicle energy consumption research. IEEE Trans. Intell. Transp. Syst. **23**(4), 3302–3312 (2022). https://doi.org/10.1109/TITS.2020.3035596
17. Overall, J.E., Tonidandel, S.: Robustness of generalized estimating equation (GEE) tests of significance against misspecification of the error structure model. Biometrical J. **46**(2), 203–213 (2004)
18. Petkevicius, L., Saltenis, S., Civilis, A., Torp, K.: Probabilistic deep learning for electric-vehicle energy-use prediction. In: 17th International Symposium on Spatial and Temporal Databases, pp. 85–95 (2021)
19. Pevec, D., Babic, J., Carvalho, A., Ghiassi-Farrokhfal, Y., Ketter, W., Podobnik, V.: Electric vehicle range anxiety: an obstacle for the personal transportation (r)evolution? In: 2019 4th International Conference on Smart and Sustainable Technologies (SpliTech), pp. 1–8. IEEE (2019)
20. Schielzeth, H., et al.: Robustness of linear mixed-effects models to violations of distributional assumptions. Methods Ecol. Evol. **11**(9), 1141–1152 (2020)
21. Shmueli, G.: To explain or to predict? Stat. Sci. **25**(3), 289–310 (2010)
22. Steinstraeter, M., Buberger, J., Trifonov, D.: Battery and heating data in real driving cycles (2020). https://doi.org/10.21227/6jr9-5235
23. Steinstraeter, M., Heinrich, T., Lienkamp, M.: Effect of low temperature on electric vehicle range. World Electr. Veh. J. **12**(3), 115 (2021)
24. Wedderburn, R.W.: Quasi-likelihood functions, generalized linear models, and the Gauss—Newton method. Biometrika **61**(3), 439–447 (1974)
25. Wu, G., Ye, F., Hao, P., Esaid, D., Boriboonsomsin, K., Barth, M.J.: Deep learning-based eco-driving system for battery electric vehicles (2019)

Vehicle Routing Problem
for an Integrated Electric Vehicles
and Drones System

Setyo Tri Windras Mara(✉), Saber Elsayed, Daryl Essam, and Ruhul Sarker

School of Engineering and Information Technology, University of New South Wales,
Canberra, ACT 2600, Australia
{s.windras_mara,d.essam,r.sarker}@adfa.edu.au, s.elsayed@unsw.edu.au

Abstract. This study explores a new research direction on the cooperation between electric vehicles (EVs) and drones in last-mile logistics in the form of *electric vehicle routing problem with drones* (E-VRPD). The primary objective of E-VRPD is to find an optimal vehicle tour to minimize the total completion time to deliver parcels to a set of customer nodes using a set of EVs, each equipped with a single drone. Due to the importance of such problems and the lack of existing techniques, in this work, we develop a sequential decomposition algorithm with an improvement phase to solve E-VRPD. This algorithm involves the development of a mathematical formulation for inserting drone sorties into an EV tour, leading to a *matheuristic* algorithm. The proposed method is evaluated on a set of instances involving up to 40 customers and 7 recharging nodes, with the experimental results showing the effectiveness and relevancy of E-VRPD.

Keywords: Electric vehicle routing problem · Last-mile logistics · Drones · Decomposition · Matheuristic

1   Introduction

The ease of getting desired items without having to go out of your house has led to the continuous growth of home deliveries in recent years. However, this rising number of customer home deliveries posses a hidden drawback for both firms and society. Although it sounds very convenient, direct deliveries to customer's houses may be costly, highly inefficient, and not environmental-friendly [1]. The inefficiency issue in last-mile logistics has been long known by researchers and practitioners. During these golden years of the E-commerce business, where the majority of parcels delivered are small-size packages [2], this issue has become more relevant than ever.

Several innovations have emerged as potential solutions in response to this particular challenge. These innovative ideas range from implementing novel delivery concepts, such as parcel lockers, to using new transportation technologies [1]. Accordingly, in this study, we aim to explore the cooperation of these innovations in last-mile logistics, particularly between electric vehicles (EVs) and drones.

© ICST Institute for Computer Sciences, Social Informatics and Telecommunications Engineering 2023
Published by Springer Nature Switzerland AG 2023. All Rights Reserved
A. L. Martins et al. (Eds.): INTSYS 2022, LNICST 486, pp. 197–214, 2023.
https://doi.org/10.1007/978-3-031-30855-0_14

Here, this cooperation is referred to as *electric vehicle routing problem with drones* (E-VRPD), where a firm must deliver parcels to a set of customer nodes using a set of EVs, each equipped with a single drone. Due to the range limitation of EVs, a set of recharging stations is available to recharge the battery of EVs, and the main purpose of E-VRPD is to find optimal vehicle tours to minimize the total completion time of delivery tasks.

E-VRPD can be seen as an extension of vehicle routing problem with drones (VRPD) [3] and electric vehicle routing problem (E-VRP) [4]. Compared to VRPD, E-VRPD considers the deployment of EVs instead of traditional internal combustion engine vehicles (ICEV). This corresponds to the pursuit of a more sustainable transportation mode amidst the realization of various negative externalities from freight transportation sectors to the environment [1]. As to E-VRP, E-VRPD practically extends E-VRP with the presence of drones as an additional transportation mode, leading to a larger solution space to be explored.

This work defines E-VRPD and develops a sequential decomposition algorithm with an improvement phase to solve E-VRPD. The algorithm involves the development of a mathematical formulation for inserting drone sorties into an EV tour, leading to the development of a *matheuristic* algorithm [5]. To this time, this is the first effort to propose an algorithm for E-VRPD, as we are not aware of previous works that deal with a similar problem. As such, we evaluate the performance of our proposed algorithm by comparing it with E-VRP solutions. Furthermore, with a set of numerical experiments, we show the relevancy of the E-VRPD as a promising research area in operations research and logistics.

The rest of this paper is structured in the following way. Section 2 presents a literature review on related studies. Section 3 describes E-VRPD. Section 4 delivers an explanation of our proposed algorithm. Then, Sect. 5 presents computational experiments and analyzes their results. Finally, in Sect. 6, we discuss some conclusions and future research directions.

2   Literature Review

The study of the cooperation between ground vehicles (e.g. trucks) and drones was introduced in [2], where the seminal mathematical formulation of coordination between a ground vehicle (GV) and a drone, namely the flying sidekick traveling salesman problem (FSTSP), was discussed. FSTSP considers a single truck assisted by a single drone to perform a parcel delivery task to a set of customer nodes in a graph. In this form of cooperation, a human operator can operate the attached drone by launching the drone from a launching node (a depot node or a customer node) to deliver a parcel to a single customer node. While the drone performs its *sortie* (drone-delivery operation), the truck can serve other customer nodes before recollecting the drone in a rendezvous node, as long as the endurance constraint of the drone is not violated. Another influential work from [6] presented an integer programming formulation for a similar model to FSTSP, namely the traveling salesman problem with drone (TSPD). By comparing their models to the classical traveling salesman problem (TSP) model, these two seminal studies successfully illustrated how using drones in last-mile logistics with GV as its 'moving hub' can reduce the time required to complete delivery tasks.

Meanwhile, within the last decade, a handful of works have discussed the optimal way to implement EVs in logistics. Among them, the most popular direction is perhaps E-VRP, which deals with the optimization of EV routes by considering the constraints of battery and charging operations. For instance, a recent survey on E-VRP from [4] reported 136 published works related to E-VRP within the last ten years, which shows that the deployment of EVs in logistics is attracting the interest of researchers and practitioners.

Unfortunately, our literature review shows that only four research works are available on the integration between drones and EVs in logistics, as most of the previous works deal with the traditional delivery system with a single type of vehicle. To the best of our knowledge, [7] is the first study to consider the cooperation between EV and drone in a TSP-variant model. They presented an EV-based transportation model where an EV is equipped with a single drone. The model presented in [7] aims to minimize the total energy consumption of the ground vehicle, and they assumed that the drone could be launched multiple times within a tour. A recent study from [8] then developed a mathematical formulation for a similar problem and named the problem the electric traveling salesman problem with drone (E-TSPD). The model presented in [8] embodied two particular differences from the problem discussed in [7], in which [8] considered the presence of recharging stations in the graph and assumed that the drone battery could be recharged using the energy from the EV after finishing a sortie. That study was then continued in [9], where the authors extended E-TSPD to consider the possibility of a partial recharging policy. In this regard, [9] relaxed the classical assumption of E-VRP variants where the EVs must be fully recharged after entering a recharging station. Another recent study [10] discussed the first scaling-up extension of E-TSPD, with a new model named E-VRPD, with the objective function of minimizing total energy consumption. In [10], a mathematical formulation of E-VRPD was presented with a hybrid ant colony optimization algorithm introduced to solve E-VRPD instances with up to 50 customer nodes. Nevertheless, we note that the E-VRPD model presented in [10] assumed that the EVs are only used as a moving hub for launching and retrieving the drones, as only drones serve all of the demand from customer nodes. Borrowing the term of [11], the E-VRPD model presented by [10] can be classified as non-simultaneous coordination between ground vehicles and drones, where this class of model is highly-related to the 2-echelon routing problems [12]. Additionally, [10] also did not consider the presence of recharging stations as they assumed that the EVs would always have enough energy to finish their tour.

In summary, the contributions of this study are twofold. Firstly, we define the E-VRPD with simultaneous coordination between EVs and drones as a new form of optimization problem. We differ our contribution from [10] by discussing a simultaneous form of E-VRPD with recharging stations throughout the graph and relaxing the assumption of unlimited energy of EVs. Secondly, a sequential decomposition algorithm with an improvement phase is proposed as the first solver for E-VRPD, as there is no existing approach for E-VRPD. This decomposition approach is executed by deconstructing E-VRPD into a set of smaller (and simpler) sub-problems that can be sequentially solved using a set of established tools. The idea of decomposition has been noted for a long time as an effective and practical way to solve any complex optimization problems, as shown by several classical decomposition techniques in operations research such as Dantzig-Wolfe, Lagrangian, and Benders decomposition [13]. In retrospect, the decomposition technique has also been noted as a traditional class of *matheuristic* approach [5], i.e. a practice of combining metaheuristic frameworks [14] with exact algorithms, which is known to be a very promising approach to solving variants of routing problems [15].

3   Problem Description of E-VRPD

This section briefly describes E-VRPD. The problem can be defined in an undirected graph $G = (V, A)$. The set $V = V_0 \cup V_S \cup V_C$ captures all the nodes within the graph, while set A comprises all arcs $(i, j) \in V, i \neq j$ between those nodes. In accordance, set $V_0 = \{0, r+n+1\}$ is presented as the set of the depot node $\{0\}$ along with its dummy node $\{r+n+1\}$, set $V_S = \{1, ..., r\}$ contains all r recharging stations available on the graph, and $V_C = \{r+1, ..., r+n\}$ represents all the n customer nodes to be served.

The E-VRPD model aims to find a set of optimized routes to serve all the customer nodes using f homogeneous fleet of EVs and drones $F = \{1, ..., f\}$. All the routes must be started from and finished at the depot node, and each customer node must be served only once, either by an EV or a drone. In the case where a certain node i is visited by both EV and drone, its demand q_i is served by the EV. Additionally, these routes are subject to the capacity constraint, where each EV and drone has a limited payload capacity, Q_t and Q_d, respectively. In some occasions, $q_i > Q_d$ is valid, therefore, we introduce a subset $V_D \subseteq V_C$ to list all the drone-eligible customer nodes.

Along the tour of EVs, the operator can launch the equipped drone from node $i \in V_L = \{0, ..., r+n\}$ to serve the customer nodes in V_D. After getting launched, the drone can then deliver the parcel of the targeted customer node $j \in V_D$ with a service time s_j, then return back to its corresponding EV at a different node $k \in V_R = \{1, ..., r+n+1\}$ before its energy capacity, E_d, runs out. Borrowing the popular terminology from [2], we call such an operation a sortie and define it as a tuple $<i, j, k>$, where $i \neq j \neq k$. Moreover, note that during a sortie of drone f, the corresponding EV can visit other customers and/or recharging nodes before visiting the rendezvous node k.

Similar to the drones, the EVs are also subject to the limitation of their battery E_t. The battery energy of EVs is drained to fuel its movement as well as recharge its drone's battery. The latter concept is borrowed from [8], as we assume that after finishing the sortie the drone batteries will be replaced with a new one, and then the used batteries are recharged using the energy from the EV. If required, the EVs can stop at the available recharging stations $i \in V_S$ to recharge their battery with a recharging rate of R. These stations can also be used as a launching and retrieval point for a sortie. In accordance, we introduce h_t as the battery consumption rate of EVs and h_d as the battery consumption rate of drones.

The objective function considered here is to minimize the total completion time required, T, to perform all the delivery tasks. Let $F_a \subseteq F$ be the subset of active tours and T_f be the completion time of tour f, the value of T then can then be calculated as in Eq. (1). Borrowing the finding of [16], the completion time of a tour f can be decomposed into three components:

1. the total travel time of the GV. Here, it comprises the sum of travel time, service time and recharging time of EVs.
2. the total setup time required to launch (s_L) and recollect (s_R) the drone and
3. the total time spent by the GV to wait for the drone.

Accordingly, the value of T_f can be calculated as in Eq. (2) by introducing A^s as the set of all possible (i, j, k) sorties and the following parameters: $d_{i,j}^t$ as the distance through arc $(i, j) \in A$ for EVs, $d_{i,j}^d$ as the distance through arc $(i, j) \in A$ for drones, v_t and v_d to represent the speed of EVs and drones, s_i to represent the service time required to serve node i, $t_{i,j}^t = \frac{d_{i,j}^t}{v_t}$ as the time required for EVs to traverse through arc $(i, j) \in A$, and $t_{i,j}^d = \frac{d_{i,j}^d}{v_d}$ as the corresponding travel time parameter of drones.

$$C = \max_{f \in F_a}(T_f) \tag{1}$$

$$T_f = \sum_{i,j \in A} (t_{i,j}^t + s_j)X_{i,j,f} + \sum_{i,j,k \in A^s} (s_L + s_R)Y_{i,j,k,f} + \sum_{k \in V_S} R_{k,f} + \sum_{k \in V_R} W_{k,f} \tag{2}$$

In addition, the value of these decisions must be taken into account to calculate the completion time of each tour in Eq. (2). These are:

1. $X_{i,j,f} \in \{0,1\}$ that sets whether EV f traverses through arc (i, j)
2. $Y_{i,j,k,f} \in \{0,1\}$ to decide whether drone f performs sortie (i, j, k),
3. $R_{k,f} \geq 0$ as the recharging time spent by EV f in recharging station k,
4. $W_{k,f} \geq 0$ to define the waiting time spent by EV f in node k to wait for the arrival of the drone,
5. $a_{i,f}^t, a_{i,f}^d \geq 0$ to respectively record the arrival time of the EV and drone f at node i, and
6. $e_{i,f}^t, e_{i,f}^d \geq 0$ to respectively record the battery state of EV and drone f when they arrive at node i

Then, the values of $R_{k,f}$ and $W_{k,f}$ can be defined as in Eqs. 3 and 4, while we also define several assumptions in E-VRPD as follows:

1. Drone can safely land at the rendezvous node before the arrival of the EV. In this regard, we define that if one vehicle arrives earlier, the early vehicle must wait for the latter.
2. Full recharging policy is applied for EVs, so they must be in a fully-charged state when departing a recharging station.
3. All customer nodes have a low-weight demand and are drone-eligible. Therefore, we can neglect the capacity constraint of EVs in this study.
4. Drones always start their sortie in a fully charged state, and the battery recharging time is negligible.
5. The battery energy of drones remains drained when the drone performs a service at drone node j, since it needs to be active during the whole service time. On the other hand, the engine of EVs is deactivated by the operator during a visit. In this regard, the battery consumption of drones within a sortie (i, j, k) can be defined as a time-based function $\left(t_{i,j}^d + s_j + t_{j,k}^d\right) h_d \leq E_d$, while the battery consumption of EVs in arc (i, j) can be calculated using a simple distance-based function $\left(d_{i,j}^t h_t\right)$ [4].
6. Every time the EV visits a node, the human operator must perform these tasks in the following order: retrieving the drone (if any), fulfilling the customer order (if any), recharging the EV (if any), and launching the drone (if any).

$$R_{k,f} = \frac{E_t - e_{k,f}^t - (E_d - e_{k,f}^d)}{R} \tag{3}$$

$$W_{k,f} = \max\left(0, a_{k,f}^d - a_{k,f}^t\right) \tag{4}$$

4   Sequential Decomposition Algorithm

This section demonstrates how to solve E-VRPD using a decomposition-based algorithm. This algorithm relies on the idea of sequential decomposition, where we deconstruct a complex optimization problem into a set of smaller (and simpler) sub-problems that can be solved sequentially [13]. The end product of these sequential decisions corresponds to the near-optimal solution of the original problem.

Accordingly, in order to deconstruct the relatively complex E-VRPD, we rely on a classic concept in developing a heuristic approach for vehicle routing problem (VRP), namely 'cluster-first, route second [13]. The core idea is that, in order to find the near-optimal solution of VRP, one can divide the customer nodes into k clusters (where $k \leq f$), then optimize the route for each cluster (that comprises a smaller set of customer nodes). Additionally, in finding the near-optimal route for a truck-drone tandem, the authors of [2] derived the idea of 'truck-first, drone-second' that states that the route of a truck-drone tandem can be developed by finding the optimal truck-only TSP tour for all the corresponding nodes first, then inserting the drone sorties to re-optimize the tour.

Algorithm 1: A sequential decomposition algorithm for E-VRPD

Input: E-VRPD instance
Result: S^*, T^*

1   $S \leftarrow \emptyset, T \leftarrow 0, m \leftarrow 1$
2   **Phase I - Decomposition**
3   $V_{CL} \leftarrow kMeans(V_C, t_{i,j}^t, f)$
4   **while** $m \leq CL$ **do**
5     $S_m^{TSP} \leftarrow MinTimeTSP(V_{C,m}, t_{i,j}^t)$
6     $S_m^{E-TSP} \leftarrow RechargingInsertion(S_m^{TSP}, V_S, t_{i,j}^t)$
7     $S_m^{E-TSPD}, T_m \leftarrow DroneInsertion(S_m^{E-TSP}, V_{C,m}, t_{i,j}^t, t_{i,j}^d)$
8   **if** $T_m > T$ **then**
9       $T \leftarrow T_m$
10   **end**
11    $S \leftarrow Merge(S_m^{E-TSPD})$
12    $m = m + 1$
13 **end**
14 **Phase II - Improvement**
15 $S^*, T^* \leftarrow RandomizedVND(S, T)$

These two ideas are utilized to build the first phase of our proposed algorithm, which comprises two phases: decomposition and improvement. Algorithm 1 presents the pseudocode of our algorithm. We denote S as a solution array and T as the objective value (of total completion time). Accordingly, S^* and T^* are the final solution and the objective value obtained from the algorithm. In the following subsections, each of these phases will be explained.

4.1 Decomposition Phase

The first phase of the algorithm decomposes an E-VRPD instance into four sub-problems: clustering with k-Means, TSP with a time minimization objective function, recharging insertion problem, and drone insertion problem. These sub-problems are visually presented in Fig. 1, where the output of each sub-problem will be used as an input for the next one.

Clustering: First, all the customer nodes, V_C, are clustered into $m \leq f$ clusters. Here, we deploy the classic k-Means clustering algorithm to create clusters using $t_{i,j}^t \in A$ as the distance function.

Notably, one major task in the k-Means algorithm is finding the appropriate value of m. From a practical standpoint, one important observation here is that deploying all available vehicles ($m = f$) tends to minimize the total completion time, as this balances the workload of each vehicle and reduces the chance of having an overloaded resource (that corresponds to an increasing value of maximum completion time). On the other hand, for cost minimization variants, limiting the value of k to be as small as possible is a logical choice, as it corresponds to the reduction of fixed vehicle cost [17].

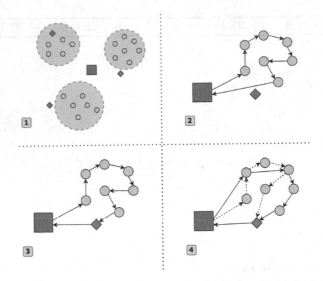

Fig. 1. Decomposing E-VRPD into four stages: (1) clustering, (2) traveling salesman problem, (3) recharging insertion, and (4) drone insertion

From the deployment of k-Means, we derive V_{CL} as the set of customer nodes that has been divided into CL clusters. In this regard, we denote $V_{C,m} \subset V_{CL}$ as the subset of customer nodes included in cluster m.

Traveling Salesman Problem: the second step of this algorithm is to find the optimal single EV tour (started and ended at the depot node) that captures all the customer nodes in each $V_{C,m}$. For each m, we define a TSP to minimize the completion time that can be defined as in Eq. (5). In this step, we simply deploy the Concorde solver [18], widely known as a state-of-the-art solver for TSP.

$$T_m^{TSP} = \sum_{i \in \{V_0 \cup V_{C,m}\} \backslash \{j\}} \sum_{j \in \{V_0 \cup V_{C,m}\} \backslash \{i\}} (t_{i,j}^t + s_j) X_{i,j,m} \tag{5}$$

Recharging Insertion: from the TSP tour of EV (S_m^{TSP}), we now aim to see whether it is required to insert any recharging stations within the tour. In this step, the battery state of EV m on its arrival at node $i \in S_m^{TSP}$ is examined. Then, a recharging station is inserted into the tour before the point where the EV's battery runs out. At this point, one might argue that inserting the drone sorties before inserting recharging stations could perhaps be more beneficial, as it could reduce the need to use any recharging stations for the EVs. Nevertheless, our pilot study during the development phase of this algorithm showed that the

Algorithm 2: A constructive algorithm for the recharging insertion problem

---

Input: $M_m, N, d_{i,j}^t, E_t, H_t$
Result: S_m^{E-TSP}

1 $S \leftarrow [0]$, $e_0^t \leftarrow E_t$, $i \leftarrow 1$, $j \leftarrow 1$
2 **while** $i \leq |M_m|$ **do**
3 $\quad$ $C_r \leftarrow \left(d_{(M_{m,j-1},M_{m,i})}^t + d_{(M_{m,i},N_{(M_{m,i})})}^t \right) H_t$
4 $\quad$ **if** $e_{j-1}^t - C_r > 0$ **then**
5 $\quad\quad$ $S \leftarrow Merge(M_{m,i})$
6 $\quad\quad$ $e_j^t \leftarrow (e_{j-1}^t - d_{(M_{m,j-1},M_{m,i})}^t H_t)$
7 $\quad\quad$ $j = j + 1$
8 $\quad$ **else**
9 $\quad\quad$ $S \leftarrow Merge(N_{(M_{m,j-1})}, M_{m,i})$
10 $\quad\quad$ $e_j^t \leftarrow (e_{j-1}^t - d_{(M_{m,j-1},N_{(M_{m,j-1})})}^t H_t)$
11 $\quad\quad$ $e_{j+1}^t \leftarrow (E_t - d_{(N_{(M_{m,j-1})},M_{m,i})}^t H_t)$
12 $\quad\quad$ $j = j + 2$
13 $\quad$ **end**
14 $\quad$ $i = i + 1$
15 **end**
16 $S_m^{E-TSP} \leftarrow S$

---

presence of a recharging station within an E-VRPD tour could potentially be beneficial objective-wise due to the possibility of launching and/or retrieving drones there (see Fig. 1). This corresponds to the finding of [19] that showed how the performance of a truck-drone logistics system could be improved by including several parking lots for launching-retrieving purposes.

Moving on, this recharging insertion task can be easily solved with a constructive algorithm. The core concept of this constructive algorithm is as follows: *"if one cannot reach the nearest recharging station from node $i+1$ (the next location in the tour), one should detour to the nearest recharging station from node i (current location) before visiting node $i + 1$"*. For this task, we define $M_{m,i}$ as the i-th node in the EV tour m and N_i as the nearest recharging station from node $i \in \{V_0 \cup V_C\}$. For a case where there are two recharging stations with the same distance from i, we simply take one of them randomly. The constructive algorithm is presented in Algorithm 2.

Drone Insertion: After obtaining the full EV tour of cluster m (S_m^{E-TSP}), which corresponds to the electric traveling salesman problem (E-TSP), the next step is to insert drone sortie(s) with the aim of reducing the completion time of tour m. In this regard, we define the drone insertion task as a mixed-integer linear program (MILP), adapting the approach of [20]. In order to build the MILP formulation, we first define L as the length of solution array and $L_m = |S_m^{E-TSP}|$, then, we label the nodes in S_m^{E-TSP} as $[1, ..., L]$ according to the order of the EV tour m, where both nodes '1' and 'L' stand for the depot node (start and finish). By defining the following notations and sets:

- A_m as the set of all (i, j) arcs in S_m^{E-TSP} where $i < j$,
- $V_{L,m} = \{1, ...L - 1\}, V_{D,m} = V_{C,m} \cap V_D$, and $V_{R,m} = \{2, ...L\}$ as the required sets to define possible sorties in cluster m,
- A_m^s as the set of all feasible sortie arcs (i, j, k) from $V_{L,m}, V_{D,m}$ and $V_{R,m}$ where $i < j < k$.

we can present the MILP of the drone insertion problem for each value of m, as in Eqs. (6)–(15).

$$\min \sum_{i,j \in A_m} \left(t_{(M_{m,i}, M_{m,j})}^t + s_{(M_{m,i})} \right) X_{i,j,m}$$
$$+ \sum_{i,j,k \in A_m^s} (s_L + s_R) Y_{i,j,k,m} + \sum_{k \in V_{R,m}} W_{k,m} \tag{6}$$

subject to:

$$\sum_{\substack{i \in |1,...,j-1| \\ i<j}} X_{i,j,m} + \sum_{i \in |1,...,j-1|} \sum_{k \in |j+1,...,L|} Y_{i,j,k,m} = 1 \qquad \forall j \in |2, ..., L-1| \tag{7}$$

$$\sum_{\substack{i \in V_{L,m} \\ i<j}} X_{i,j,m} \leq 1 \qquad \forall j \in V_{R,m} \tag{8}$$

$$\sum_{j,k \in A_m^s} Y_{i,j,k,m} \leq \sum_{\substack{i \in \{1,...,L\} \\ i<j}} X_{i,j,m} \qquad \forall i \in V_{L,m} \tag{9}$$

$$\sum_{i,j \in A_m^s} Y_{i,j,k,m} \leq \sum_{\substack{i \in \{1,...,L\} \\ j<k}} X_{j,k,m} \qquad \forall k \in V_{R,m} \tag{10}$$

$$\left(t_{(M_{m,i}, M_{m,j})}^d + s_{(M_{m,j})} + t_{(M_{m,j}, M_{m,k})}^d \right) Y_{i,j,k,m} \leq E_d \qquad \forall (i, j, k) \in A_m^s \tag{11}$$

$$\sum_{q,r \in A_m^s} Y_{p,q,r,m} \leq \sum_{\substack{i,j,k \in A_m^s \\ i<p,k \leq p}} Y_{i,j,k,m} \qquad \forall p > 0, p \in V_{L,m} \tag{12}$$

$$Y_{i,j,k,m} + Y_{p,q,r,m} \leq 1 \qquad \forall (i, j, k) \in A_m^s, (p, q, r) \in A_m^s, \begin{matrix} i \leq p, k > p \\ q \neq j \end{matrix} \tag{13}$$

$$Y_{i,j,k,m} + Y_{p,q,r,m} \leq 1 \qquad \forall\, (i,j,k) \in A_m^s,\ (p,q,r) \in A_m^s, \overset{i<r, k \geq r}{q \neq j} \qquad (14)$$

$$0 \leq \left(t^d_{(M_{m,i}, M_{m,j})} + s_{(M_{m,j})} + t^d_{(M_{m,j}, M_{m,k})} \right) Y_{i,j,k,m}$$
$$- \sum_{\substack{p \in V_{L,m} \\ p < q}} \sum_{\substack{q \in V_{R,m} \\ i \leq p, q \leq k}} \left(t^t_{(M_{m,p}, M_{m,q})} + s_{(M_{m,q})} \right) X_{p,q,m} \leq W_{k,m} \qquad \forall\, (i,j,k) \in A_m^s$$

$$(15)$$

The objective function (6) aims to minimize the total completion time of tour m, by reducing the sum of travel time, setup time, and waiting time of the EV. Equation (7) ensures that each customer node is visited at least once, either by the EV or drone. Equation (8) sets the direction of an EV tour. Equations (9) and (10) guarantee that the launching and rendezvous nodes of a sortie of a certain drone are also visited by the corresponding EV. Equation (11) is the endurance constraint of drone sorties. Equations (12)–(14) guarantee the continuity of a drone sortie, such that the drone could not be launched before it is retrieved back from the previous sortie. Lastly, Eq. (15) defines the value of $W_{k,m}$.

4.2 Improvement Phase

The previous decomposition phase is executed iteratively for each cluster m. The solution of each cluster then corresponds to an E-TSPD solution, and obviously, those m E-TSPD solutions are together a feasible solution for an E-VRPD instance. This solution set can be used as an input for any improvement-based metaheuristics, such as variable neighborhood search, tabu search, or genetic algorithm [14]. Here, we are interested to examine the suitability of this two-stage concept for E-VRPD. Thus, we append a simple local-search improvement phase to further improve the quality of the solution produced by the decomposition phase. In this regard, we employ a *randomized variable neighborhood descent* (VND) with eight neighborhood moves: (1) swap node, (2) swap whole, (3) insertion node, (4) insertion whole, (5) reverse node, (6) reverse whole, (7) remove sortie node and (8) add sortie node. This VND procedure and its neighborhood moves are adopted from [21]. Additionally, interested readers can check the work of [22] to read the complete explanation of the VND procedure.

5 Numerical Experiments and Analysis

This section describes the numerical experiments executed in this study, alongside the results from these experiments.

Table 1. Summary of problem parameters

Parameter	Value	References
EV	Renault Kangoo Z.E	[24]
Drones	DJI Matrice 300 RTK	[25]
Charger	Alpitronic Hypercharger HYC 300 kW	[26]
$d^t_{i,j}$	Calculated by Manhattan distance	[2]
$d^d_{i,j}$	Calculated by Euclidean distance	[2]
s_i	1 min	[2]
E_t	33 kWh	[24]
E_d	55 min	[25]
v_t	35 mph	[3]
v_d	50 mph	[3]
h_t	0.159 kWh/km	[24]
h_d	0.01 kWh/min	[25]
R	300 kWh	[26]
s_L, s_R	1 min	[2]

5.1 Experiments Settings

All experiments were implemented on a personal computer with AMD Ryzen 5 1600 Six-core Processor 3.2 GHz, 16 GB DDR4 memory, NVIDIA Quadro K-1200 GPU and Windows 11 operating system. The algorithm is coded in Julia language and executed as a single-thread code. Both k-Means and Concorde solver were implemented using available wrapper packages in the Julia environment, while whenever a MILP formulation needs to be solved, we deploy Gurobi as a solver using the JuMP environment [23]. The runtime limit of Gurobi is set as 10 min (600 s), while the improvement phase of our algorithm is executed for 3 min (180 s). In addition, constraint checking for each E-VRPD solution is performed with a penalty function technique. In this regard, whenever a solution violates the E-VRPD constraints (i.e. drone endurance, continuity of tours and/or sorties), a large penalty value is incurred to the objective value.

5.2 Benchmark Problems

In order to evaluate the performance of our algorithm, we derived a set of test instances for E-VRPD. These instances are adapted from the popular E-VRP instances from [17], in which we take the location demography of the nodes (depot, recharging stations, and customer nodes). We generate 30 instances in total with various combination values of customer nodes $n \in \{5, 6, 7, 8, 10, 15, 20, 25, 30, 40\}$, recharging stations $r \in \{3, 4, 5, 7\}$, and available vehicles $f \in \{2, 3, 4\}$. Then, to develop a more realistic dataset for E-VRPD, we modify the instances with several parameters presented in Table 1, where several of them are based on real-life data (i.e. E_t, E_d, h_t, h_d, and R).

5.3   Comparison to Existing Techniques

Then, in order to show the relevancy of E-VRPD, we compare the E-VRPD solutions from our proposed algorithm with E-VRP solutions. This comparison is selected to gauge the gap of quality that can be attained from implementing drones into an E-VRP system. In this regard, the hybrid variable neighborhood search/tabu search (VNS/TS) algorithm [17] was selected as a solver for E-VRP.

We implemented VNS/TS by carefully following the design and parameter settings presented in [17]. Nevertheless, our pilot study showed that the quality of E-VRP solutions produced by VNS/TS is largely influenced by its initial solution. In the original design of [17], the initial solution of VNS/TS was produced with the classic nearest-neighbor algorithm. However, we note that [17] aimed to minimize total transportation cost in their study, while we consider to minimize total completion time instead. Due to the difference in these objective functions, in this study, we feed VNS/TS with S^{E-TSP} solutions to ensure the quality of the produced E-VRP solutions.

5.4   Experimental Results and Analysis

Here, we present and discuss the experiment results. These discussions are driven by the two research questions (RQs) listed below:

RQ 1: "Is the proposed algorithm effective for solving E-VRPD instances?"

RQ 2: "What are the benefits to obtain from implementing drones into an electric vehicles-based transportation system?"

First, Fig. 2 presents the full numerical experiment results. Each sub-graph in Fig. 2 corresponds to each instance, which is presented as a combination of n-r-f. From Fig. 2, we can observe the effectiveness of the proposed algorithm in finding quasi-optimal solutions for E-VRPD, as the final solution values from our algorithm are always superior to the E-VRP solution from VNS/TS for all instances. In addition, it is also observed that the solutions produced by the first phase (decomposition phase) of the proposed method are comparable to the E-VRP solutions. Nevertheless, from Fig. 2, it is clear that the effectiveness of our algorithm is enhanced by the addition of a local-search procedure in the second stage. By comparing the quality of the solutions produced by the first stage to those of the second stage, our experiments show that the presence of the VND procedure reduces the objective value by around 22% on average. This corresponds to the classic adage that optimizing each sub-system (E-TSPD tour of each vehicle) does not always correspond to the optimal solution of a complex system (full E-VRPD instances) [27].

Then, addressing the second RQ, Fig. 2 also shows that the inclusion of drones into an EV-based delivery system could improve the performance of the system. This is indicated by the reduction in the total completion time, which can be seen from the comparison between the quality of E-VRPD final solutions with the final solutions for E-VRP. In this regard, the total completion time of E-VRPD final solutions is consistently lower than E-VRP, as E-VRPD is able to exploit the faster travel time of drones to provide services to a set of drone-eligible customer

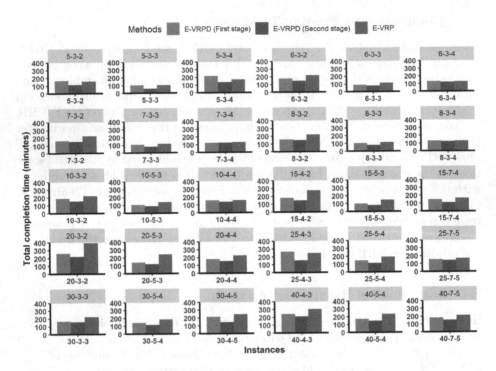

Fig. 2. Mean of total completion time for each method

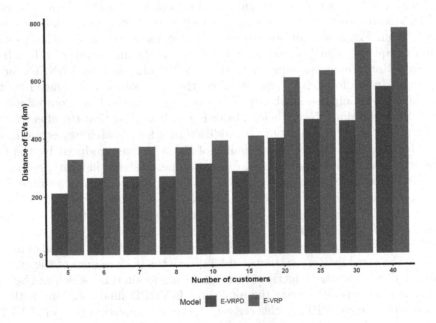

Fig. 3. Comparison of total distance traveled by EVs

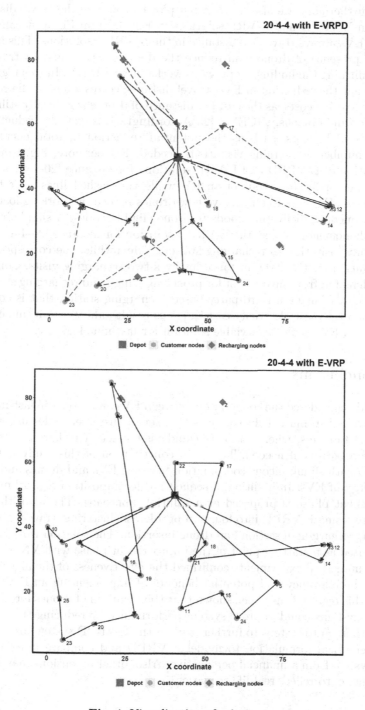

Fig. 4. Visualization of solutions

nodes. Furthermore, we also derive a bar plot to compare the travel distance of EVs from E-VRPD and E-VRP solutions in Fig. 3. From Fig. 3, it can be seen that the EVs always travel less distance in the E-VRPD solutions. This indicates that the presence of drones can reduce the distance that must be traveled by EVs, confirming the findings of previous works in VRPD [21]. In this regard, it is evident that the reduction in EVs' travel distance corresponds to the reduction of transportation costs, as the cost per distance of drones is generally still smaller than EVs (and obviously, ICEVs) [2]. Accordingly, this distance reduction may bring several benefits, such as the potential reduction in total energy usage and the number of charging visitations needed. Furthermore, Fig. 4 presents a visualization of E-VRPD and E-VRP solutions for instance '20-4-4', where the straight lines refer to a tour of an EV while the dashed lines refer to drone sorties. From Fig. 4, one can observe how drones reduce the working load of EVs by simultaneously delivering goods to drone-eligible nodes. A simple indication of this phenomenon is that the E-VRPD solution for instance '20-4-4' does not require any visitation to recharging stations. Meanwhile, the corresponding E-VRP solution for the given instance involves two recharging visits. Considering the burden of upfront investment for procuring a high-end recharging station [28] and the cost of using a third-party-based recharging station that is commonly larger than the basic electricity cost [29], this result indicates that implementing drones with EVs could be a viable solution for last-mile logistics.

6   Conclusions

This study considered the cooperation between EVs and drones in last-mile logistics. Here, a firm must deliver parcels to a set of customer nodes using a set of EV-drone tandems, where the EVs could visit a set of recharging stations to recharge a battery if needed. The main contribution of this study is to define E-VRPD with simultaneous coordination between EVs and drones and the limited energy of EVs. In addition, a sequential decomposition algorithm with an improvement phase is proposed as a solution approach. The algorithm works by decomposing E-VRPD into four sub-problems: clustering, traveling salesman problem, recharging insertion and drone insertion. The solution from this phase is then used as a starting point of the improvement phase with VND.

Our numerical experiments confirmed the effectiveness of the algorithm and showed the relevancy and potential benefits of implementing an E-VRPD system. In this regard, it has been shown that the inclusion of drones into EV-based delivery systems could improve system performance by reducing the total completion time. Future steps to further explore the E-VRPD system are to develop a mathematical formulation to model E-VRPD and compare it to an ICEV-based system from a financial perspective. Also, other extensions may be added to the model to reflect real-life scenarios.

References

1. Boysen, N., Fedtke, S., Schwerdfeger, S.: Last-mile delivery concepts: a survey from an operational research perspective. OR Spectr. **43**(1), 1–58 (2021)
2. Murray, C.C., Chu, A.G.: The flying sidekick traveling salesman problem: optimization of drone-assisted parcel delivery. Transp. Res. Part C: Emerg. Technol. **54**, 86–109 (2015)
3. Sacramento, D., Pisinger, D., Ropke, S.: An adaptive large neighborhood search metaheuristic for the vehicle routing problem with drones. Transp. Res. Part C: Emerg. Technol. **102**, 289–315 (2019)
4. Kucukoglu, I., Dewil, R., Cattrysse, D.: The electric vehicle routing problem and its variations: a literature review. Comput. Industr. Eng. **161**(July), 107650 (2021)
5. Boschetti, M.A., Maniezzo, V.: Matheuristics: using mathematics for heuristic design. 4OR **20**(2), 173–208 (2022)
6. Agatz, N., Bouman, P., Schmidt, M.: Optimization approaches for the traveling salesman problem with drone. Transp. Sci. **52**(4), 965–981 (2018)
7. Baek, D., Chen, Y., Chang, N., Macii, E., Poncino, M.: Energy-efficient coordinated electric truck-drone hybrid delivery service planning. In: 2020 AEIT International Conference of Electrical and Electronic Technologies for Automotive, AEIT AUTOMOTIVE 2020 (2020)
8. Zhu, T., Boyles, S.D., Unnikrishnan, A.: Electric vehicle traveling salesman problem with drone (2022). http://arxiv.org/abs/2201.07992
9. Zhu, T., Boyles, S.D., Unnikrishnan, A.: Electric vehicle traveling salesman problem with drone with partial recharge policy (2022). http://arxiv.org/abs/2205.13735
10. Kyriakakis, N.A., Stamadianos, T., Marinaki, M., Marinakis, Y.: The electric vehicle routing problem with drones: an energy minimization approach for aerial deliveries. Cleaner Logist. Supply Chain **4**(March), 100041 (2022)
11. Moshref-Javadi, M., Winkenbach, M.: Applications and Research avenues for drone-based models in logistics: a classification and review. Expert Syst. Appl. **177**(March), 114854 (2021)
12. Cuda, R., Guastaroba, G., Speranza, M.: A survey on two-echelon routing problems. Comput. Oper. Res. **55**, 185–199 (2015)
13. Ball, M.O.: Heuristics based on mathematical programming. Surv. Oper. Res. Manage. Sci. **16**(1), 21–38 (2011)
14. Martí, R., Pardalos, P.M., Resende, M.G.: Handbook of Heuristics, vol. 1–2. Springer, Cham (2018). https://doi.org/10.1007/978-3-319-07124-4
15. Archetti, C., Speranza, M.G.: A survey on matheuristics for routing problems. EURO J. Comput. Optim. **2**(4), 223–246 (2014). https://doi.org/10.1007/s13675-014-0030-7
16. Dell'Amico, M., Montemanni, R., Novellani, S.: Drone-assisted deliveries: new formulations for the flying sidekick traveling salesman problem. Optim. Lett. **15**(5), 1617–1648 (2019). https://doi.org/10.1007/s11590-019-01492-z
17. Schneider, M., Stenger, A., Goeke, D.: The electric vehicle-routing problem with time windows and recharging stations. Transp. Sci. **48**(4), 500–520 (2014)
18. Applegate, D.L., et al.: Certification of an optimal TSP tour through 85,900 cities. Oper. Res. Lett. **37**(1), 11–15 (2009)
19. Gomez-Lagos, J., Candia-Vejar, A., Encina, F.: A new truck-drone routing problem for parcel delivery services aided by parking lots. IEEE Access **9**, 11 091–11 108 (2021)

20. Es Yurek, E., Ozmutlu, H.C.: A decomposition-based iterative optimization algorithm for traveling salesman problem with drone. Transp. Res. Part C: Emerg. Technol. **91**(July 2017), 249–262 (2018)
21. Kuo, R.J., Lu, S.H., Lai, P.Y., Mara, S.T.W.: Vehicle routing problem with drones considering time windows. Expert Syst. Appl. **191**, 116264 (2022)
22. Duarte, A., Sánchez-Oro, J., Mladenović, N., Todosijević, R.: Variable neighborhood descent. In: Martí, R., Pardalos, P.M., Resende, M.G.C. (eds.) Handbook of Heuristics, pp. 341–367. Springer, Cham (2018). https://doi.org/10.1007/978-3-319-07124-4_9
23. Dunning, I., Huchette, J., Lubin, M.: JuMP: a modeling language for mathematical optimization. SIAM Rev. **59**(2), 295–320 (2017)
24. Collie, S.: Renault Kangoo ZE: electric van priced from $52,527 for private buyers. (2021). https://www.drive.com.au/news/renault-kangoo-ze-price/
25. DJI: DJI Matrice 300 RTK (2022). https://www.dji.com/au/matrice-300/specs
26. Randall, C.: Alpitronic's hyperchargers pass plug & charge audit (2022). https://www.electrive.com/2022/08/05/alpitronics-hyperchargers-pass-plugcharge-audit/
27. Meadows, D.H.: Thinking in Systems: A Primer. Chelsea Green Publishing, Hartford (2008)
28. LaMonaca, S., Ryan, L.: The state of play in electric vehicle charging services - a review of infrastructure provision, players, and policies. Renew. Sustain. Energy Rev. **154**(November 2021), 111733 (2022)
29. Davis, W.: Australia's largest electric car charging network hikes prices (2022). https://www.drive.com.au/news/australias-largest-electric-car-charging-network-hikes-prices/

Integrated Passenger-Freight Transportation Model: Metro of Quito (Ecuador) as a Case Study

Michel Barán[1], Fernando Sandoya[2,3], Jorge Chicaiza-Vaca[4,5], and Benjamín Barán[6(✉)]

[1] Catholic University of Asunción, Cordillera de Amambay casi, Asunción, Paraguay
mbaran@cba.com.py

[2] ESPOL Polytechnic University, Vía Perimetral km 30.5, Guayaquil, Ecuador
fsandoya@espol.edu.ec

[3] Universidad de Guayaquil, Av. Delta s/n y Av. Kennedy, Guayaquil, Ecuador
fernando.sandoyas@ug.edu.ec

[4] Center for International Migration (GIZ/CIM), Dag-Hammarskjöld-Weg 1-5, Eschborn, Germany

[5] Pichincha Chamber of Freight Transport, Av. El Inca Oe1-70, Quito, Ecuador
investigacion@ctpp.org.ec

[6] Comunera University, Dr. Juan Eulogio Estigarribia, Asunción, Paraguay
bbaran@cba.com.py

Abstract. This paper explores the potential of a collaborative passenger and freight transportation system as a sustainable option for urban logistics. A novel multi-objective optimization model is proposed for packages delivery services using the capacity of a mass public passenger transport network, considering the Quito Metro (Ecuador) as a study case, in which metro stations are used to pick up and deliver packages. This would be a new efficient model for mixed distribution for last mile delivery. The model considers several objectives linked to the interests of different stakeholders: cargo transport costs, delivery times and the passenger service level. The integration of freight and passenger transportation will promote greater efficiency in the passenger transport network, reducing the number of commercial fossil fuel vehicles that circulate exclusively for freight transport within the city limits, and will improve life conditions in metropolitan areas. In this study, a mixed linear integer multi-objective programming model is proposed to represent this problem of joint transportation of passengers and packages, including some criteria and restrictions that represent real rules of operation and business. Finally, to solve the proposed model, a genetic algorithm based on the well-known NSGA-II is implemented for a real world case study of the metro of Quito for validation.

Keywords: Freight on public transport · Urban Logistics · Integrated Passenger Freight Transportation · Multi-objective optimization

This work was partially supported by the Center for International Migration (GIZ/CIM) Grants - Return Expert programme.

A. L. Martins et al. (Eds.): INTSYS 2022, LNICST 486, pp. 215–230, 2023.
https://doi.org/10.1007/978-3-031-30855-0_15

1   Introduction

While the COVID-19 crisis brought passenger traffic to a standstill, freight traffic by air, sea and truck continued to run to keep the world's economies going and to deliver vital goods. Car trips to crowded city centers and shopping malls were replaced by an explosion of online shopping and doorstep deliveries. Cargo boxes stuffed between the seats of passenger planes replaced tourists and conference attendees flying to distant lands. The crisis also caused severe disruptions in the movement of goods, and the world saw the consequences of the system's weaknesses: delays and empty shelves.

Demand for freight transportation will undoubtedly plummet in the economic aftermath of COVID-19, but the balance between passenger and freight transportation has shifted, perhaps forever [1]. The crisis is an opportunity for a mobility transformation that considers an approach that addresses both passenger and freight transport. Such an approach could channel resources into building an efficient system that also addresses the climate crisis that has already begun. In this context, this work emphasizes the urgent need for better integration of passenger and freight transportation to make our entire mobility system more resilient and sustainable.

Urban planners often consider ridership when allocating road and building space. This fact is clearly reflected in the growing interest in 'tactical urbanism' (a term coined for the action-oriented approach involving short-term, low-cost and scalable interventions in existing road infrastructure). On the one hand, cities such as Brussels or Hong Kong are creating more space for pedestrians and cyclists and prioritizing access for electric vehicles [2,3]. These changes help improve the quality of life in urban areas and make the transport system work better for people. However, such urban planning often does not include freight or urban freight transport, even though, a quarter of the world's population shops online. In the U.S., online purchases are up 44.0% in 2020 compared to 2019 [4]. That's the highest annual e-commerce growth in at least two decades. It's also nearly triple the 15.1% increase in 2019 [5].

The transportation of freight has a major impact on the economy; both large and small businesses rely on the collection and transportation of goods on a daily basis. Ecuador cities are no exception. For example, due to the topology of the city of Quito, the vast majority of goods are delivered from the south to the north and vice versa, traveling more than $70\ km$ from their point of origin. Industrial areas are located at the extreme ends of the city, but consumption points are located in the center.

There have been some studies on the potential impact of using rail systems such as inner-city subways and trams to transport goods within urban areas. Very few of these studies are conducted in Latin America and there is no study in Ecuador. Jansen et al. [6], Ghilas et al. [7], and Li et al. [8] show how the entire freight transportation sector (manufacturers, shippers and carriers, as well as receivers) generally derives economic benefits from transporting goods by public transportation. They consistently find that public transportation agencies realise economic benefits when they make their spare transportation capacity available to transport parcels and/or small units of goods. In addition, public agencies can benefit financially from greater sustainability of transit operations. There are also benefits in the social sphere. Less burdensome transportation operations pave the way for delivery and passenger services. This new paradigm in the Ecuadorian context implies a significant change in the current operational and theoretical approach to mobility. Another point is the need to make both public and private investments and adjustments. At a minimum, a consolidation facility and pick-up and delivery points must be made available at selected transit hubs to initiate an integration process. An acceptance model (targeting public administrations, private and public companies, actors of the transport and logistics systems in general) needs to be merged with an integrated business model that should take into account all stages of the innovation process: from concept and planning to implementation, monitoring and evaluation.

Many cities in Latin America have special geographical conditions, in the Andean region cities embedded in valleys between mountains, or on the coast cities follow the flow of a river. Many times, the main characteristic of these cities is an elongated design, longer than wide, which makes them suitable to having a main line of mass public transportation, for example, with a single metro line that allows to go quickly from the top to the bottom of the city, managing to significantly minimize costs, time and negative externalities in passengers' transportation. In other cases, establishing a single line for mass passenger may be a cheaper option for some Latin American countries, within the reach of the state budget, instead of a complex and expensive network. Examples of cities where this type of transportation system has been established in Latin America are Guayaquil (Ecuador), Quito (Ecuador), Panama City (Panama), Caracas (Venezuela), Medellín (Colombia), Santo Domingo (Dominican Republic), among others. It can be seen in Fig. 1 that a single line runs through the entire city or at least sectors of the city with high traffic congestion.

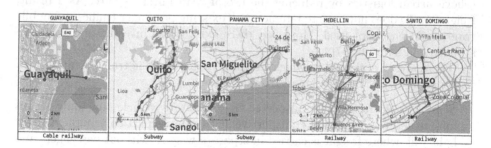

Fig. 1. Mass transit system that crosses the Metropolitan Area of several Latin-American cities

All these systems have some similarities. In Guayaquil (Ecuador) the Aerovía is a suspended aero public transportation system that connects the economic center of the metropolitan area of Guayaquil, usually overcrowded, and the neighboring industrial city of Durán with 5 km in length. The project entered into operations in 2020 [9], allowing a safe and fast crossing, from one side of the river to the other in 15 min, as an alternative crossing to the bridge through which, to travel the same stretch, would take 40 to 60 min [10]. Panama Metro is the only Central American Metro System, inaugurated in 2014. It has 30 stations, with a total length of 37 km [11]. Medellin Metro transportation system (Colombia) began operations in 1995 with a single line 25.8 km long [12]. Santo Domingo Metro is the public road transport system, or metro, that helps the city of Santo Domingo, capital of the Dominican Republic. It is the largest metropolitan rail system in the Caribbean with a 15 km route on its line 1 [13].

The present research aims to contribute with the development of a multi-objective optimization model [14] and its corresponding solution method based on simulations and metaheuristics for the integrated passenger and urban freight transportation problem applied to a public transportation system. A mathematical model is proposed and solved using evolutionary algorithms. Due to the nature of the studied system, algorithms for the treatment of multiobjective optimization problems can be identified. It is proposed to computationally solve the model using algorithms specifically designed for this task it, validating this innovative proposal by carrying out experiments considering real instances, using the new metro of Quito as a case study.

2   Related Work

Ranieri et al. [15] explore innovative approaches to last-mile freight transportation and also look at collaborative and cooperative logistics. Cleophas et al. [16] analyze vertical and horizontal approaches to collaboration in urban transport. They classify public freight transportation as a form of vertical collaboration. Another innovative approach is the so-called underground logistics system (ULS) [17]. These underground systems, which are mostly for freight transport, can relieve urban logistics by reducing the use of road infrastructure. As a result, freight traffic does not have to interact with existing passenger traffic, and public transportation is not used. Moreover, there exist works investigating how ULS systems can be built [17].

There are several ways in which freight can share public transportation with passengers, with varying degrees of integration:

1. *Shared track*: freight is transported in a separate vehicle that only shares infrastructure with public transport vehicles. This is particularly the case for light rail, where freight is carried in separate wagons without passengers and with its own traction unit. It is necessary to ensure that freight vehicles do not interfere with the timetable of passenger vehicles. Examples of this least integrated type of shared transport can be found in Dresden, Frankfurt or Zurich [18].

2. *Shared vehicle*: freight is transported in a separate wagon (light railways) or an attached trailer (e.g. bus). People and freight share the same travel route, time and distance. Dependencies exist mainly in loading, unloading and transhipment. For examples, see Shen et al. [19] and Behiri et al. [20].

3. *Shared Wagon*: freight is transported in the same wagon or compartment as passengers. Passengers and freight do not only share the travel route, time and distance, but also the space. In particular, peak periods of transport demand for both passengers and freight must be taken into account, as the available space must be divided between the two. In addition, design and safety considerations must be taken into account [21].

Ji et al. [22] envision a multimodal passenger-and-package sharing (PPS) network for urban logistics that integrates subways, taxis, and trucks. A "hub-and-spoke" structure is designed that includes nodes at subway stations and service shops connected to the hubs. Packages are transported by subway on the backbone links between the hubs and carried by taxis or trucks between the service shops and the hubs, depending on the unit cost of these two modes and the capacity constraint of taxis. A mixed integer linear programming model for hub location problems - a combination of the multi-assignment p-hub median problem without capacity constraints and the capacitated multi-assignment p-hub covering problem - is formulated to optimize the multimodal PPS network. They propose a modified genetic algorithm (GA) to solve the large hub location problem (HLP). The HLP model consists of binary variables indicating hub locations and non-negative continuous variables indicating package flows. A modified GA considers the set of binary variables as individuals.

Romano-Alho et al. [23] introduced a concept called cargo hitching. The solution is to use spare capacity in passenger traffic. This paper contributes to the existing literature on cargo hitching in the following dimensions: a) Application of an agent-based simulation framework to systematically study the impact of cargo hitching from the perspective of travellers, carriers, and regulators. The simulation framework includes detailed modelling of mobility-on-demand services on the supply and demand side, explicitly capturing the interactions between supply and demand; b) Conduct extensive simulations to cover different freight demand allocation strategies to special vehicles using a city-wide model of Singapore in 2030 and gain insights into the potential impacts of cargo hitching. The authors used SimMobility, a high resolution agent and activity-based simulation platform for flows of people and goods.

Zheng et al. [24] proposed a framework for integrating metro for urban logistics delivery to avoid conflicts with ground transportation and reduce delivery costs, transportation distance, and vehicle delivery times. By integrating a metro-based underground logistics system with ground-based delivery vehicles (GDVs), an optimization model for urban logistics delivery route based on a single metro line was developed to improve delivery efficiency. In the processing of this model, the total transportation cost was used as objective function, considering the capacity constraints of GDVs and a soft customer time window. In addition, the vehicle routing problem with time windows was considered.

Villa et al. [25] investigated the potential of a metro system in a large city like Madrid to offer delivery services by using existing transportation capacity and using the metro stations to collect parcels in lockers. This would be a new mixed distribution model for last mile e-commerce delivery. To this end, the paper assesses the costs and impacts of two alternative scenarios for managing unused rolling stock space (shared trains) or dedicated enforcement services (dedicated trains) on existing routes. The external costs of the proposed scenarios are compared with the current scenario for e-commerce delivery (parcel delivery by road). This study presents the quantification of the economic, environmental and social cost analysis of a new model for e-commerce parcel delivery using the public transportation network in a large city. The study focuses on evaluating and comparing the total estimated costs for the two proposed alternatives. The results show that underground transportation of parcels could significantly reduce the costs of congestion, accidents, noise, greenhouse gas emissions, as well as air pollution.

In Sun et al. [26], a metro prototype is developed that integrates retrofitted metro stations and newly built capsule pipelines to support automated delivery from urban logistic, gateways to inner-city destinations. Based on four indicators (i.e., freight flow unit, regional accessibility, environmental cost savings, and order priority), an entropy-based fuzzy TOPSIS evaluation model is proposed to select appropriate origin/destination flows for underground freight transportation. Then, a mixed-integer programming (MIP) model with a well-tuned solution framework combining a multi-objective Particle Swarm Optimization (PSO) algorithm and the location-allocation routing (LAR) of the M-ULS network is developed. The simulations are based on Nanjing metro for validation. Results confirm that the proposed algorithm is able to make high-quality Pareto-optimal [14] LAR decisions. Moreover, the Nanjing M-ULS project demonstrates strong economic feasibility and benefits to society and the environment.

3   Mathematical Formulation

The linear scheme of the transport system is represented in Fig. 2, with the stations and travel time tt_s from the departure station for demand i, d_i to the arrival station a_i. Demands are a set of goods that suppliers send to final customers. These demands must be packed at the departure station in load units, which we denote as boxes. Once these demands are delivered by the supplier, they are temporarily stored in departure stations with a cost, until they can be shipped in a train to their destination station, where each cargo is picked up by the final customer. We assume that the demands must be transported integrally, that is, the same demand cannot be divided to be sent in different trains.

Bearing in mind the aforementioned, in order to formulate a multi-objective model for the integrated passenger and freight transport, the following expressions are derived, with model sets in Table 1, parameters in Table 2 and decision variables in Table 3:

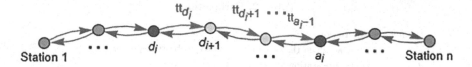

Fig. 2. Conceptual model for the integrated passenger-freight transportation of Quito Metro

Table 1. Model Sets.

Set	Description
$i : 1, ..., I$	Demands
$j : 1, ..., J$	Vehicles (Trains)
$s : 1, ..., S$	Stations
$f : 1, ..., F$	Transportation Fares

Objective functions

$$Minimize \; f_1 = \sum_{i=1}^{I} \sum_{j=1}^{J} (R_i - r_i \, x_{ijd_i}) \tag{1}$$

$$Minimize \; f_2 = \sum_{s=1}^{S} \sum_{i \in II_s} \sum_{j=1}^{J} h_j \, Q_i x_{ijs} \tag{2}$$

$$Minimize \; f_3 = \sum_{i=1}^{I} UC_1 Q_i \, (R_i - r_i \,) + \sum_{i=1}^{I} \sum_{f=1}^{F} \sum_{j \in F_f}^{J} UC_{2j} Q_i \left(E_i - \sum_{s \in I_s} tt_s \right) \tag{3}$$

Equation (1), (2) and (3) give the three objective functions namely:

- Minimization of total time of demand permanence in the stations waiting to be loaded (1).
- Minimization of total time during the loading, unloading and transport operations of the boxes (2). It should be noted that the time required by the boxes during their movement from the train are the same regardless of the way in which the loads are assigned to the trains, therefore, only the loading or unloading time differ according to the schedule in which the loads are assigned.
- Minimization of total transport and storage cost incurred from the time the demands arrive at their departure stations until they are transported and delivered to their destination stations (3).

The aim of this multi-objective model is to determine a set of time in which the demands are loaded without violating the constraints (4) to (18). i.e., subject to

Table 2. Parameters.

Parameter	Description
r_i	Time at which the demand i is ready to be transported
d_i	Departure station for demand i
a_i	Arrival station for demand i
End_i	Time expected for the delivery of demand i
UC_1	Unitary cost involved in storing a box / unit of time in a station (\$ /box/unit of time)
$UC_{2,j}$	Unitary cost involved in send a box on train j (\$ /box)
F_f	Set of trains in which the f fare is applied
l_j	Train j's departure time from the station 1
SC_s	Storage capacity at station s
tt_s	Travel time from station s to the next one
I_s	Set of demands needing to pass by station s on their way
II_s	Set of demands departing from or arriving at station s
D_i	Set of demands departing from the same station as demand i and ready for departure earlier than i: $D_i = \{ k \ /r_k \le r_i \& d_k = d_i \}$
Vol_i	Volume of demand i
We_i	Weight of demand i
CVB	Boxes volume capacity
CWB	Boxes weight capacity
Q_i	Number of boxes containing demand i
cap_j	Boxes transport capacity of train j
W_{max}	Maximum waiting time of trains at any station s
W_{min}	Minimum waiting time of trains at any station s
h_j	Time needed for handling (loading/unloading) a single box at train j
M	Big positive real number

$$\sum_{j=1}^{J} x_{i,j,d_i} = 1, \quad i = 1, 2, \ldots, I \tag{4}$$

Constraint (4) assures that each demand is loaded onto a single train exactly once.

$$x_{i,j,s} - x_{i,j,s+1} = 0, \quad \forall s \in [d_i, a_j - 1], i = 1, 2, \ldots, I \tag{5}$$

Constraint (5) enforces that the demand, once a train is assigned, goes through all stations from its departure station to its arrival station.

$$\sum_{i \in I_s}^{J} x_{i,j,s} Q_i \le cap_j, \quad j = 1, \ldots, J, \ s = 1, \ldots, S \tag{6}$$

Constraint (6) forces the transport capacity of each train.

$$x_{i,j,d_i} r_i \le l_j + \sum_{s=1}^{d_i-1} (C_{j,s} + tt_s), \quad i = 1, \ldots, I, \ j = 1, \ldots, J \tag{7}$$

Table 3. Decision variables.

Variable	Description
$x_{i,j,s}$	1 if demand i is in train j at station s, 0 otherwise
$y_{k,i}$	1 if $k \in D_i$ and k is not yet loaded when i becomes ready for departure
$C_{j,s}$	Waiting time of train j at station s
R_i	Time at which demand i is loaded (at station d_i)
E_i	Time at which demand i arrives at its destination station (at station a_i)

Constraint (7) assures the arrival time of demands, so that a demand can only be assigned to a train that arrives later than the demand's departure station.

$$C_{j,s} \geq W_{min}, \quad j = 1, \ldots, J, \ s = 1, \ldots, S \qquad (8)$$

$$C_{j,s} \leq W_{max}, \quad j = 1, \ldots, J, \ s = 1, \ldots, S \qquad (9)$$

Constraints (8) and (9) ensure that the minimum and maximum waiting times are satisfied at each station.

$$C_{j,s} \geq \sum_{i \in II_s} h_j \, x_{i,j,s} \, Q_i, \quad j = 1, \ldots, J, \ s = 1, \ldots, S \qquad (10)$$

Constraint (10) determines the feasibility of the waiting time of each train at each station.

$$Q_i = Max \left\{ \left\lceil \frac{Vol_i}{CVB} \right\rceil, \left\lceil \frac{We_i}{CWB} \right\rceil \right\} i = 1, \ldots, I \qquad (11)$$

Equation (11) is designed to represent the number of boxes needed to pack each demand.

$$R_i \geq l_j + \sum_{s=1}^{d_i-1} (C_{j,s} + ll_s) - M(1 - x_{i,j,d_i}), \quad i = 1, \ldots, I, \ j = 1, \ldots, J \qquad (12)$$

Constraint (12) determines the earliest time at which each demand is loaded into a train.

$$R_k \leq r_i + M \, y_{k,i}, \quad k \in D_i, \ i = 1, \ldots, I \qquad (13)$$

Constraint (13) forces the consistency of the definition of binary variables y.

$$\sum_{k \in D_i}^{J} y_{k,i} \, Q_k \leq SC_{d_i} - Q_i, \quad i = 1, \ldots, I \qquad (14)$$

Constraint (14) forces the storage capacity at each station.

$$x_{i,j,s} \in \{0,1\}, i = 1, \ldots, I, \ j = 1, \ldots, J, \ s = 1, \ldots, S \qquad (15)$$

$$C_{j,s} \geq 0, R_i \geq 0, \ j = 1, \ldots, J, \ s = 1, \ldots, S \tag{16}$$

$$R_i \geq 0, i = 1, \ldots, I \tag{17}$$

$$y_{ki} \in \{0,1\}, \ k \in D_i, i = 1, \ldots, I \tag{18}$$

The last block of constraints (15) to (18) define the binary decision variables $x_{i,j,s}$ and $y_{k,i}$ in addition to the no negative real variables R_i and $C_{j,s}$.

4   Case Study

The Metro of Quito city, capital of Ecuador, will be the underground public transport network of the city. The system's first line, which will include 15 stations, extends from Quitumbe (south of the city) to El Labrador (north of the city) with a length of 22.6 km (see Fig. 3). Its operation is expected to start in December 2022, according to its promoters. It will allow to cross almost the entire city in 33 min, a section that normally takes between 90 to 120 min through the current congested roads of the city [27].

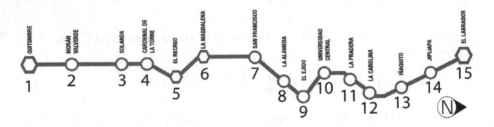

Fig. 3. Metro of Quito line

The presented model for integrated passenger and freight transport is applicable in environments such as the Metro of Quito transport system, whose first Metro Line is based on a linear system of mass transportation, with stations where merchandise may be loaded and unloaded. In this type of transport system, trains may be thought as doing a circular route, i.e. they start from station 1 (Quitumbe), go through all the stations located on the line, arriving at station 15 (El Labrador) and returning back to station 1 in the opposite direction using a parallel line.

The studied model represents this situation and considers simultaneously several objective functions, each of them representing the interests of different stakeholders: cargo owners, customers, passengers, and government. Several constraints that reflect possible real situations may also be considered: system operation rules and business conditions for load management.

The following Schedule Table (see Table 4) reflects the behavior assumed for the operation of the Quito metro. Table 4 presents an unique *ID*, with the corresponding *Station name*. The table also presents the *Station stay at regular time*, and the *Station stay at rush hour*, both of this waits inside the station are for the loading and unloading of merchandise or passengers, (times are defined in minutes) and finally the *Schedule Table* indicates a *Traveling time to the next station* (also in minutes).

Table 4. Schedule Table.

ID	Station name	Station stay at regular time	Station stay at rush hour	Traveling time to next station
1	QUITUMBRE	4 min	2 min	3 min
2	MORáN VALVERDE	4 min	2 min	4 min
3	SOLANDA	3 min	1 min	4 min
4	CARDENAL DE LA TORRE	3 min	1 min	3 min
5	EL RECREO	3 min	1 min	3 min
6	LA MAGDALENA	3 min	1 min	3 min
7	SAN FRANCISCO	4 min	2 min	4 min
8	LA ALAMEDA	4 min	2 min	3 min
9	EL EJIDO	3 min	1 min	4 min
10	UNIVERSIDAD CENTRAL	3 min	1 min	4 min
11	LA PRADERA	3 min	1 min	3 min
12	LA CAROLINA	3 min	1 min	3 min
13	IÑAQUITO	4 min	2 min	3 min
14	JIPIJAPA	4 min	2 min	4 min
15	EL LABRADOR	4 min	2 min	-

Since the route is circular in this approach, the next station of station S_n will be the station S_{n+1} (n = 1,...,14). In the last station (El labrador) where the metro begins the returning path until the metro reaches the initial station (Quitumbre), the real next station of S_n would be S_{n-1}, but the traveling time will be assumed the same in both directions.

Table 5 presents the demand used as a didactic example. This demand is conformed by an Source Station that indicates in which station the interested party deposits his shipment (demand), a Destination Station, which represents where the shipment will be received, the number of boxes to be sent using box as unit of measure, the Time of arrival of the shipment at the source station (in minutes), which indicates at what time interval this demand was deposited at the station of origin and a desired deadline, all in minutes, indicating until what time the shipment should be received.

Table 5. Demand Table.

ID	Source Station	Destination Station	Number of Boxes	Time of arrival at the station	Desired cut-off time
1	4	8	6	604	843
2	1	6	3	840	958
3	3	8	5	592	922
4	4	7	6	520	1027
5	2	7	3	772	1005
6	1	7	6	506	1257
7	2	12	1	692	740
8	4	11	5	799	973
9	1	10	6	591	1257
10	2	4	5	624	926
11	5	10	7	632	854
12	1	7	5	782	971
13	4	1	4	646	1240
14	4	11	4	605	1173
15	2	12	3	763	1313

5   Problem Statement

To solve the proposed problem, a multi-objective genetic algorithm NSGA-II (see Algorithm 5) was implemented. This well recognized evolutionary algorithm proposes a procedure to efficiently classify the individuals of a population in several non-dominated fronts and using elitist principles, the best solutions of a population have the opportunity to be chosen for the next generation using an explicit diversity preserving mechanism called Crowding distance [28].

Algorithm 5 begins reading the Schedule and the Demand Table at step 1, the population is initialized and the restrictions are checked to make sure that population P has only feasible solutions. If no feasible solution is found, a error message is printed.

After assessing individuals of population P and using genetic operator, an offspring population Q is generated and the main loop begins at step 6. The parent and offspring population are combined in R which is sorted lexicographically according to no-dominance and crowding distance. The best individuals of R are selected to generate a new evolutionary population P. Then, a new offspring population Q is generated applying genetic operators to P.

After fulfilling a stop criterion, the loop ends and the final P is returned.

6   Case Study Results

Solving the case study with this proposed NSGA-II algorithm, Table 6 presents the obtained Pareto set.

Algorithm 1. *Non-dominated Sorting Genetic Algorithm version 2 (NSGA-II)*

1: Read demand and schedule data
2: $t=0$ //Initialize generation counter
3: Initialize evolutionary population P_t //set of feasible candidate solutions. If no feasible solution is found, print error message.
4: Assess individuals of P_t
5: Apply genetic operators to P_t to generate Q_t
6: **while** Stopping Criterion not met **do**
7:     $R_t = P_t \cup Q_t$ //combine parent and offspring populations
8:     **if** an individual (solution candidate) does not meet the constraints
9:         Erase it
10:     Sort R_t lexicographically according to no-dominance and crowding distance
11:     Select best elements of R_t to generate a new evolutionary population P_{t+1}
12:     Choose offspring population Q_{t+1} by applying genetic operators to P_{t+1}
13:     $t=t+1$
14: **return** P_t

Table 6. Chromosomes of each individual of the Pareto set for the Case Study.

Solution 1

| 4 | 42 | 14 | 5 | 5 | 6 | 25 | 36 | 15 | 18 | 17 | 37 | 8 | 16 | 36 |

Solution 2

| 4 | 42 | 14 | 5 | 5 | 6 | 25 | 37 | 15 | 18 | 17 | 36 | 8 | 16 | 36 |

Solution 3

| 4 | 42 | 14 | 5 | 6 | 6 | 25 | 36 | 15 | 18 | 17 | 37 | 8 | 16 | 36 |

Solution 4

| 4 | 42 | 14 | 5 | 6 | 6 | 25 | 37 | 15 | 18 | 17 | 37 | 8 | 16 | 36 |

A chromosome is a representation of a solution, in this case a vector with dimension I = 15 (see Table 6) where each position of the vector corresponds to a demand (see Table 5). An element of a chromosome represents the ID of the metro (see Table 4) where the corresponding shipment should be loaded.

For didactic purposes, consider solution 1 of Table 6, where an example could be the demand with ID 5 of 3 boxes that departs from station 2, which must be loaded on the metro with ID 5 to be sent to its destination at station 7.

Table 7. Pareto front for the Metro of Quito case study.

	F_1: Time in station	F_2: Transportation time	F_3: Total cost
solution 1	106	353.4	122.548
solution 2	90	353.4	125.428
solution 3	82	381	133.504
solution 4	82	381	133.504

Table 7 presents the corresponding *Pareto front* showing the values of the three objective function for each solution of the Pareto set. First of all, it is worth noting that even though there are 4 solutions in the Pareto set, only 3 different points will be seen in the Pareto front since solutions 3 and 4 have the same values in the objective space; therefore, we will not consider solution 4 in the following analysis.

Solution 1 is clearly non-dominated since it has the lowest value of F_3 (total cost). Similarly, solution 3 (or solution 4) is non-dominated since it has the lowest F_1 (Time in station). On the other hand, solution 2 is a compromise solution having a value for F_1 (Time in station) and for F_3 (total cost) between the values for solutions 1 and 3, while F_2 (Transportation time) is not lower than solution 1 but it is better than solution 3.

In short, the analyzed Case Study has no single best solution considering simultaneously all three objective function. Four possible non-dominated solutions were found from which a decision maker can choose the one that best fit his criterion. Any solution of the Pareto set would be a good option in a pure multi-objective context.

7   Final Considerations

Performing certain logistical activities, such as moving goods within a crowded city using available capacity in underground passenger transportation networks, is an efficient approach. However, there are very few applications in Latin America and none in Ecuador. In this context, it is worth promoting sustainable urban development that benefits the environment and improves urban logistics by diverting some freight traffic to the metro network. This paper analyzes the combined passenger and freight transport with a line network configuration, as found in some mass transportation systems in Latin American cities, using as a case study the metro system in Quito, whose stations can still be converted for the subway transport of urban delivery orders.

First, a novel multi-objective optimization model is proposed that considers three objectives to evaluate the feasibility of transporting urban delivery orders that incorporate the interests of different stakeholders: a first objective related to freight owners: the total waiting time for loading at stations; a second objective related to the level of service to passengers: the cost of loading and unloading; and a final objective related to transport network managers: the total cost of transporting the entire logistics operation.

Second, the presented mathematical model is solved using the well-known NSGA-II algorithm. The implemented algorithm was executed in a reasonable time, which proves that the algorithm can be used for practical purposes in planning the loading of goods in real transportation networks. The numerical results show that the considered objectives are in conflict; therefore, the Pareto front provides the decision maker with good quality information for further analysis and final decision making.

This work has some limitations in terms of modeling and network diversity topologies, for example, we simply specify a structure in which stations are centered around a line, rather than other types of more complex configurations, such as multiple lines with interchange stations, which are common in many metro transportation systems, left as a future work. The development of a model for combined passenger and freight transportation in an underground transportation system such as the metro of Quito also needs to consider important aspects such as the ETL (extract, transform, and load) process of several databases and the business model behind. On the one hand, the ETL approach requires a data management system with records and reports to collect, organize, present, and use the logistics data collected at all levels of the system. On the other hand, the business model requires a comparison between traditional freight transportation and the model based on an integrated passenger and freight transportation system.

In addition, an analysis of several technical requirements is needed: packaging boxes for demand response, parcel lockers, sections of metro wagons conditioned to receive goods, the coordination required between shippers, logistics companies, and crowd-shipping platform providers, as well as an analysis that examines the full range of economic, legal, social, and psychological issues involved.

Finally, among other practical considerations, the impact of uncertain demand and delays in the arrival times of goods and trains at stations should be taken into account. Of course, other objective functions and constraints could also be considered to obtain a holistic model that takes into account the interests of passengers, merchants, transit operators, and city administrators.

References

1. Karam, A., Eltoukhy, A.E., Shaban, I.A., Attia, E.A.: A review of COVID-19-related literature on freight transport: impacts, mitigation strategies, recovery measures, and future research directions. Int. J. Environ. Res. Public Health **19**(19), 12287 (2022)
2. Walking and cycling: latest evidence to support policy-making and practice. https://www.who.int/europe/publications/i/item/9789289057882. Accessed 11 Nov 2022
3. Pedestrianisation - Transport Department. https://www.td.gov.hk/en/transportinhongkong/pedestrians/pedestrianisation/index.html. Accessed 11 Nov 2022
4. DigitalCommerce, Digital-commerce 360. United States e-commerce grows 44%. https://www.digitalcommerce360.com/article/us-ecommerce-sales. Accessed 4 May 2022
5. Weforum.https://www.weforum.org/press/2020/01/urban-deliveries-expected-to-add-11-minutes-to-daily-commute-and-increase-carbon-emissions-by-30-until-2030-without-effective-intervention-e3141b32fa/. Accessed 24 June 2022
6. Jansen, T.A.M.: Development of a design model for integrated passenger and freight transportation systems. Ph.D. thesis. Master's thesis, Eindhoven University of Technology, the Netherlands (2014)

7. Ghilas, V., Demir, E., Van Woensel, T.: The pickup and delivery problem with time windows and scheduled lines. INFOR: Inf. Syst. Oper. Res. **54**(2), 147–167 (2016)
8. Li, B., Krushinsky, D., Reijers, H.A., Van Woensel, T.: The share-a-ride problem: people and parcels sharing taxis. Eur. J. Oper. Res. **238**(1), 31–40 (2014)
9. Aerovia Guayaquil. https://aeroviagye.com/. Accessed 24 June 2022
10. AFD. Proyecto de Teléferico Aereo de Guayaquil. https://www.afd.fr/es/ressources/proyecto-de-telelerico-aerovia-en-gayaquil. Accessed 24 June 2022
11. Metro de Panama. https://www.elmetrodepanama.com/. Accessed 24 June 2022
12. Metro de Medellín. https://www.metrodemedellin.gov.co. Accessed 24 June 2022
13. Metro de Santo Domingo. https://www.metrosantodomingo.com/. Accessed 24 June 2022
14. Von Lüken, C., Barán, B., Brizuela, C.: A survey on multi-objective evolutionary algorithms for many-objective problems. Comput. Optim. Appl. **58**(3), 707–756 (2014)
15. Ranieri, L., Digiesi, S., Silvestri, B., Roccotelli, M.: A review of last mile logistics innovations in an externalities cost reduction vision. Sustainability **10**(3), 782 (2018)
16. Cleophas, C., Cottrill, C., Ehmke, J.F., Tierney, K.: Collaborative urban transportation: recent advances in theory and practice. Eur. J. Oper. Res. **273**(3), 801–816 (2019)
17. Dong, J., Xu, Y., Hwang, B.G., Ren, R., Chen, Z.: The impact of underground logistics system on urban sustainable development: a system dynamics approach. Sustainability **11**(5), 1223 (2019)
18. Marinov, M., et al.: Urban freight movement by rail. J. Transp. Lit. **7**, 87–116 (2013)
19. Shen, J., Qiu, F., Li, W., Feng, P.: A new urban logistics transport system based on a public transit service. In: CICTP 2015, pp. 650–661 (2015)
20. Behiri, W., Belmokhtar-Berraf, S., Chu, C.: Urban freight transport using passenger rail network: scientific issues and quantitative analysis. Transp. Res. Part E Logist. Transp. Rev. **115**, 227–245 (2018)
21. Kelly, J., Marinov, M.: Innovative interior designs for urban freight distribution using light rail systems. Urban Rail Transit **3**(4), 238–254 (2017)
22. Ji, Y., Zheng, Y., Zhao, J., Shen, Y., Du, Y.: A multimodal passenger-and-package sharing network for urban logistics. J. Adv. Transp. 6039032 (2020)
23. Romano-Alho, A., et al.: A simulation-based evaluation of a Cargo-Hitching service for E-commerce using mobility-on-demand vehicles. Futur. Transp. **1**(3), 639–656 (2021)
24. Zheng, C., Gu, Y., Shen, J., Du, M.: Urban logistics delivery route planning based on a single metro line. IEEE Access **9**, 50819–50830 (2021)
25. Villa, R., Monzón, A.: A metro-based system as sustainable alternative for urban logistics in the era of e-commerce. Sustainability **13**(8), 4479 (2021)
26. Sun, X., Hu, W., Xue, X., Dong, J.: Multi-objective optimization model for planning metro-based underground logistics system network: Nanjing case study. J. Ind. Manag. Optim. (2021). https://doi.org/10.3934/jimo.2021179
27. Metro de Quito. https://www.metrodequito.gob.ec/. Accessed 24 June 2022
28. Von Lücken, C., Hermosilla, A., Barán, B.: Algoritmos Evolutivos para Optimización Multiobjetivo: Un Estudio Comparativo en un Ambiente Paralelo Asíncrono. In: X Congreso Argentino de Ciencias de la Computación (2004)

Author Index

Printed in the United States
by Baker & Taylor Publisher Services